CARETAKING DEMOCRATIZATION

COMPARATIVE POLITICS
AND INTERNATIONAL STUDIES SERIES

Series editor, Christophe Jaffrelot

The series consists of original manuscripts and translations of noteworthy manuscripts and publications in the social sciences emanating from the foremost French researchers.

The focus of the series is the transformation of politics and society by transnational and domestic factors—globalisation, migration and religion. States are more permeable to external influence than ever before and this phenomenon is accelerating processes of social and political change the world over. In seeking to understand and interpret these transformations, this series gives priority to social trends from below as much as to the interventions of state and non-state actors.

RENAUD EGRETEAU

Caretaking Democratization

The Military and Political Change in Myanmar

UNIVERSITY PRESS

Oxford University Press is a department of the University of Oxford. It furthers the University's objective of excellence in research, scholarship, and education by publishing worldwide.

Oxford New York
Auckland Cape Town Dar es Salaam Hong Kong Karachi
Kuala Lumpur Madrid Melbourne Mexico City Nairobi
New Delhi Shanghai Taipei Toronto

With offices in
Argentina Austria Brazil Chile Czech Republic France Greece
Guatemala Hungary Italy Japan Poland Portugal Singapore
South Korea Switzerland Thailand Turkey Ukraine Vietnam

Published in the United States of America by
Oxford University Press
198 Madison Avenue, New York, NY 10016

Library of Congress Cataloging-in-Publication Data is available
Renaud Egreteau.
Caretaking Democratization: The Military and Political Change in Myanmar.
ISBN: 9780190620967

Printed in India on acid-free paper

To Doi Ling

CONTENTS

LIST OF TABLES

FOREWORD AND ACKNOWLEDGMENTS

This study draws on a familiarity with Myanmar's contemporary affairs tentatively acquired since I first set foot in the country as a fresh graduate student, in 2002. More specifically, however, it is the product of regular field research I have carried out in the country since early 2011. In a rapidly changing domestic environment, I have seldom declined the opportunity to sit and share a conversation over a *lah peh ye* (sweetened milk tea) in a teashop in Yangon's suburbs, in Myitkyina's markets or in the guesthouse of the elected parliamentarians in Naypyitaw. In fact, this is something one did at one's peril before "change" happened in Myanmar. Many Burmese veteran politicians, social workers, journalists, religious leaders, community activists, civil servants and retired army officers have spent countless hours with me over the past four years, relentlessly discussing, challenging—and diversifying—my vision of the contemporary Burmese social and political realms. I've learned much from the improvised, yet regular, debates I have had since 2011 with Burmese lawmakers in Naypyitaw, the eerie capital, or with Kachin teachers in the country's northern mountains, as well as with members of prominent Burmese political families in Yangon, and the growing local NGO and "capacity-building" crowd there. The numerous personal briefings I received from Burmese political party leaders, ministerial officials and members or spokespersons of various ethnic and political organizations, based in Myanmar or along its borderlands, have also been extremely beneficial to my ongoing studies and understanding of the complex societies that form Myanmar.

The present work also benefited from countless discussions with fellow "Burma-watchers", in the more or less comfy lounges of hotel and guesthouse lobbies, during international conference panel discussions, and in local street teashops inside Myanmar. Among the many colleagues who helped this research grow by providing regular or specific input, by commenting on earlier drafts and chapters, or simply by suggesting new directions for research, I would like to thank David I. Steinberg, Christina Fink, Andrew Selth, Tin Maung Maung Than, Mary P. Callahan, Maung Aung Myoe, Robert H. Taylor, Larry Jagan, Derek Tonkin, Morten Pedersen, Khin Zaw Win, Ian Holliday, Mael Raynaud, Romain Caillaud, Carine Jaquet, David Camroux, and Christophe Jaffrelot, my former PhD supervisor at Sciences Po Paris. All were tremendously supportive. This monograph takes its cue from a research paper I initially prepared in 2013 for the Center for International Research (CERI), Sciences Po Paris, and Christophe Jaffrelot proposed early on that I morph that paper into a book-length manuscript.[1] Miriam Perier, also from CERI, as well as Michael Dwyer at Hurst and his editorial team, provided more than useful insights to improve the manuscript. Ambassador Thierry Mathou and the French embassy crew in Yangon have also facilitated many of my on-site research interviews with top-ranking Myanmar officials. Finally, I am indebted to my wife, Doi Ling, just because it is her, and because it is me.

This manuscript uses the vernacular terms "Myanmar" and "Yangon" without any political connotation. Burma will be used for pre-1989 events. The vernacular term "Bamar" is also used to distinguish the mainly Buddhist ethnic majority of the country—also known as "Burman" in the American scholarship—from the numerous other ethnic minorities such as the Shan, Karen (Kayin in the vernacular), Arakanese (Rakhine), Karenni (Kayah), Chin, Naga and Kachin, among others. The non-Bamar communities of contemporary Myanmar reportedly make up a third of its total population. This manuscript, however, prefers the English adjective "Burmese" to indicate the nationality of all citizens of Myanmar, as this avoids the grammatically incorrect adjective "Myanmarese" (which reads as awkwardly as "Americanese"), and the less inclusive adjective "Myanmar", which literally—and more commonly—refers to the Bamar community.

Map of Myanmar

ACRONYMS

AAPP	Assistance Association for Political Prisoners
AFPFL	Anti-Fascist People's Freedom League
Akha NDP	Akha National Development Party
ALD	Arakan League for Democracy
AMRDP	All Mon Regions Democracy Party
ANP	Arakan National Party (=RNP)
ASEAN	Association of South East Asian Nations
BIA	Burma Independence Army
BNA	Burma National Army
BSPP	Burma Socialist Program Party
CNDP	Chin National Democratic Party
CNF	Chin National Front
CNP	Chin National Party
CPB	Communist Party of Burma
CPP	Chin Progressive Party
DKBA	Democratic Karen Buddhist Army
DP(M)	Democratic Party (Myanmar)
DSA	Defense Services Academy
ENC	Ethnic Nationalities Council
EU	European Union
INDP	Inn National Development Party
IPU	Inter-Parliamentary Union
KDUP	Kokang Democracy and Unity Party
KIA	Kachin Independence Army
KIO	Kachin Independence Organization
KNP	Kayan National Party

KNU	Karen National Union
KPP	Kayin People's Party
KSDDP	Kayin State Democracy and Development Party
KSDP	Kachin State Democracy Party
Lahu NDP	Lahu National Development Party
Lisu NDP	Lisu National Development Party
MNP	Mon National Party
MPC	Myanmar Peace Center
NDF	National Democratic Force
NDSC	National Defense and Security Council
NLD	National League for Democracy
NPP	National Progressive Party
NUF	National Unity Front
NUP	National Unity Party
OTS	Officers' Training School
PNO	Pa'O National Organization
PSDP	Phalon-Sawaw Democratic Party
RNDP	Rakhine Nationalities Development Party
RNP	Rakhine National Party (=ANP)
SNDP	Shan Nationalities Democratic Party
SNLD	Shan Nationalities League for Democracy
SLORC	State Law and Order Restoration Council
SPDC	State Peace and Development Council
SSA-S	Shan State Army-South
TNDP	Tai'Leng Nationalities Development Party
TNLA	Ta'ang National Liberation Army
TPNP	Ta'aung (Palaung) National Party
UDPKS	Unity and Democracy Party (Kachin State)
UEC	Union Election Commission
USDA	Union Solidarity and Development Association
USDP	Union Solidarity and Development Party
UWSA	United Wa State Army
WDP	Wa Democratic Party
WNUP	Wa National Unity Party
ZCD	Zomi Congress for Democracy

CHRONOLOGY

1941	A group of Burmese nationalists led by Aung San, future architect of Burma's independence, forms the Burma Independence Army (BIA) with Japanese support.
1943	Burma gains nominal independence under Japanese control. Aung San is appointed defense minister; Ne Win becomes commander of the Burma National Army (BNA).
27 March 1945	The BNA joins the Allied forces to fight against the Japanese occupation.
27 January 1947	The Aung San-Attlee Agreement paves the way for Burma's independence.
5 February 1947	The Karen National Union (KNU) is formed and starts to lobby for the creation of an independent Karen state, separate from the Bamar heartland.
12 February 1947	Signature of the Panglong Agreement, providing for the creation of a loose federal union after the country's independence.
19 July 1947	Assassination of Aung San in Rangoon.
24 September 1947	Adoption of Burma's first constitution.
4 January 1948	The Union of Burma gains independence from Britain as a parliamentary republic with a limited federal system. U Nu becomes prime minister.
1949	The KNU begins a large-scale armed rebellion.

June 1951	Launch of the first post-independence legislative elections.
January 1952	With 60 per cent of the vote, Prime Minister U Nu's Anti-Fascist People's Freedom League (AFPFL) wins the polls. U Nu forms a new government in March.
April 1956	Second general elections. The AFPFL wins 55 per cent of the vote, but a group led by Aung San's brother and the National Unity Front (NUF) obtain more than 37 per cent.
June 1956	U Nu resigns and leaves the premiership to Ba Swe.
April 1957	Ba Swe resigns and U Nu is once again nominated prime minister.
April 1958	The AFPFL splits into two rival factions: the AFPFL "Stable" (led by Ba Swe and Kyaw Nyein) and the AFPFL "Clean" (led by U Nu and Thakin Tin).
26 September 1958	Following several months of political instability, the Burmese armed forces are called upon to lead a caretaker government.
April 1959	Ethnic Shan princes (*sawbwas*) renounce their privileges.
February 1960	Third post-independence general elections, organized under military supervision. U Nu's 'Clean' faction, renamed Pyidaungsu Party, wins and forms a new government.
April 1960	The armed forces retreat to their barracks.
February 1961	The Christian-dominated Kachin Independence Organization (KIO) is founded.
August–September 1961	New legislation imposes Buddhism as the state religion.
2 March 1962	General Ne Win seizes power through a coup d'état and forms a seventeen-member Revolutionary Council. U Nu and his cabinet are arrested.
July 1962	Crackdown on student demonstrations. Ne Win

	founds the Burma Socialist Program Party (BSPP), or *lanzin pati*.
Febuary 1963	Series of economic nationalizations.
March 1964	Creation of the Shan State Army, fighting for an independent Shan entity.
April 1964	The BSPP becomes the sole legal political party.
April 1966	U Nu and his colleagues are released in a general amnesty.
June 1967	Anti-Chinese riots in the main Burmese cities.
April 1969	U Nu leaves for Thailand seeking asylum.
April 1972	General Ne Win resigns from the army.
4 January 1974	Burma's second constitution is adopted, allowing a transfer of power from the Revolutionary Council to a People's Assembly (Pyithu Hluttaw) under BSPP domination.
December 1974	Series of demonstrations on the occasion of former UN Secretary General U Thant's funeral in Rangoon. Massive crackdown on protesters and students.
1976	Purges in the military. Tin Oo, former commander-in-chief, is jailed in January 1977.
February 1978	Start of Operation Naga Min in Rakhine State. Exodus of 250,000 Muslim refugees (or Rohingyas) into Bangladesh.
July 1980	General amnesty ordered by Ne Win. U Nu returns from exile; Tin Oo is released.
August 1981	Ne Win resigns from his post of Union president and is succeeded by San Yu.
October 1982	Adoption of a new citizenship law.
May 1983	Series of purges in the military intelligence services. Colonel Khin Nyunt is tasked with their reorganization.
September 1987	Demonetization of 25, 35 and 75 kyat banknotes; creation of 45 and 90 kyat banknotes.
March 1988	Brawl in a teashop in northern Rangoon. Street

	protests while Aung San Suu Kyi, daughter of Aung San, incidentally returns to Rangoon to nurse her ailing mother.
July 1988	Following waves of protests and crackdowns, Ne Win resigns as BSPP chairman.
8–12 August 1988	Massive crackdown on student and worker demonstrations, in which over 3,000 people are killed by anti-riot forces and army troops.
18 September 1988	The armed forces seize power in a military coup. A new junta is formed under the name of the State Law and Order Restoration Council (SLORC). Its new leader, General Saw Maung, annuls the 1974 constitution.
27 September 1988	Aung San Suu Kyi and Tin Oo found the National League for Democracy (NLD).
April 1989	The underground Communist Party of Burma (CPB) collapses and splits into four ethnic-based armed militias, including the powerful United Wa State Army (UWSA).
June 1989	The country's official name in English is changed from Burma to Myanmar.
19 July 1989	Aung San Suu Kyi is placed under house arrest.
27 May 1990	First multi-party general elections held since 1960. The NLD wins 392 of 485 seats. The SLORC rules out a transfer of power, arguing a new constitution is first needed.
14 October 1991	Aung San Suu Kyi is awarded the Nobel Peace Prize in Oslo.
December 1991	Massive exodus of Rohingyas from western Myanmar into Bangladesh.
23 April 1992	General Than Shwe replaces General Saw Maung as head of the SLORC, with General Maung Aye as deputy.
April 1992	Agreement on the repatriation of 250,000 Rohingyas back into Rakhine State.
26 September 1992	Martial law is lifted after four years.

9 January 1993	A National Convention tasked with drafting a new constitutional text convenes; it gathers about 700 military-appointed delegates.
June 1993	A US embargo on arms to Myanmar is signed.
15 September 1993	Creation of the Union Solidarity and Development Association (USDA).
February 1994	A ceasefire is reached between the Tatmadaw and the KIO.
December 1994	A Buddhist-led Karen faction breaks away from the KNU and forms the Democratic Karen Buddhist Army (DKBA).
February 1995	Death of U Nu in Yangon.
10 July 1995	Aung San Suu Kyi is released from house arrest.
28 November 1995	The NLD pulls out of the National Convention.
January 1996	The National Convention is indefinitely adjourned.
8 November 1996	The EU adopts a common position on, and develops a series of international sanctions against, Myanmar.
March 1997	US President Bill Clinton signs an executive order that prohibits any new US investments in Myanmar.
July 1997	Myanmar joins the Association of South East Asian Nations (ASEAN).
15 November 1997	After an internal purge, the SLORC changes its name to the State Peace and Development Council (SPDC). Than Shwe remains its chairman and military intelligence chief; General Khin Nyunt becomes Secretary 1.
27 March 1999	Michael Aris, husband of Aung San Suu Kyi, dies of cancer in the UK.
22 September 2000	Aung San Suu Kyi is once again placed under house arrest in Yangon.
2 March 2002	Ne Win's son-in-law and three grandsons are arrested for high treason.
6 May 2002	Aung San Suu Kyi is released from house arrest.
2 December 2002	Death of Ne Win in Yangon.

30 May 2003	Aung San Suu Kyi and her supporters are attacked by thugs in Depayin, northern Myanmar. She is placed under "protective custody".
July 2003	The US adopts the Burma Freedom and Democracy Act, imposing a new round of financial sanctions against Myanmar.
August 2003	Khin Nyunt is appointed prime minister and announces a seven-step roadmap to a "discipline-flourishing" democracy.
17 May 2004	The National Convention reconvenes (step one of the roadmap) with about 1,100 delegates appointed by the SPDC. The NLD opts for a boycott.
October 2004	An EU Common Position strengthens diplomatic and commercial sanctions against Myanmar.
18 October 2004	Lt.-Gen. Khin Nyunt and thousands of his military intelligence officers are purged. Khin Nyunt and Foreign Minister Win Aung are placed under house arrest.
July 2005	Myanmar pressured into turning down its right to the ASEAN chairmanship.
6 November 2005	Transfer of the national capital from Yangon to Naypyitaw.
3 September 2007	The National Convention proposes the first draft of a new constitution to be adopted (step three of the roadmap).
26 September 2007	Buddhist monk-led demonstrations gain momentum but are crushed by anti-riot and police forces; at least thirty-one people are killed, sparking international outrage.
2 May 2008	Cyclone Nargis ravages the Irrawaddy delta and Yangon, leaving at least 140,000 casualties.
10 May 2008	A referendum is held to adopt the new constitution (step four of the roadmap). Officials announce that 92 per cent of voters backed the constitution.
May 2009	John Yettaw swims across Yangon's Inya Lake and enters Aung San Suu Kyi's property.

August 2009	Aung San Suu Kyi is tried and sentenced to eighteen more months under house arrest.
14 August 2009	US Senator Jim Webb visits Yangon, signaling a policy change decided by the Obama administration.
March 2010	The SPDC publishes election laws and appoints a Union Election Commission (UEC) to oversee the forthcoming polls (step five of the roadmap). The NLD maintains its boycott, leading to a party split and the formation of the National Democratic Force (NDF).
7 November 2010	General elections are held in all but five constituencies.
13 November 2010	Aung San Suu Kyi is freed from house arrest.
17 November 2010	The names of the election winners are announced.
8 December 2010	The UEC publishes the final results; the USDP wins 388 of the 492 seats in the Union parliament.
20 January 2011	Senior-General Than Shwe appoints 166 military officers to the Union parliament.
31 January 2011	The two chambers of the Union parliament convene and elect Thura Shwe Mann as speaker of the lower house and Khin Aung Myint as speaker of the upper house.
4 February 2011	The parliament convenes in congress and elects former SPDC prime minister Thein Sein as president of the Union and head of state.
30 March 2011	The SPDC disbands while Than Shwe and Maung Aye retire.
June 2011	The KIO breaks its seventeen-year long ceasefire and resumes its struggle against Burmese troops.
19 August 2011	Aung San Suu Kyi meets President Thein Sein in Naypyitaw.
27 September 2011	President Thein Sein suspends the Chinese-funded dam project in Myitsone, Kachin State.
November 2011	The NLD drops its boycott policy and votes to re-register as a legal party.

1 December 2011	US Secretary of State Hillary Clinton meets Aung San Suu Kyi in Yangon.
12 January 2012	Former intelligence chief Khin Nyunt is released from house arrest, along with ethnic leader Hkun Htun Oo and several leaders of the 1988 uprising, such as Min Ko Naing and Ko Ko Gyi.
1 April 2012	By-elections are held; the NLD wins forty-three of the forty-five seats contested.
26 April 2012	The EU suspends all sanctions against Myanmar for a year.
June 2012	Anti-Muslim riots in Rakhine State.
September 2012	The censorship bureau is abolished.
November 2012	First ever visit of a US President to Myanmar; President Obama meets both his Burmese counterpart and Aung San Suu Kyi.
March 2013	Rioting between Muslim and Buddhist mobs in Meiktila, central Myanmar.
May 2013	President Thein Sein visits Washington, D.C. and meets with President Obama.
July 2013	A parliamentary committee for the revision of the 2008 constitution is formed.
December 2013	Myanmar organizes the twenty-seventh South East Asian Games in Naypyitaw.
February 2014	A thirty-one-member parliamentary committee for constitutional revision is formed.
10–11 May 2014	As ASEAN chair, Myanmar hosts the twenty-fourth ASEAN Summit in Naypyitaw.
12–13 November 2014	Myanmar hosts, back to back, the twenty-fifth ASEAN Summit and an East Asia Summit; US President Obama travels to Naypyitaw.
February 2015	Fighting resumes between Burmese troops and ethnic Kokang militias near the Chinese borders.
30 March 2015	The draft of a national ceasefire agreement is accepted by President Thein Sein and sixteen ethnic political and armed groups.
June 2015	A first set of constitutional amendments is discussed in parliament and vetoed by the military.

15 October 2015	The final text of the national ceasefire agreement is signed by eight armed groups and the government.
8 November 2015	General elections are successfully held. The NLD wins an outright majority in both houses of the Union parliament.
1 February 2016	The new Union legislature convenes in Naypyitaw.

INTRODUCTION

DEMOCRATIZATION FROM ABOVE?

In May 2009, Aung San Suu Kyi faced a public trial at the North Yangon District Court. She had been under house arrest for the past six years, after she and a convoy of her supporters were attacked by hoodlums in Depayin, a town in northern Myanmar. Earlier in the month, a fifty-three-year-old American eccentric, John W. Yettaw, had swum into her Yangon lakeside house compound, where she was confined.[1] The district court, near the Insein prison where the daughter of Myanmar's independence hero was detained during the trial (along with her two aides), ruled that she was guilty of having illegally sheltered a foreigner, and of having accepted unlawful documents from him. The Burmese authorities—the State Peace and Development Council (SPDC, or the "junta")—deemed this an unacceptable breach of her detention conditions. On the day the district judge was to make his decision public, he had a flabbergasted audience of fifty-odd foreign diplomats and journalists in front of him.[2] For those seeking to grasp the politics of the absurd and resiliently ludicrous despotism of contemporary Myanmar, a "country unlike any other" as Rudyard Kipling once put it, this farcical trial was a fine illustration.

Less than three years later, however, Aung San Suu Kyi was triumphantly elected to Myanmar's newly formed Union legislature. After boycotting the November 2010 general elections—the first in twenty years—her party, the National League for Democracy (NLD), was re-legalized in November 2011. When the new administration, formed after the controversial 2010 polls, announced that by-elections would be held on 1 April 2012, the icon of Myanmar's pro-democracy struggle seized the opportunity to run for office.

Her electoral campaign was celebrated jubilantly by the Burmese people throughout the country's central plains, which she toured for weeks in February and March 2012. The party won forty-three of forty-five contested seats. Soon after her pivotal victory, Aung San Suu Kyi was provided with a passport, and allowed to leave the country—and return—for the first time in twenty-four years. Thus, after two decades, she was finally able to receive in person the Nobel Peace Prize she had been awarded in Oslo back in 1991. Furthermore, she tacitly green-lighted the dismantling of the international sanctions incrementally imposed on Myanmar by the Western-led international community since the early 1990s. In Yangon, world leaders and international policymakers—including UN Secretary General Ban Ki-Moon in April 2012 and US President Barack Obama in November of that year—started lining up to pay courtesy calls complete with photo-ops. Her colonial residence on 54 University Avenue was no longer an off-limits compound closed to Burmese, foreigners and swimmers alike. The muse of Myanmar's democratic opposition was poised to return to the forefront of her country's politics.

To many outsiders, Myanmar's political scene seems to have been entirely reconfigured at the turn of the 2010s. The military junta that had ruled the country under different political incarnations[3] since the last coup d'état (18 September 1988) was officially disbanded in March 2011, five months after the controversial elections it supervised on 7 November 2010. This gave way to a new hybrid regime, headed by an elected civilian president. Thein Sein, himself a former three-star army general and ex-prime minister of the SPDC (2007–11), was made Myanmar's new head of state, replacing Senior-General Than Shwe. Thein Sein and his new government gradually reached out to various opposition groups, starting with Aung San Suu Kyi herself and a cluster of ethnic armed insurgencies. Smiling and shaking hands for bemused photographers, these erstwhile arch-rivals were seemingly attempting to rebuild bridges long destroyed. It was a case of "history in the making", as Hillary Clinton argued during her landmark visit to Yangon in December 2011—the first by a US Secretary of State since 1955.

Aung San Suu Kyi's tactical decision to enter parliamentary politics in 2012 after years of iconic opposition, and her patience with the most reluctant members of her own party, was soon rewarded even further. On 8 November 2015, three-and-a-half years after the triumphant 2012 by-elections, the NLD finally won a resounding electoral victory at the national level. The 2015 polls were designed to renew the national and fourteen provincial assemblies first formed five years earlier. In contrast to the 2010 elections, which were fully controlled by the SPDC, this time Burmese voters straightforwardly, and freely, turned against the elites who had dominated the transitional landscape since 2010. Chiefly drawn from the military and the old junta bureaucracy, these political forces were almost all wiped out. The November 2015 vote was an unambiguous nationwide plebiscite on Aung San Suu Kyi herself, and a clear rejection of the five-year rule of the Union Solidarity and Development Party (USDP). The NLD took 79 per cent of the elected seats in the Union parliament, and 57 per cent of the total votes.[4] Deprived of its first electoral victory in May 1990, when the junta refused to honor the poll results that followed the 1988 student and pro-democracy uprising, the party now saw its historical legitimacy reaffirmed. It was a "fair return" on two decades of "sacrifices", said Tin Oo, the NLD emeritus patron and former commander-in-chief of the Tatmadaw, the Burmese armed forces.[5]

How was it possible to go from Aung San Suu Kyi's farcical trial in 2009 to her thundering electoral victory in 2015? How, and why, could such a profound transformation of Myanmar's political process be triggered after the 2010 polls—and convincingly confirmed by the NLD's electoral triumph five years later? Why does the transition from direct military rule to a hybrid parliamentary system, in which Myanmar's armed forces effectively agree to share power, seem (so far) to have proved successful in a country so routinely ruled by men in uniform? How and why could this transitional process be conceivable, and achievable, in the early 2010s, when a similar attempt at transferring power twenty years earlier, in 1988–90, had clearly been a failure? This monograph intends to look at some of the underlying determinants behind the tortuous process of political change that has been at work in Myanmar since 2010. It takes the view that the transition from direct military rule to "something else",[6] which unfolded in Myanmar between 2010 and 2015, is a *sui generis* case. The transition has been driven from above, by ruling Burmese elites—especially military ones—in a clear position of strength since the early 2000s, yet willing to see Myanmar's state structures morphing into a new type of regime, in which the armed forces could be in a position to remain on board, but rethink their own political role.

Unlike in the Arab world during the early 2010s, or in the case of the various "color" revolutions that have shaken Eastern Europe throughout the 2000s, political change in Myanmar has neither emerged from popular street protests, nor been imposed by the outside world. Startlingly, the key institution driving the transitional process was neither the traditional pro-democracy opposition led by Aung San Suu Kyi, nor an interfering international community seeking, since the first Western sanctions imposed in the 1990s, to encourage—if not force—a regime change. Rather, as this book will highlight, it was the unapologetically interventionist Tatmadaw itself. Why was this so? Why have the Burmese armed forces decided to start this transformation at this very moment? Why did their leadership opt for gradual withdrawal from the forefront of politics in the 2010s, and not twenty years earlier? What were their motivations after more than two decades of direct and almost unchallenged military rule?

By effectively instituting a well-thought-out transitional opening in 2011, the Tatmadaw leadership merely chose to move down a notch on the scale of political intervention. It remained much in control of the first phase of the early 2010s' transitional process. This partial disengagement from day-to-day politics was first outlined after the coup d'état that propelled the State Law and Order Restoration Council (SLORC) to power on 18 September 1988. The withdrawal had, however, been carefully—and openly—planned since the announcement in August 2003 of a seven-step roadmap towards a "discipline-flourishing democracy",[7] best epitomized by the enactment of a new, military-inspired constitution in 2008—the third since independence from the British in 1948. As this book will argue, the Tatmadaw, by far Myanmar's most historically and pervasively dominant institution, has thus merely been "caretaking" most of the political process at work in the early 2010s, without facing much pressure during its course.

Does this necessarily mean that Myanmar will become the unexpected poster child of a successful transition from military rule to a stable multiparty democracy? How does the Burmese case fit into the extensive body of research on democratic transitions and post-military political change? What can the process at work in the country in the early 2010s tell us more broadly about transitions, especially elite-driven ones? What are the prospects for evolution of the constitutional order unveiled in 2008 and the "transit" regime (to follow Samuel Finer's expression) that succeeded the junta in 2011? The multiplicity of labels qualifying this post-SPDC political and constitutional system—"semi-civilian" or "quasi-civilian", "hybrid", "transitional" and so on—reflects how the interpretation of post-junta events remains highly contested, at home and abroad. How has Myanmar's new state nomenclature functioned since 2011, and which are the key new institutions it relies on? What kind of civil-military relations does the future hold for the country, especially after the resounding 2015 electoral victory of Aung San Suu Kyi's NLD, which must share power with the Tatmadaw? This study will probe this set of questions in order to persuasively assess the initial phases of Myanmar's latest transitional moment and its prospects—beyond the effusive praise of a so-called "Burma Spring". Indeed, at a time when a myriad of foreign observers, investors and consultants is flocking in, we need to pay more attention to Myanmar's domestic contexts and internal political dynamics.

A Cautionary Tale

Both key figures on the national political scene and foreign observers have been puzzled by the rapid transformations taking place under the aegis of a new Burmese state leadership, sworn in on 30 March 2011. After twenty-three years of fierce military authoritarianism under the SLORC and then the SPDC, the impetus from the former SPDC prime minister himself, Thein Sein, proved to be a decisive factor. Indeed, he was elected in February 2011 to occupy Myanmar's highest institutional position for the first five years of the new post-junta political system. Inducted into his new presidential function on 30 March 2011, Thein Sein and his new government—comprising over eighty ministers and deputy ministers—were subsequently able to initiate large-scale political, economic and social reforms, while reaching out to the ethnic and democratic opposition, in particular to Aung San Suu Kyi. In this, Thein Sein had the support of an entourage of Burmese experts, technicians and academics—including dissidents returning from exile.

Thein Sein was also assisted in this vast enterprise of political change by other key personalities, state and local institutions, and broader social forces. Among them, the former Tatmadaw joint chief-of-staff, "Thura" Shwe Mann, played a significant role. Like Thein Sein, turning in his military uniform to enter parliamentary politics, the former four-star general was elected in November 2010 to the lower house (Pyithu Hluttaw) of the Union parliament, and was ultimately appointed its speaker in January 2011. During his five year mandate (he lost his parliamentary seat in the 2015 elections), the ambitious retired officer openly aimed to strengthen the country's resurgent legislature, or simply to make the revived legislative branch "exist" in the face of the powerful executive led by Khin Aung Myint, a former minister of culture during the later SPDC era and another retired general, similarly and actively took the speakership of the upper house (Amyotha Hluttaw). From 2011, another retired military intelligence official, Aung Min, led the government team that has initiated new rounds of ceasefire and peace talks with the majority of the armed ethnic groups still at odds with the Bamar-dominated central authorities and the Burmese military. Ex-admiral Soe Thane, a former commander-in-chief of the Myanmar Navy, has also joined the presidential entourage and has been in charge of various economic portfolios.

Under the impetus of these former senior army officers and their teams of civilian counselors, as well as with the tacit support since 2011 of the new Tatmadaw supreme commander, Senior-General Min Aung Hlaing, the new civilian administration has engaged the country in a stunning reform process. This process has in turn largely been influenced by a revitalized Burmese civil society. Surprising in its swiftness and scope, the resolutely reformist liberalization initiated in 2011 seems to have rekindled hopes for a country so routinely viewed as underdeveloped, ostracized and under the constant yoke of brutal men in khaki uniform. New forums for public expression have emerged, for Myanmar's ordinary citizens as well as for the civil society that has developed rapidly since the tragic passage of Cyclone Nargis in 2008 and the domestic mobilization it engendered. Trade unions and opposition parties have been re-legalized. Strikes and public demonstrations are now commonplace. A national human rights commission was created in September 2011. A year later, the censorship board was dissolved. The Internet is no longer fully controlled by the state, and the laptop and smartphone industries are booming.[8] The vast majority of the 2,500 political prisoners counted in 2009 have been released—by early 2016, only a few dozen were said to remain behind bars (or to have been arrested since).[9] Ever since Aung San Suu Kyi was first placed under house arrest in July 1989, the release of prisoners of conscience has been one of the principal crusades championed by junta opponents throughout the world.[10] Aung San Suu Kyi herself was freed on 13 November 2010, a week after polls were held by the SPDC. She has since been allowed to travel internally and abroad without restriction, for the first time since her return to the country in 1988.

Furthermore, since the early 2010s, an emerging private sector, advocacy groups, artistic circles, a revived local intelligentsia and hip urban youth have all gradually transformed the country's social and political space, influencing it through their increased political involvement. This is thanks to an impetus and a tolerance never before seen among the central authorities in Naypyitaw, Myanmar's capital since 2005. Today, the phenomenon is particularly noticeable in the wholesale transformation underway in Yangon, the former capital, and it is spreading gradually, albeit timidly, to other urban areas in the country. Foreign journalists and critics seldom face problems when applying for visas, and Asian and Western tourists have been flocking in. Yangon's airport handled one million visitors in 2014, against a mere 200,000 five years previously. Burmese dissidents in exile have begun to return in order to take part in the rebuilding of an economy still on the sidelines of globalization. Foreign investors and multinational corporations started in the early 2010s to prospect in a "gold rush" atmosphere, as one of Asia's richest regions in natural resources appeared to be opening up. However, traffic-jams, an appalling drainage and sewage system—vividly observed during heavy monsoon days—and extremely prohibitive rents have started to plague plague the ramshackle Yangon, Myanmar's main port of entry.

As Western governments began to review their sanctions policy as early as 2012—once Aung San Suu Kyi was first elected to parliament—the wider diplomatic community reopened its doors to a Burmese state long treated as a pariah. The major international financial institutions gradually attempted to reintegrate the Burmese economy—so underdeveloped and with such inadequate structures and institutions—into world trade and global flows. In June 2013, Naypyitaw welcomed with great fanfare a thousand international delegates of the World Economic Forum. In 2014, Myanmar presided over the Association of South East Asian Nations (ASEAN), having been pressured to forgo its turn at the chairmanship in 2006. The country appears to be gradually regaining a key position on the regional, and even world, stage. A euphoria and a sense of bold optimism have rapidly emerged, not only among the various Burmese populations, but also among foreign observers who experienced life in Myanmar "before". Drawing parallels with the popular yet chaotic and bloody revolts of the Arab world in the early 2010s and the Eurasian colored revolutions of the 2000s, a flurry of new books, reports and magazine covers appeared, praising the unexpected advent of a non-violent "Burmese Spring".[11]

There have been, however, large segments of Burmese society, especially in the remote rural areas and the ethnic-dominated peripheries, where change has proved rather elusive, if not completely absent. The further one moves from Yangon or Naypyitaw, the more difficult it becomes to reconcile the optimistic narratives about positive change and liberalization with the political realities of regions where militarization, insurgent warfare and trafficking of all sorts remain a way of life. In light of the NLD's formidable electoral success in November 2015, the value and pace of the Thein Sein government's 2011–15 reform agenda and the legislative performance of the parliament formed after the 2010 polls (and dominated for five years by members of the old junta nomenclature), have likewise increasingly been questioned, at home and abroad.[12] The extent of the state, bureaucratic and military transformations promised after 2010, as well as fundamental changes in the state leadership, have appeared more limited than was initially claimed. The wider costs and implications of the 2010–15 transitional moment have thus gradually prompted criticism, if not naïve disenchantment, among local and international commentators. The Burmese electorate massively voted for Aung San Suu Kyi's party in November 2015 has in a sense emphasized even further the reluctance to take for granted the casually optimistic narratives about "change" and the "New Myanmar" that emerged in the early 2010s from the stately avenues of Naypyitaw and Yangon's comfy hotel lounges, crowded with foreign businessmen and international consultants.

The post-junta developments have, progressively, shaped a new environment of social and political uncertainty. Unrealistic expectations about the depth of the social, political and economic restructuring have been too routinely formulated. Unreasonable hopes have blinded domestic and international observers to feasible reforms in a country so long under the sole and untested management of its armed forces. The process of change at work since the late 2010s has not proved free of glitches, frustrating delays and setbacks. Behind rosy pictures of Aung San Suu Kyi drawing thousands of admirers during electoral meetings in 2012 and 2015, or uniformed Tatmadaw officers laughing with Karen and Shan rebels like gentlemen around a tea table, the continuing existence of deeply entrenched ills in present-day Myanmar points to an enduring reality: the country, its society and polity, have not undergone any major revolutionary moment since 2010. There has been no sweeping rupture, no sudden revolution, but rather an incremental process of relative change—for better or worse—and a series of transformative forces at work.

Whilst startling top-down reforms outlined by seemingly progressive elites in Naypyitaw have dominated recent news, deep social, cultural and economic transformations have also been at work in Myanmar since the early 2000s. The rapid political transition of the 2010s should not, therefore, overshadow the profound and protracted changes that have occurred in Burmese society since the turn of the twenty-first century. Other scholars have delved into these phenomena.[13] Without dismissing the various current metamorphoses, this book focuses on social and political forces observed in the first half of the 2010s. It does not, however, pretend to offer a comprehensive treatment of events from 2010 to 2015. Nor will it offer a definitive assessment of the ongoing military/civil transition, which might be interpreted in different ways by authors who have had different encounters from mine with the Burmese polity and society over the past decade or so. The advent of democracy always generates popular disenchantment and a high degree of uncertainty, as Adam Przeworski once rightly put it.[14] There are always winners and losers in a process of transition. This process can often reach such a fluid, if not volatile, state that it is imperative to decipher it carefully, with hindsight. Such is the aim of this book.

The Transition's Opening: Why Now? A Scholarly Review

There is a wide diversity of opinions about what prompted the Burmese junta to mutate into a semi-civilian regime in 2011 and to crack open the doors of political and economic liberalization at this particular moment in time.[15] Contrary to a flurry of news reports and political analyses jubilantly depicting an unfolding "Burma Spring", seasoned scholars of the Burmese polity have been cautious in their examination of the ongoing incremental process of change—a process, as a matter of fact, which they seldom label as "democratic". For example, Trevor Wilson, a former Australian ambassador posted in Yangon in the early 2000s, cautioned analysts early on to be level-headed in their appreciation of the latest political developments in a country that has drawn myriad field-leading newcomers in the past few years.[16] To interrogate what lies behind the process of incremental change observed between 2010 and 2015, one may need to examine the most recent literature, which has attempted to decipher Myanmar's transitional moment as events have unfolded. A careful review of the emerging body of research soberly excludes any single explanation for Myanmar's change from direct military rule to a hybrid political system.

A handful of long-standing Burma-watchers have argued that nothing that has happened in or to Myanmar since the 2010 elections has come as a surprise. The whole post-2010 transitional process, from a military rule to a "transit" regime (Finer), was in fact outlined by the Tatmadaw leadership early on. The junta born of the last coup d'état, staged in 1988, had already planned its own disbanding upon forming. As a former student activist of 1974—and son of a former minister in Premier U Nu's 1950s cabinets—put it, "like good generals, they retreat[ed] in order" at the very moment when the SPDC was at its peak, just "sitting on a sofa".[17] Robert H. Taylor has frequently emphasized the fact that the Burmese military leadership has always sought to control the pace, timing and extent of its own withdrawal from politics after each of its interventions.[18] The post-2011 political transformations, he recently underlined, had been announced as early as August 1988.[19] Such developments had already been observed twice in the country, when the Tatmadaw retreated to the barracks in 1960 (after less than two years of a caretaker administration) and in 1974 (after twelve years of an army-led Revolutionary Council).

The Tatmadaw leadership has indeed always considered its political intervention, each time it has seized power, as "transitory" or "temporary"—even if "temporary" meant for two decades. As claimed by one senior government official, who happened to be a member of both the *ancien régime* and the new administration formed by President Thein Sein after 2011, "our government was a *de facto* government. We knew we would have to introduce political changes if we really wanted to develop the country".[20] Other political scientists have been similarly unsurprised by the change. For Mary P. Callahan, the armed forces have straightforwardly controlled a process they themselves had clearly outlined. As she explains, the military's "hands have not been forced by popular protests, a defeat in war, or crippling intramilitary factionalism. On the contrary, they have been acting from a position of strength".[21] Dan Slater too highlights what he calls a "multifaceted confidence game" played by the junta in the 1990s and 2000s to its own advantage.[22] The military regime followed its own set of rules, and thus only started to mutate when it considered it was in a clear position of strength in relation to both its domestic and its international opponents. Only then could it safely initiate what Slater further describes as a "double-edged détente" with both the internal opposition camp and a highly critical international community.

Thus, after the 1988 coup, only the pace and timing of the retreat to the barracks was unknown, even to the Tatmadaw top brass. Tellingly, General Saw Maung, who had led the army takeover in September 1988, argued soon afterwards that it was the military's duty to allow and monitor (yet not take charge of) a constitution-making process that would codify the post-intervention regime and prepare the ground for the military's own disengagement.[23] However, unlike their predecessors, the post-Ne Win generation of military officers considered that the well-executed and self-imposed guardianship role of the armed forces ought to be enshrined in a new constitutional text. As an army ideologue asserted in 1993, when a first national convention tasked to draft a new constitutional text was convened:

> neither the 1947 Constitution nor the 1974 Constitution had given a definite role to the Tatmadaw in national political leadership [...] the country has now inescapably come to a stage where a definite role would have to be given to the Tatmadaw in the nation's political leadership [...] all those who have the welfare of the country at heart should concentrate their attention on providing the Tatmadaw with a leading role in national politics in writing a new constitution.[24]

As early as 1992, six core political objectives were defined.[25] They were later supplemented with 104 institutional principles that the army leadership would consider non-negotiable in order to launch its disengagement from the forefront of politics and pave the way for a "post-SLORC", multiparty political system codified by a new constitution. The appointment of a national convention in January 1993, tasked with drafting an initial constitutional text, was meant to present a loose, if not farcical, commitment to a participatory process. The constituent body was under full control of the regime, and soon after Aung San Suu Kyi's party left the assembly in November 1995, it was adjourned. The drafting process was revived in August 2003, when the recently appointed SPDC[26] prime minister General Khin Nyunt proposed a new policy initiative, outlining a seven-point roadmap to a "discipline-flourishing democracy".[27] The latter was intended to lay the groundwork for the restoration of a functioning parliamentary system in which the army's tutelage was to be acknowledged.

Thus the post-SPDC hybrid system shaped after the 2010 elections was to be construed as a logical mutation of the Tatmadaw's political role and control over state institutions. It corresponds to the Tatmadaw's enduring praetorian ethos and "institutional character", as recently argued by Burmese academic Maung Aung Myoe; and there should be no surprise here.[28] Realistically, the policy relevance of the Burmese armed forces in the new post-junta regime, to be defined once the seven steps of the 2003 roadmap were completed, could not be questioned too far, given the Tatmadaw's position of strength throughout the 1990s and 2000s.[29] Besides, continues Maung Aung Myoe, as long as a tacit mutual understanding persisted between the Tatmadaw hierarchy and the new semi-civilian administration, the stability of the post-junta "transit" regime would not be challenged.[30] And, indeed, between 2010 and 2015, it was not.

Taking a conceptual approach, Aurel Croissant and Jil Karmerling have claimed that the Tatmadaw's carefully-planned constitution-making process—spanning fifteen years—was the only plausible "survival strategy" for the army leadership, if it intended to remain a relevant policy actor.[31] Marco Bünte agrees; only through the institutionalization of a "power-sharing agreement" between civilian and military elites, he shows, could the Tatmadaw keep its political significance in the post-junta system and therefore safely instigate a gradual withdrawal in the 2010s.[32] Paul Chambers develops the same argument on the "transformative bargain" that the Tatmadaw needed to negotiate before disengaging in 2011.[33] All these views, however, implicitly convey the idea that the Tatmadaw leadership has always aimed to hold on to power. The "survival strategy" argument indeed implies that, from its inception, military rule in Myanmar was conceived by the military itself as the most efficient mode of governance, and that the Burmese generals who stepped in with the 1988 coup d'état merely intended to take control and keep power for the sake of it. As explained above, official Tatmadaw propaganda says something different. Military rule in Myanmar has rather been construed by the army ideologues as transient and momentary, not definitive. Thus there should be no quest for "survival", since the armed forces, its leadership has routinely claimed, would always (partially) disengage from the political realm in the end. Whether or not one takes this propaganda at face value is another matter.

For most observers, the transitional process has always been elite-driven and top-down. Institutional change has been initiated both "from within" (that is, inside Myanmar, not by the outside world) and "from above" (by the ruling military elites).[34] Priscilla Clapp, a former US *chargé d'affaires* in Yangon, further argues that the military leadership's "original intent" and careful planning were essential conditions for the successful beginning of the transition.[35] A few scholars have nonetheless insisted on the decisive role of the traditional opposition and pro-democracy forces, both inside and outside Myanmar—but they are in a minority.[36] What most long-standing specialists of Myanmar underline is the lack of influence over the transitional process of political forces completely external to the country's polity or society—the international community in particular. Robert H. Taylor, among others, insists on the fact that the reforms launched by Thein Sein's quasi-civilian government in 2011 have not been designed under pressure of international sanctions, contingent events such as Cyclone Nargis in May 2008 or "trips abroad to see air-conditioned shopping malls" that might hypothetically have enlightened Burmese military rulers about their country's poor state of affairs.[37]

As for the timing of the current transition, Morten Pedersen and Lee Jones have tentatively explored some of the determinants of this long-awaited process. Why now? In their respective works, they have argued that the Tatmadaw was enabled to initiate incremental disengagement in the early 2010s chiefly by the containment, if not diminishment, of the traditional threats and fears that have recurrently prompted its intervention in Burmese politics.[38] In other words, the Tatmadaw leadership felt secure enough to start its withdrawal from day-to-day politics in the early 2010s—once the opposition of various segments of the Buddhist monastic community (Sangha) had been stifled after the misnamed "Saffron Revolution" of 2007; once the many ethnic armed rebellions had been marginalized and the international community safely kept at bay after its post-Nargis intervention efforts in 2008. Pedersen further explains that the metamorphosis of Myanmar's political landscape has been made possible by the gradual evolution of the Tatmadaw's own perceptions of international and domestic security threats to the nation.[39]

For Narayanan Ganesan, with this process of change and gradual disengagement from day-to-day politics, the Burmese armed forces have also sought to recover a "political legitimacy" lost during the 1990s and 2000s—a legitimacy lost, at least, in the eyes of the many Burmese who have considered the political intervention of the Tatmadaw as either a historical right, or at best a necessary evil needed to heal the postcolonial wounds of a fragmented Burmese society. With the tightly controlled 2010 polls, Ganesan continues, the military was provided with the opportunity to change the course of the country's policymaking in ways that could be deemed "legitimate", acceptable and legal—at least from the standpoint of its own partisans, including those most disappointed by years of mismanagement and autocratic rule.[40] In so doing, the Tatmadaw could hope to rebuild its public image. This is an argument commonly made by disillusioned retired military officers in Myanmar.[41]

Like Pedersen and Taylor, Marco Bünte considers exogenous factors—a mere structural background, as he puts it—to be far less significant than endogenous ones.[42] Myanmar's transition of the early 2010s appears *sui generis*. Likewise, Lee Jones has claimed that the trajectory of the ongoing state-led reforms is primarily conditioned by the country's internal political economy, the complex social power relations forged over recent decades and the present domestic political situation.[43] Rather than external powers, the "struggles between social forces for power and control over resources, [have shaped] the extent of 'reform' and its actual implementation".[44] The longstanding economic dominance of a small number of "cronies" well-connected to the SLORC-SPDC could have limited the scope of domestic reforms. An opening up and a liberalization of the national economy were needed. Only Maung Zarni recognizes at work, in and around Myanmar, strong global capitalistic forces that may have accelerated the former regime's decision to crack the doors open in the 2010s.[45] Min Zin and Brian Joseph have argued that the willingness of the Burmese political and military elites to move out of China's shadow and re-engage with the United States has to be taken into account.[46]

There is no single explanation as to what prompted the end of a direct form of military governance at a very specific moment, in 2010 and 2011. Some observers remain rather perplexed. Among them, Khin Zaw Win—a former Burmese political prisoner, now a leading community and policy activist—has cautioned that the control and planning of the transition at the turn of the 2010s had in fact been far from absolute. The leadership that succeeded the SPDC in March 2011 was, he contends, not ready to govern or to initiate such a rapid and multifaceted reform process in the early 2010s.[47] Many decisions were made *ad hoc*, and even the pace of the reform activity may have worried many senior officials, particularly within the army leadership. As Christina Fink has similarly stressed, the "political reforms [may] have already gone farther than some in the military expected or are comfortable with".[48] So, if the start of the process and the transitional opening of 2010 and 2011 were planned and well thought-out, their later developments were left undefined. As Richard Horsey puts, the hybrid regime formed after the 2010 elections and the reformist agenda of its first leadership should be understood only as the early stages of what one should expect of a classical transition from authoritarian rule.[49]

Structure of the Book

This book discusses the new form of rule and governance taking shape in post-SPDC Myanmar in the first half of the 2010s, when the military has still been an influential policy actor but has increasingly strived to shift its involvement in politics toward a less direct approach, tolerating relative criticism and opposition, granting civilians a greater role in conducting state business, but still holding onto numerous preserves and "caretaking" most of the political process. Drawing on civil-military relations and praetorianism,[50] the first chapter will argue that the main policy actor at the core of the transitional process has remained the secretive Tatmadaw. Consistent with the observations of scholarship on military intervention, it was the armed forces and their uncontested leadership that allowed the "opening" to unfold soon after the 2010 elections, by officially disbanding the "junta" and morphing into a hybrid "transit regime". In a sense, as previously in 1960 and 1974, the military institution has acted as "caretaker" of the transition. The literature on praetorianism, as we shall see, has investigated at length the "caretaking" role long enjoyed by many coup-prone armed forces around the world, imposing their guardianship over the state and the nation through their military might. But in the case of Myanmar, it has been possible to avert violence and bloodshed, as one of the key players of the transitional process has proudly argued: ex-general Khin Aung Myint, who was elected speaker of the upper house in 2011.[51]

Yet, even if the armed forces' partial disengagement from politics since 2011 was carefully planned by the military leadership—just as when the Tatmadaw previously retreated to the barracks in 1960 and 1974—an institutional and political "elite pact" was nonetheless needed thereafter, to pursue the initial procedural transition allowed by the military top brass. The existing scholarship on elite-driven transitions calls this a "pacted transition", between some elements of the old state nomenclature and a handful of newly empowered interlocutors found outside the *ancien régime*—first among them, in the Burmese case, Aung San Suu Kyi, a set of ethnic-minority leaders and high-profile civil society groups. The conceptually grounded first chapter will thus go on to explore why and how relatively constructive, yet very fragile and incomplete, political bargaining took place in 2011 and 2012 between a few key Burmese elites, military and civilian. This allowed the transitional process to unfold a few years after the 2011 disbanding of the junta without any major political challenges, and to continue thus until the second post-junta electoral exercise was held in November 2015, five years after the contentious 2010 polls. In contrast with previous attempts to establish a significant dialogue between the Tatmadaw and the various civilian oppositions in the 1990s and 2000s, since 2011 most political actors have proved open to dialogue with one another, although not always meaningfully. But Burmese elites have always been sulkily divided, recalls bitterly a former leader of the 1988 uprising.[52] Furthermore, the scholarship on democratization tells us that intra-elite negotiated pacts seldom last. Thus a successful outcome to Myanmar's ongoing transition, as it was pacted in 2011, is far from pre-ordained, despite the peaceful organization of the 2015 electoral process and the resounding victory of Aung San Suu Kyi's party.

Chapter Two will analyze the patterns of Myanmar's sudden opening up of the political and social space in the early 2010s. The new climate that emerged under Thein Sein's semi-civilian presidency (2010–15) appears to have nurtured an unprecedented level of optimism, at home and abroad. Opposition to the authorities has been more or less allowed, dissent relatively tolerated, civil society expanded, while censorship has been considerably eased. New labor, media and foreign investment laws have been prepared. Trade unions, political parties, and workers' strikes have been legalized. The transitional moment was accompanied by obvious environmental, institutional and political changes. At the same time, new forms of radicalism and contentious politics have (re)surfaced, benefiting from the relaxation of military and state control. All these changes have posed new challenges to the country's social cohesion and its prospects for peaceful democratization, but also to the transition as it was initially pacted.

Further demonstrating the transformative processes at work, Chapter Three focuses on one of the most unexpectedly positive developments of the past few years in Myanmar: the resurgence of parliamentary politics in a country long deprived of any meaningful legislative activity. The first post-junta legislature, crafted after the controversial 2010 elections, has promptly gained heightened political status—even more so since the subsequent 2012 by-elections that witnessed a triumphantly elected Aung San Suu Kyi entering the lower house. However, still in its infancy, Myanmar's new parliamentary institutions remain vulnerable and the second post-SPDC legislature, formed after the successful November 2015 elections, is bound to face formidable challenges in the second half of the 2010s. This chapter will evaluate the initial performance and functioning of the first post-SPDC legislature (2010–15), and identify its most obvious weaknesses.

Chapter Four will tone down the euphoric optimism that emerged soon after the transition—and was reaffirmed after the NLD's triumph in the 2015 legislative polls—by highlighting one of the more enduring realities of contemporary Myanmar: the persistence of "praetorian" behaviors and the continuing dominance of the military institution beyond the disbanding of the junta, or SPDC, in 2011. The Tatmadaw remains a key policy actor and, as this chapter will demonstrate, is still the "last resort decision-maker" in the new post-SPDC hybrid system. As crises emerge, as threats escalate, as local contentious politics grow uncontrollable, in Myanmar the size of the basic decision-making unit still seems limited to a few men in uniform. When political tensions rise in ethnic-dominated areas, it is the representatives of the Tatmadaw who step in. When Aung San Suu Kyi won the 2015 general elections, it was with the commander-in-chief that she sought to establish a meaningful dialogue. The military has also secured an official post-junta role in the legislature. The 2008 constitution has reserved a quarter of all parliamentary seats for the armed forces. The various legislative functions performed by the army-appointed lawmakers since 2010 must be thoroughly assessed in order to evaluate the lawmaking influence the military leadership may seek to retain in future legislatures, especially those dominated by its historical opponents, such as the NLD.

Chapter Five explores the deepening of religious and ethnic cleavages in the 2010s, and attempts to evaluate their impact on the course and the pace of the ongoing transitional process. The struggle for ethnic rights and interethnic peace, indeed, predates the struggle for democracy in Myanmar. The question of distributing economic and political resources between the ethnic Bamar majority, which represents about two thirds of the 2015 Burmese population (approximately 52 million people), and a myriad of ethnic minority groups, has been the unresolved source of violent conflicts and disputes since independence. Continuing internal migration (whether forced or voluntary) and evolving ethnic identities have further complicated the country's ethnic landscape over the past couple of decades. On the one hand, Thein Sein's administration embarked on a new round of inter-ethnic peace parleys since 2011, which this chapter will investigate. On the other, religion, moral values, and the place and influence of "outsiders" in Myanmar's society have resurfaced as major themes of public debate, along with occasional and localized communal violence, particularly in 2012 and 2013. A handful of radical Buddhist associations have started to regain a voice in the public space and have imposed a debate on state involvement in religious affairs, in ways that would not have been possible a decade ago. Monastic organizations have re-emerged as powerful actors seeking to shape public values and influence policymakers, especially within the walls of the new parliament in Naypyitaw.

Finally, beside the ethno-religious conundrum, Chapter Six attempts to develop a realistic assessment of other long-term challenges and troubles that the Burmese polity and society will continue to face in the second half of the 2010s, and beyond. While most are not necessarily hindering democratization, all nonetheless pose considerable threats to the stability of the country and the long-term processes of reconciliation within a society at war with itself for so many decades. Prominent among these are the pervasive and multifaceted political and social clientelisms solidly entrenched in Burmese society; the oligarchical structuration and weaknesses of the national economy; and the influence of Myanmar's peculiar geography. The country, indeed, cannot avoid taking into consideration the impact that its geopolitical situation has long imposed on its domestic development. Lying between two emerging giants—China and India—as well as in a Southeast Asian region where politics remain volatile and democratic consolidation is an endlessly moving target, can be as much a boon as a burden, and offers a perfect incentive for the military to remain involved in broader policy roles.

1

MILITARY GUARDIANSHIP AND THE SEARCH FOR A PACTED TRANSITION

Transitional openings from military rule to civilian-led governance can take many forms. Military rulers can be forced out by a popular revolt—a common catalyst for regime change, as observed in various Arab countries in the early 2010s.[1] They can also be overthrown by, or in the aftermath of, a foreign intervention, as were Manuel Noriega in Panama (1989–90), Saddam Hussein in Iraq (2003) and Muammar Gaddafi in Libya (2011). There can also be a "planned withdrawal" of the old military nomenclature. The latter simply aims to control the transition and either to secure a safe post-junta retirement, or to mutate into a hybrid regime and assume new types of civilian function after the withdrawal of armed forces. Several African military rulers—in Zaire, Ethiopia and Nigeria—as well as the Brazilian and Chilean armed forces attempted to use this approach, more or less successfully, during the 1970s and 1980s.[2]

Myanmar offers a quasi-unique case in point. On the very day that the former SPDC prime minister, ex-general Thein Sein, was sworn in as the new president of the Union of Myanmar, a new hybrid regime took shape in Naypyitaw. On 30 March 2011, the Burmese "junta" was no more; but the passing of the torch was only the beginning of a new phase. Unlike the street revolutions of the Arab world and Eurasia, the powers that be in Myanmar were ousted neither by popular will, nor by an external intervention. Quite significantly, it was the junta leadership that was in a position, throughout the

1990s and 2000s, to calculate and control from above the pace and modalities of its own gradual breakdown.

Two propositions may help understand why. First, each time the Tatmadaw has initiated a disengagement from politics in its recent history, it has been in a position of political strength, be it after the eighteen-month-long "caretaker" administration of 1958–60, after the adoption of the 1974 constitution, or in the wake of the 2010 elections. Second, the "praetorian ethos" shaped and re-shaped by its own ideologues and top ranking officials since the 1950s has imposed on several generations of Burmese soldiers such a vision of their essential role in society and politics that praetorian and interventionist behaviors appear firmly entrenched in the mindset of past, present and would-be Tatmadaw officers.[3] Drawing on two sets of scholarship, on praetorianism and "pacted" democratic transitional processes, this chapter begins by exploring how and why the Burmese armed forces have operated since independence on a scale of "praetorian" intervention. The chapter shows that in initiating a transitional opening in 2011, the Burmese military leadership simply opted to move down a notch on this scale. Refusing to reach the bottom of the scale—which would imply a complete withdrawal from civilian and state affairs, a configuration unseen in Myanmar for almost sixty years, and probably never even envisioned by the military ideologues—the Tatmadaw has hitherto secured key policy prerogatives in a well-thought-out post-junta constitutional order for the 2010s, and possibly beyond.

Yet even if the military's partial withdrawal from politics in 2011 was, as in 1960 and 1974, carefully planned, an institutional and political pact was needed thereafter to pursue the initial transition "offered" by the Tatmadaw. As this chapter claims, one loose, incomplete and fragile "pact" was thus sought by a group of Burmese elites soon after the SPDC was disbanded in March 2011. Different sets of actors drawn from the old military nomenclature, the rejuvenated top brass of the armed forces, the historic pro-democracy opposition and a few leaders of Myanmar's many ethnic minorities indeed engaged in a form of dialogue. In doing so, they have attempted to reach a—quite limited, as we will argue—political settlement to allow consolidation of the country's liberal moment a few years after Senior General Than Shwe, who had ruled the country since 1992, finally relinquished power in March 2011. This was needed to at least "let the people breathe", as a former political prisoner underlined,[4] after two decades of blunt military dictatorship, and to open up a new phase of intra-elite political bargaining.

Moving Down on the Praetorian Scale: A Post-Junta Constitutional Order

In the discipline of comparative politics, social scientists have proposed various theoretical tools and analytical frameworks since the 1950s to understand the recurring intrusion of armed forces into a country's political, social and economic spheres, to describe their behavior once in power (or in a position to greatly influence it), and to map out the patterns of their subsequent disengagement, voluntary or forced, from the political and civilian realms. Beginning in the late 1950s, Samuel P. Huntington was one of the first to propose an interpretative framework of military modes of political intervention.[5] Morris Janowitz, Samuel Finer, Amos Perlmutter and Eric Nordlinger, among others, completed—and criticized—Huntington's work in the 1960s and 1970s.[6] In particular, Perlmutter and Nordlinger drew up a typology of a military's political role according to its degree of control over the political arena, government bodies and, more generally, over political decision-making.[7] Muthiah Alagappa has further developed their typology for the early 2000s.[8] To better grasp the Tatmadaw's grip on postcolonial Myanmar's policymaking, I will hereafter use their combined models, and base my argument on the differentiation between three main types of military intervention in politics: (1) the "arbitrator" or "moderator" type of armed forces, (2) the "guardian" or "participant-ruler", and (3) the "praetorian ruler".

In general, this body of scholarship claims that when the military positions itself in the political arena as an "arbitrator" (which Alagappa labels a "referee"),[9] it does not take part in the government but, rather, acts as a powerful professional force with a broad network of policy and economic influences, attempting recurrently to weigh in on the country's political scene. The arbitrator or moderator-type of military commonly seeks to act as a "mediator" within the political realm, strongly impacting on the formation of successive civilian governments. Through its often prestigious legacy, the second type of military institution, the "guardian" army (or "participant-ruler", for Alagappa),[10] often plays a more leading role, because it has established itself as a "protector" of the nation and its state institutions. It has also proved to be more effectively and regularly interventionist, either by repeatedly taking power for a limited period (a *coup d'état* to promptly "restore order"), or by laying claim to some of the legal instruments of political or legislative intervention. This is done in a sustainable way: reserved seats in parliament, legal parachuting of active officers into state governments and local administrations, etc. The third type, the "praetorian" ruler, is a military institution that directly assumes all governmental functions and occupies a position of force in prescribing a dictatorial type of political-military order, sometimes (but not always) accompanied by an ideological revolution in which civilian institutions are totally subordinated to an independent, yet clientelistic, political organization created by a corps of military officers—a "junta".

Thus, according to this literature, there is a spectrum of possible military intervention in politics, or various "levels of intervention"[11] by the armed forces. There is a "scale of praetorianism" that a military institution can go up or down, depending on its political ambitions and degree of involvement in state and civilian affairs, one end of this "scale" being a full retreat to the barracks and submission to civilian control, the other being full command of the state structure.[12] I would argue that since Myanmar won its independence from the British in 1948, the Tatmadaw has never ceased to go up, down and back up these various echelons of interventionism. James F. Guyot has preferred the metaphor of "praetorian cycles", rather than that of a "scale".[13] But his analysis conveys the very same idea of an extraordinarily resilient military interventionism—in one form or another—in postcolonial Myanmar.

A closer examination of the official Tatmadaw literature and propaganda, as well as public speeches made by successive high-ranking Burmese military leaders since the 1950s, reveals a striking paradox.[14] The Burmese officer corps never really presented itself as the "ruling class", but rather as an elite tasked with "guarding" the country's fragile post-independence institutions and protecting the nation's integrity whenever needed—including against internal forces. The Tatmadaw has therefore long considered itself—or at least has deliberately given the impression that it considers itself—as an actor in government and society with an exceptional rather than a permanent role. Intriguingly, as previously mentioned, each time the military seized power—in 1958, 1962 and 1988—it strived to underline the "transitional", and never the definitive, nature of its political interventions. It routinely justified the latter by citing the weakness, incompetence and corruption of the civilian government of the day, as well as the persistence of constantly renewed domestic and external threats. Thus, for the successive Burmese senior officer corps of the post-independence Tatmadaw, these repeated intrusions did not seem to reflect a systematic willingness to seize government institutions or to stand in for the state—although the facts obviously speak to the contrary. Indeed, between 1948 and 2015, the Tatmadaw exerted absolute control over Myanmar's state institutions for a total of thirty-six years (54%) and partial control for eighteen and a half years (27.5%), and was under very loose civilian control only for twelve and a half years (18.5%).

It is worth recalling the dynamics of the Tatmadaw's first direct political intervention, which was orchestrated in September 1958, ten years after independence. A month later, the national parliament, which was not dissolved by the military intervention, allowed General Ne Win, commander-in-chief of the Tatmadaw since 1949, to form a "caretaker" administration. This army-led government—a perfect example of a military's short-lived praetorian intrusion into state politics—lasted for a year and a half. The military hierarchy soon kept its initial promises to prepare and hold national elections, in February 1960. The party led by U Nu, who then regained his post as prime minister, won these legislative polls with a large margin. The Tatmadaw then promptly returned to its barracks as of April 1960.[15] At the time—in a Cold War context—the community of international observers saluted this "model" of transition by a military institution whose leaders, save a few, publicly asserted their disinterest in continuing to remain in control of the state.[16] What is more, the success of this 1958–60 praetorian interlude is still frequently cited by contemporary Burmese military ideologues.[17]

Nevertheless, the Tatmadaw was soon back in control after the coup d'état of 2 March 1962. In power once again, General Ne Win formed a Revolutionary Council composed only of high-ranking officers, who were all loyal to him. Unlike the caretaker government of 1958, this time the new "junta" gradually endeavored to transform the country's political and social landscape through a socialist "revolution" (*taw-hlan-ye-khit*) in which the Tatmadaw was to be the ideological spearhead.[18] In the late 1960s, however, the Ne Win-inspired Revolutionary Council in turn initiated its own gradual mutation. To prepare the Tatmadaw's withdrawal once again, Ne Win ordered a debate within the military as well as in the party he had created in 1962 (and which became the sole legal party two years later), the Burma Socialist Program Party (BSPP, or *lanzin pati*). A new constitutional order had to be established in which the military was only to be a distant arbitrator of the political domain and not the revolutionary mastermind it had become after 1962.[19] The "civilianization" of the second Ne Win military regime was thus codified by the country's second constitution, adopted by referendum in December 1973, which came into effect the following month.[20]

An autocrat from the ranks of the army, of which he remained commander-in-chief until 1972, Ne Win kept his distance from his active-duty officer corps and its internal rivalries during the 1970s and gradually favored the BSPP's civilian political structures, as well as its personnel, in order to govern. Thus, after twelve years of direct military administration under the auspices of the Tatmadaw (1962–74), the Burmese regime had evolved toward an autocratic civilian system that was only "moderated" by the military in the background. The Tatmadaw merely delegated the direct management of public affairs to the BSPP (whose ranks were filled with active and retired military officers), and above all to the figurehead, Ne Win.[21] Both the party and its unchallenged chairman have thereafter exerted a quasi-absolute sway over the unicameral parliamentary assembly (Pyithu Hluttaw) created by the 1974 constitution. For the second time, the Burmese armed forces handed power back to the civilian sphere in a transition that its high command, at the time unified under the aegis of Ne Win (who gave up his uniform to become the new civilian head of state), had designed on its own terms in the 1970s.

The third "transition", as experienced since 2011, seems to follow the same praetorian logic as those in 1960 and 1974. After taking back the reins of power in 1988, the Tatmadaw systematically tried to shape the ideal conditions for its gradual disengagement. Ne Win having resigned in July 1988, the coup d'état of 18 September 1988 propelled a new junta, the State Law and Order Restoration Council (SLORC), onto the center stage. General Saw Maung became its leader after a bloody crackdown on the August 1988 protest movement. Like his predecessors, Saw Maung insisted on the "transitional" nature of the new junta. The SLORC was indeed officially founded with the aim of pacifying the political scene shaken up by the pro-democracy uprising and, since 1987, by renewed ethnic rebellions in peripheral areas of the country. The mission it assigned itself, as a model interventionist and authoritarian "praetorian" ruler, was to restore order, allow for the drafting of a new constitution,[22] and thereby create the legal and political conditions for the army's eventual restitution of power to civilian authorities.

The SLORC rapidly presented six objectives and 104 principles that it considered non-negotiable for the launch of constitutional reforms and the pending transition to a so-called civilian regime, along the lines of what the constitution crafted in 1974 by Ne Win had planned for the Revolutionary Council, born in March 1962. A National Convention entrusted with drafting a third constitutional text was thus convened by the junta in January 1993. But it was suspended in 1996 after the main opposition party, Aung San Suu Kyi's National League for Democracy (NLD), walked out in November 1995, judging its discussions to be unashamedly undemocratic. In August 2003, the newly appointed SPDC prime minister, General Khin Nyunt, proposed a new initiative. He announced a seven-point "roadmap to discipline-flourishing democracy" that laid the groundwork for the transitional regime and the restoration of a parliamentary, democratic, and above all civilian republic of Myanmar.[23] The second National Convention was convened in May 2004 under the auspices of Lieutenant-General Thein Sein, at the time Secretary-1 of the SPDC. This represented steps one and two of the roadmap. After three years of centralized and top-down discussions, Thein Sein and the 1,000-odd delegates of the National Convention presented a constitutional text, skillfully drafted according to the objectives and principles initially formulated by the Tatmadaw in the early 1990s (step three). The text was adopted in May 2008 by referendum (step four), despite heated controversy surrounding the regime's strict supervision of the polls shortly after Cyclone Nargis struck the Irrawaddy delta and Yangon on 2 May.

In order to remain relevant, and thus influential, in the upcoming post-junta context, the Tatmadaw felt it needed to preserve the legal instruments that enabled it to intervene as a "guardian" in the political arena. The constitution of 2008 provided it with such instruments.[24] Thus, within the new government formed by the president of the Union, three ministers, their affiliated deputy ministers and the whole bureaucratic apparatus under the command of these ministries were to be appointed directly by the commander-in-chief of the armed forces (Articles 232b and 234b)—the ministries of defense, home affairs and border affairs. In March 2011, President Thein Sein thus welcomed to his cabinet Major-General Hla Min, Lieutenant-General Ko Ko—two former senior SPDC officials—and Lieutenant-General Thein Htay, a former leading administrator of the Tatmadaw's defence and arms industries.[25] All three were assisted by deputy ministers who also remained in uniform and had no constitutional obligation to retire from the armed forces in order to participate in the government.[26] Moreover, the 2008 constitution having envisaged a theoretical form of decentralization, the same reasoning can be found at the local level in each of the fourteen decentralized governments of the country's seven states and seven regions (Article 262a). Thus, fourteen ministers of security and/or border affairs were named directly by the supreme commander of the Tatmadaw in 2011, with no prior consultation with the elected chief ministers of these local governments—nor with the central government in Naypyitaw, much less the local parliamentarians themselves. Since 2011, all the ministers of security and border affairs have held the rank of colonel. Furthermore the 2008 Constitution allowed the Tatmadaw a quarter of all parliamentary seats in the country's new legislative bodies.

Finally, the 2008 constitution provided for the creation of a National Defense and Security Council (NDSC). Five of its eleven members are active military personnel: the commander-in-chief and his deputy, and the three Union-level "army-ministers" (Article 201). It seems that this council, the object of much speculation due to the degree of secrecy surrounding the tenor of its internal debates, met every week in the first months of its existence.[27] From then until the 2015 elections, it still convened regularly. Nearly all appointments of the most prominent state officials appear to require its approval.[28] It has also intended to play a centralizing role, enabling the hierarchy of the active-duty Tatmadaw—under Senior-General Min Aung Hlaing since 2011—to maintain a permanent dialogue with the executive and legislative bodies of the first post-junta transitional regime led by the two speakers of the Union parliament and Thein Sein's presidential entourage.

It therefore took the SLORC-SPDC establishment some twenty-three years to initiate the long-promised transitional process to a quasi-civilian administration in 2011. After the adoption of a new constitution (step four of the roadmap), national and local elections had to be held (step five—in August 2010, elections were set for 7 November 2010) and a national parliament convened (step six—the parliament's gates opened on 30 January 2011), and a government led by a newly-elected president of the Union had to be formed out of the parliamentary elections before the successor regime could emerge (the seventh and last step). So it was not until March 2011 that the last two survivors of the 1988 coup d'état, Senior-General Than Shwe and Vice Senior-General Maung Aye,[29] withdrew from public life. But, as in 1960 and in 1974, it was the armed forces that "granted" the withdrawal, when—and only when—its leadership deemed that sociopolitical and legal conditions had been met. For the military hierarchy, which had learned from General Ne Win's era, the transition had to be controlled from the outset, through its own supervision of the immediate transitory regime that would succeed the SPDC.

Thus, after being a "moderator" of the political arena in the 1950s, the Tatmadaw became the "guardian" of order from 1958 to 1960, and then a "praetorian" absolutist ruler after the revolutionary coup of 1962, when it proved capable of imposing a murky xenophobic and socialistic ideology meant to transform society and its people. It then launched into a new process of "civilianization" in the early 1970s, asserting itself as more paternalistic and reverting to "guardianship" of the socialist revolution. Then, suddenly, the Tatmadaw became "praetorian" again, and even dictatorial, after the 1988 coup, when it regained power through a junta (SLORC-SPDC), taking control of all the country's institutions. Since 2011, it has gone back down a notch on the scale of praetorianism and once again sees itself as a "guardian" of the new institutions it has attempted to forge since 1993, arguing that this is perfectly consistent with its rhetoric and the responsible image it wants to project—an image that has, however, been radically damaged by over two decades of violent dictatorship. Nonetheless, the Tatmadaw evidently aims to remain relevant in the new political order shaped after 2011. It does not yet seem ready—or even willing—to join the other end of the praetorian spectrum and become a mere mediator on the political scene, far less an institution entirely subject to civilian and democratic control, as in all firmly consolidated Western, Indian or Japanese democracies, for instance. This doesn't ever seem to have been envisioned in the commanding ranks of the military sphere.

Intra-Elite Negotiation

O'Donnell and Schmitter's suggestion (1986) seems particularly accurate when considering Myanmar today: that the political process underway since the November 2010 general elections is a transition "toward an uncertain 'something else'. That 'something' can be the instauration of a political democracy, or the restoration of a new, and possibly more severe, form of authoritarian rule. The outcome can also simply be confusion".[30] The self-disbanding of the SPDC "junta" in March 2011 was a key moment in a process of institutional change long promised by the Burmese military leadership. After two decades of direct military rule following the 1988 coup d'état, this process opened new space in which an evolutionary political process could finally unfold. Though the outcome of that incremental process—still in its very early stages in the mid-2010s—remains frustratingly unknown, and its trajectory hedged with uncertainty, the process itself has at last begun.

During the first phase of the post-SPDC transition, bracketed by the two elections of November 2010 and November 2015, what could have been done and negotiated for post-junta rule? How should the new civil-military relations be defined in post-junta Myanmar, knowing that the Tatmadaw had no intention to withdraw fully from national politics? What kind of political settlement could be reached, and between whom, at the turn of the 2010s? Could there be a pluralist and inclusive form of post-military bargaining, or would the political arrangement merely be discussed among a highly exclusive group of Burmese political and army-driven elites and social actors compliant with the 2008 constitutional order? Would the settlement be the outcome of a broad compromise or an imposition from and for the leadership above? How would the "transit regime" be shaped and function after the official disbanding of the junta in March 2011? Would it survive the tentatively "pacted" transition beyond the second electoral exercise proposed in November 2015?

As demonstrated above, the transitional opening in Myanmar was made possible by the decision of the armed forces to dissolve the SPDC in 2011 and start their partial disengagement from day-to-day politics, as codified by the 2008 constitution. Nevertheless, for the process to continue beyond this (quite limited) military withdrawal, Myanmar's new ruling elites emerging from the old SPDC nomenclature needed to find other legitimate interlocutors with whom they could play by the constitution's new set of political and institutional rules. As O'Donnell and Schmitter have argued, if a process of transitional change is to be considered meaningful, the opening up of an authoritarian or military regime must be met with concomitant developments in the opposition camp.[31] Thus one needs to find one or several willing partners with whom to negotiate the continued transitional process under a post-authoritarian "transit regime". This is the "pacted transition" discussed in the Introduction of this book, between the old nomenclature and a handful of newly empowered interlocutors outside the old authoritarian regime.[32] Without it, the old rule would simply continue under new political structures. This pact—unlike other modes of transition such as popular revolutions, the collapse of an autocratic government through internal splits, or military defeat due to an external intervention—is construed as the "explicit, but not always publicly explicated or justified, agreement among a select set of actors which seek to define (or better, redefine) the rules governing the exercise of power on the basis of mutual guarantees".[33]

The unfolding of a "pacted" transition requires a political and institutional compromise between contending elites (or "players", for Linz and Stepan)[34] who must bargain over policymaking and power-sharing in the transitory political system. However, as discussed, the process of change remains highly elite-ascendant. It comes from elements within the *ancien régime* (the 'pragmatics' or the 'soft-liners'), but is pursued thanks to the co-optation of essential actors external to the outgoing regime—usually historical opponents—but also willing to play the same game.[35] Pacts can nonetheless be bargained through undemocratic means, as Frances Hagopian has asserted, using post-authoritarian Brazil as a key example. An oligarchic elite can bring together a handful of members of the old authoritarian regime with only a few of their erstwhile opponents, those with whom they feel they can dialogue and establish a non-competitive political system, to the exclusion of all other sets of potential players or actors.[36] A form of semi-authoritarian or semi-democratic regime can then emerge. But pacted transitions have proved relatively successful in several contexts: amongst others, Post-Franco Spain, post-communist Poland and Hungary and post-Pinochet Chile. Others, however, have dragged on and proved a strong barrier to further democratization, as observed in post-Soviet Russia or Bolivarian Venezuela. The initially negotiated political settlement, intended as only "temporary", quite often becomes "permanent". The risk is that post-authoritarian elites, "locked in[to]" new privileges acquired directly after the transition, will not choose to extend the initial pact beyond their clientelistic entourage, and thus will fail to further redistribute power and engage in broader democratization.[37]

In Myanmar, a "pacted transition" has long been encouraged by foreign and domestic experts alike. Many long-standing observers of the country have argued that only a compromise among at least three core Burmese sociopolitical forces could put an end to the post-1988 exclusively military-led regime.[38] These three main sets of actors are as follows: first, the ruling military establishment more or less in power since the early 1960s; second, the democratic opposition shaped after 1988 around the iconic figure of Aung San Suu Kyi; and third, the cohorts of Myanmar's politicized, if not insurgent, non-Bamar ethnic communities. Yet, environmental conditions were not met for a full tripartite dialogue until the early 2010s. The pact could only be negotiated once the Tatmadaw unilaterally initiated its withdrawal from day-to-day state politics after the 2010 general elections and the appointment of Senior-General Than Shwe's successor as supreme head of the armed forces in March 2011. In the year following the disbanding of the SPDC, three major developments indicated that both the new Tatmadaw leadership and elements of the old SPDC regime overseeing the ongoing transition were inclined to strike some sort of a deal.

The first development was the return of Aung San Suu Kyi to the forefront of politics after her release from house arrest in November 2010. Barred from contesting elections that she had, in any case, decided to boycott, she was freed just a week after the polls were held and their results announced, on 13 November 2010. She was subsequently allowed to consult and debate with her party colleagues and supporters during the first half of 2011. This unfolded almost a decade since she had last had the opportunity to freely discuss policy with her entourage or with foreigners. Under her supervision, the NLD then produced its first official statement on international sanctions against Myanmar, in February 2011.[39] In July 2011, Aung San Suu Kyi met for the ninth time with ex-major general Aung Kyi, a minister in both the old SPDC and the new government who had been assigned to liaise with her in the aftermath of the 2007 Sangha revolt. For the first time, a feeling of optimism was palpable as Aung Kyi and Aung San Suu Kyi offered a joint press briefing.[40]

A month later, the NLD leader was brought to Naypyitaw to have a one-on-one meeting with President Thein Sein. The official picture of the meeting, showing a portrait in the background of Aung San, hero of the nation and father of Aung San Suu Kyi, best epitomized the negotiated pact underway. During the SLORC/SPDC's heyday, images and allusions to Aung San were kept minimal—his face was even withdrawn from all the country's banknotes and stamps. Symbolically re-introducing both the father and the daughter in August 2011 thus conveyed a clear message.[41] After that strategic meeting in Naypyitaw, it was considered that the opportune moment had arisen to establish a healthy collaboration between the pro-democracy opposition's leading figure and the new presidency. As Burmese academic-turned-policy-advisor Kyaw Yin Hlaing has underscored, Aung San Suu Kyi still has enormous—even irrational—influence over a substantial majority of the Burmese people as well as an international community still much in awe of her.[42] Having her on board soon after the start of the transition, then, was an absolute condition for the continuation of the process.

The second major element that helped foster a political compromise at the very top level was the holding of by-elections in April 2012. In November 2011, Thein Sein's government amended the political party registration law, paving the way for the National League for Democracy to re-establish itself as a legal party. Having boycotted the 2010 elections, the NLD hadn't been able to register, and had subsequently been considered an "unlawful association" for more than a year.[43] Aung San Suu Kyi herself went to Naypyitaw to re-register her party with the Union Election Commission in November of that year.[44] Forty-odd legislators elected in 2010 to the Union parliament had been appointed to local and national ministerial positions by Thein Sein; their seats in both chambers of the Union legislature had thus remained vacant since early 2011.[45] This provided Thein Sein's administration with an opportunity to hold crucial by-elections, and so bring the NLD back to the fore. Under the impulse of Aung San Suu Kyi herself, this time around, the party's central executive committee opted to participate in the polls.[46] These by-elections—provided their organization was free and fair—would give the NLD a unique chance at another triumphant endorsement by the Burmese people, following on from the NLD's overwhelming victory in the 1990 polls, subsequently annuled. In the event, the by-elections held on 1 April 2012 proved remarkably free, if not fair. The NLD's landslide victory—forty-three of forty-five contested seats—was euphorically praised by the international community. It rekindled the latter's perceptions about the value of the transitional process in play in Myanmar since the far less acclaimed legislative elections of 2010.[47]

Lastly, in parallel with the political bargaining at work among Bamar-dominated political and military elites, a third condition was deemed vital to the success of the "pacted" transition. In fact, almost all observers of Burmese postcolonial affairs concur: to foster a stable, peaceful and developed Myanmar, its leaders need to find an appropriate degree of cooperation and understanding between the country's numerically and politically dominant ethnic group (the Bamars, of whom the NLD and the military establishment are the most visible figures) and all the other ethnic minorities resident in Myanmar under the internationally recognized boundaries of 1948. A new round of peace talks between the Bamar-led political center in Naypyitaw and a myriad of peripheral ethnic groups was thus initiated by the presidential entourage in late 2011. President Thein Sein charged a former military intelligence officer and railroad minister, ex-Major General Aung Min, with conducting negotiations between his government and the ethnic communities still engaged in armed struggle against the Tatmadaw.

As was the case with the ceasefire policies promoted by former Lieutenant-General Khin Nyunt between 1989 and 1993, these new initiatives met with rapid, and surprising, success. Several historic ceasefire agreements were concluded by Naypyitaw, including with General Saw Mutu Sae Poe's Karen National Union (KNU), General Yawd Serk's Shan State Army-South (SSA-S), and even the All Burma Students' Democratic Front (ABSDF), a transnational outfit formed in the aftermath of the 1988 uprising. None of these three had entered into any substantial military truce since they took up arms years, if not decades, ago.[48] However, beyond the conclusion of "cease-fires"—a policy objective routinely pursued by the Tatmadaw since the late 1950s—further inter-ethnic political dialogue, promised by the government purportedly to shape a Union based on federal and democratic principles, has not materialized. Furthermore, since 2011 not all ethnic communities engaged in an enduring struggle for recognition with Myanmar's successive postcolonial central authorities have chosen the path of dialogue. Indeed, as Chapter Five will further detail, several groups have openly rejected any form of political pact with a post-SPDC administration they've found extremely challenging to deal with.[49] Prominent among these are the Kachin Independence Organization (KIO), which rebooted its armed struggle against the Tatmadaw in June 2011, the ethnic Kokang militia stationed in the Sino-Burmese borderlands, and the Ta'ang National Liberation Army (TNLA), a rebel outfit drawn from the Palaung ethnic community in northern Shan State. The diverse Muslim leaderships of the country were also neglected. The ethnic dimension of Myanmar's much sought-after "elite pact" of the early 2010s therefore appeared the weakest of the three core conditions.

For some foreign thinkers, including democratic-transition pundit Larry Diamond, there was in fact no "pact" of any sort agreed by the Burmese elites in 2011. What was then bargained in Myanmar soon after the retirement of Senior-General Than Shwe did not resemble the kind of highly sophisticated political agreement needed to consolidate a fragile democratic transition.[50] If history is indeed any guide, Myanmar does not appear ready for the prompt negotiation of a complex set of institutional pacts among its dominant political actors. Compromises have seldom been reached since civil war erupted in the country in 1947, and whenever a pact has been sealed, it has too often, and too quickly, been unsealed, if not consigned to oblivion. For instance, the Panglong Agreement, a promising inter-ethnic pact agreed in February 1947, did not survive General Aung San's assassination six months later. The SLORC's and later SPDC's repeated promises of meaningful dialogue with the opposition after Aung San Suu Kyi's successive releases from house arrest in 1995 and 2002 were never fulfilled with substantial changes. Similarly, the late 1980s and early 1990s ceasefire agreements, concluded with ethnic armed groups by General Khin Nyunt's military intelligence services, were not followed by meaningful talks on federalism, resources or power-sharing. Since Ne Win's era, the consolidation of "ceasefire pacts" negotiated early on among Burmese elites seems to have been continually and indefinitely deferred.

Nevertheless, as Mary Callahan has argued, the elite-level discussions held in 2011, though not fully inclusive, helped to frame a kind of "loose settlement" for a "post-junta, constitutional" Myanmar to emerge.[51] A tentative settlement to move forward and play the political game according to the 2008 constitution was effectively brokered, and further confirmed when the by-elections and the ethnic peace talks both proved relatively successful in 2012. The "pact" hitherto negotiated, though, has remained without clear-cut parameters. Most of its contents have remained unknown to outsiders—including the key potential players at state or local level, deliberately sidelined by the dominant negotiators of the pact. As a matter of fact, though, the scholarship on transitional politics tells us that such is the prevailing logic of most political deals negotiated by a society's well-established and highly oligarchical political elites.[52]

The motivation behind elements of the old Burmese junta initiating a new dialogue in 2011—one intended to be more meaningful than the many conversations with Aung San Suu Kyi promoted by Than Shwe, his deputy Maung Aye and Khin Nyunt in the late 1990s and early 2000s—may have many underlying determinants. Most remain shrouded in mystery. One of the key determinants, though, may have been the increasing influence of certain Burmese individuals, intellectuals, peripheral politicians and dissidents in exile—all civilians standing outside Myanmar's inner core of army-centered power and military-led policymaking networks, yet influential enough to be heard by these networks. Sons and daughters of former prominent Burmese leaders, renowned prisoners of conscience released in the course of the 2000s, leaders of ethnic communities in exile and a handful of well-connected Burmese academics and business people progressively outlined new ideas and opinions about a "negotiated" transition during the 2000s, long before the transition started.[53] Transnational militant groups lambasted many of these figures for their views, which broke with the simplistic portrayal of a bipolar struggle between the military-led Burmese powers and the pro-democracy movement personified by Aung San Suu Kyi. Among others, this movement came to be known as a "Third Force" in the making, yet a movement still widely criticized for being brazenly subcontracted by the ruling elite.

Among these "Third Force" personalities, Nay Win Maung held particular influence until his death in January 2012. Born into a military family, he was the founder of *Living Color Magazine* and editor of *The Voice*, a popular newspaper, in which he managed to distil his civil-society-focused activism for several years. In 2006, together with Hla Maung Shwe, Tin Maung Thann and a few other members of the Burmese intelligentsia, he started Myanmar Egress, a non-profit organization that has acted as both a policy think-tank and an educational center.[54] Myanmar Egress' leadership, and some other high-profile Burmese militants—including Ma Thanegi, a former personal aide to Aung San Suu Kyi—have emerged as increasingly influential policy thinkers in the aftermath of the repression of the 2007 Sangha demonstration. In particular, in the midst of the 2008 constitutional referendum campaign, they openly promoted a "yes" vote for the new constitution drafted by the SPDC. This campaign was followed a year later by a second, urging the Burmese elites and ordinary people to support the electoral process scheduled for 2010—despite its acknowledged and obvious flaws, and its full control by the SPDC.

This prompted intense internal debate inside the country in the late 2000s, to the point of several veteran NLD politicians withdrawing from the party—

at a time when Aung San Suu Kyi was under house arrest, and almost incommunicado—to form new movements willing to contest the 2010 elections. Among them were the National Democratic Force (NDF) formed by Khin Maung Swe and Thein Nyunt, two long-standing pillars of the NLD,[55] as well as the Democratic Party-Myanmar (DP-M), led by Thu Wai, a veteran politician who started his career in the 1950s as the personal secretary of Deputy Prime Minister Kyaw Nyein.[56] Khin Zaw Win, a former political prisoner freed in 2005, also spearheaded the movement encouraging broader popular participation and support of a pacted transition, and therefore participation in the 2010 polls "offered" by the SPDC.[57] He had already, in a 2007 paper, sought to remind the international community that there were "other democrats" in Myanmar—read "beside Aung San Suu Kyi"—all of whom were willing to redefine and extend rule over the potential democratization process beyond the NLD opposition and its iconic leader.[58] His views have been met with strong hostility, especially, of course, in the NLD ranks.[59]

The US-born grandson of U Thant, former secretary general of the United Nations (1961–71), also belongs to this highly educated, renowned and well-connected Burmese elite increasingly attempting to offer the international scene a different voice on Burmese affairs. Educated at Harvard and Cambridge, Thant Myint-U has worked for the UN and authored several acclaimed books on his country of origin. He too has long defended the idea of a necessarily incremental transition from military rule.[60] Back in Yangon since 2011, he has led a preservation-focused organization (the Yangon Heritage Trust) while acting as a key policy advisor to the government of President Thein Sein.

Among the high-profile Burmese dissidents and former student leaders who fled Myanmar for Thailand or various Western countries in the years following the 1988 coup, only a few have advocated another way forward.[61] Unsurprisingly, several have returned to Myanmar after two decades in exile. These include Aung Naing Oo, a former ABSDF member, and Nyo Ohn Myint (nephew of ex-general Tin Oo, a prominent military associate of Ne Win); both have joined the Myanmar Peace Center (MPC).[62] Zaw Oo, a former director of the Washington-based Burma Fund, and Bo Kyaw Nyein, the son of ex-AFPFL minister Kyaw Nyein (1915–86), also returned to Yangon.[63] Many have since been accused of cozying up to the post-SPDC ruling elites, and of having opportunistically enjoyed the financial largesse of an international community willing, from 2011, to pour millions of dollars into the country.[64] Most have joined President Thein Sein's more or less close entourage of policy advisors.

Thus, remarkably, of the high-profile democratic opponents and student leaders who have returned to Yangon since 2011, or been freed from jail after 2012, very few—if any—have joined the ranks of the NLD to serve and advise Aung San Suu Kyi.[65]

Although less numerous, a handful of high-profile leaders drawn from Myanmar's various ethnic minorities have also proved influential. Harn Yawnghwe, descendant of a Shan royal family and the son of Myanmar's first president and later speaker of the upper house, Sao Shwe Thaike, has used the Euro-Burma Office he created in Brussels in 1997 to promote whatever democratization processes can be encouraged inside his native country. Lian H. Sakhong, an exiled Chin activist and former member of the outlawed Chin National Front (CNF) has chaired the Ethnic Nationalities Council (ENC). Both have often opted for academic venues to promote their views on a "pacted", yet sustainable, national reconciliation process.[66] They were to play a major liaising role between Thein Sein's government and a dozen ethnic armed groups after 2011. Naw Zipporah Sein, daughter of the late general Tamla Baw, who was chair of the KNU, has lead several rounds of discussion between the presidential team of Aung Min and the historic Karen movements she has represented as vice-chair since 2012. Other key leaders drawn from Myanmar's burgeoning ethnic-based civil society have also facilitated the 2011–15 peace parleys. To give one example, Ja Nan Lahtaw, head of the Shalom Foundation and daughter of a Kachin pastor, Saboi Jum, has also been leading peace talks between the Kachin rebels and the Burmese military establishment since 1980.[67]

All of these Burmese academics, veteran politicians, former student leaders, scions of Burmese personalities and dissidents in exile have, throughout the 2000s, instilled new ideas among the ruling military elites, and gradually strengthened the probability and feasibility of a "pacted transition". The impact of their opinions, although much debated, increased after the 2007 Sangha revolt and the tragic passage of Cyclone Nargis in May 2008. New reflections about a negotiated solution emerged at the turn of the 2010s in order to pave the way for what Matthew Mullen has labeled "reconstructive politics" in a post-junta Myanmar.[68] At the same time, these new elite-driven agendas were highly criticized, in particular by dominant Burmese pro-democracy forces, both inside and outside the country. The most prominent actors of this so-called "Third Force" were commonly accused of colluding with the military regime itself, and of neglecting the suffering of the Burmese people—especially the ethnic and religious minorities—and the many struggles and sacrifices of historic political opponents such as Aung San Suu Kyi.[69] Regardless, the "Third Force" has participated in the shaping of the "environmental conditions" necessary to the bargaining of a loose "pact" once the SPDC was disbanded in 2011.

After the retirement of Senior-General Than Shwe—a *sine qua non* condition for catalyzing "change" in post-junta Myanmar—a pacted solution could be worked on among various, though not all, Burmese elite groups. A handful of leading Bamar and ethnic-minority players agreed to further the opening of March 2011 and work on an innovative settlement. This helped to smooth the 2011–15 transitional process, and allowed the doors at last to be opened after years of direct military rule. A sense of *glasnost* was palpable in the subsequent months of the negotiated pact, as the following chapters will highlight. The behind-the-scenes negotiations seemingly led by Aung San Suu Kyi soon after her landslide victory in the 2015 elections have also indicated that the very same political and military elites are attempting to take the transitional process beyond the electoral rout of the pro-military Union Solidarity and Development Party (USDP). Within two months of the November 2015 polls, almost no electoral complaints had been filed by defeated candidates, several face-to-face meetings had been set up between Aung San Suu Kyi and the Tatmadaw commander-in-chief, Senior-General Min Aung Hlaing, and the NLD had reached out to several tycoons and ethnic strongmen of nefarious reputation.[70]

There is no guarantee, though, that the transition as it was tentatively "pacted" in 2011–12 will move beyond the initial agreements and survive in the post-2015-election landscape. The heightened tensions and political shenanigans observed on the stately avenues of Naypyitaw during the buildup to the polls have shown how fragile dialogue and compromises can be in Myanmar. Aung San Suu Kyi herself has, for instance, been reluctant to endorse the way inter-ethnic peace parleys have been carried out since 2011 by the presidential team and armed forces delegates. She even refused to attend the much-hyped signing ceremony of the National Ceasefire Agreement proposed by Thein Sein on 15 October 2015.[71] A consolidation of the transition beyond the NLD's 2015 electoral victory will surely need, in the near future, a series of other strategic "pacts" among a broader spectrum of Myanmar's contending elites.

Furthermore, as in many other intra-elite pacts observed across the world in the past, many Burmese actors and potential players were manifestly sidelined as early as 2011. Others were excluded by the NLD's crushing victory in the 2015 polls. Among the ethnic and religious minorities, the Christian-dominated Kachins have clearly been neglected, despite the crucial role played by a few prominent Kachin NGO leaders based in Yangon and a handful of Kachin parliamentarians in Naypyitaw. Since the June 2011 resurgence of open war between the Tatmadaw and the Kachin Independence Army (KIA, the armed branch of the KIO), political dialogue has been at a stalemate between a resurgent KIA and the new Burmese central authorities. The constitutional rule imposed after 2008 has also long been strongly critized by various Shan leaders, such as Hkun Htun Oo, head of the Shan Nationalities League for Democracy (SNLD), which, like the NLD, won a sweeping electoral victory in 1990 and re-entered parliament after the 2015 elections. Hkun Htun Oo, himself a former political prisoner released in 2012, has proved reluctant to break with the past and negotiate a compromise with the still Bamar-dominated military elites.[72] Lastly, the country's various Muslim leaders have also been completely left out of the transitional picture since 2011. A representative of the United National Development Party, registered with the Union Election Commission since January 2013, recently deplored the fact that Myanmar's Muslim communities have seldom been consulted by the post-2011 government and the major political parties, not to mention Aung San Suu Kyi herself.[73] Thus, if emboldened policy actors sidelined after 2011 do emerge as strong contenders in the "transition" as pacted between 2011 and 2015, or in post-2015 politics as defined by the victorious NLD, the "pact" may not last long in its initial form. A broader and more inclusive political settlement will soon be needed.

2

THE BROADENING OF SOCIOPOLITICAL SPACES

The dynamics of a transition, even a top-down one from authoritarian rule to "something else", are not just a matter of elite-driven individual initiatives. According to transitologists, mass-level forces and civil societies also commonly play a significant role.[1] The new social and political environment that emerged under Thein Sein's presidency after 2011 appeared to have nurtured an unprecedented level of optimism among many Burmese people throughout the country, or at least in its most urbanized centers. As Khin Zaw Win, who now leads a policy and capacity-building organization in Yangon, wrote in 2013, "it is like a breath of fresh air after being cooped up in the confines of dictatorship for nearly half a century".[2] Although not as transformative or even as revolutionary as many would have wished, the transitional opening was accompanied from late 2011 onwards by greater freedoms and the rediscovery of a limited set of civil liberties. A bold optimism has been clearly palpable in Yangon, Mandalay and Naypyitaw—though far less so in remote rural areas or ethnic-dominated peripheries. Nevertheless, in November 2015, this "breath of fresh air" was eventually, and resoundingly, epitomized by Burmese voters' freedom to reject the incumbent Union Solidarity and Development Party (USDP) leadership in the second post-junta legislative polls.

Far from being a done deal when initiated, the post-junta regime—Thein Sein's government, seconded by a resurgent parliament under the leadership of two ex-generals between 2011 and 2015—has gradually allowed the scope of collective action to expand in the early 2010s. Dissent has once again become tolerated, public contention permissible; newly legalized political parties have extended their activities and mobilization, and state censorship has been considerably eased. These decisions were meant to build confidence among ordinary Burmese people and non-military elite circles, but also to restore comity with the world after two decades of isolation imposed by the West. This chapter highlights the sudden broadening of Myanmar's political and social space in the first half of the 2010s, and grapples with the new questions and controversies that have subsequently emerged. Indeed, with the expansion of the public sphere, not only have opposition forces been revived, but new types of political dissent and contention have increasingly challenged the post-junta state of affairs, social cohesion and peaceful democratization. These have been increasingly visible in the build-up to the 2015 elections, and include new forms of radicalism. Their emergence, enabled by the "pacted" transition, now threatens that very transition as it was conceived by a handful of elites in 2011–12.

Dissent (Re)tolerated

Only too logically, following two decades of broken promises of democracy, the regime change in March 2011 aroused little more than modest enthusiasm among activists, academics and the international policy community. Yet, the reforms undertaken by the new executive and legislative branches after 2011 were a clear attempt to wear down what was considered the "old regime", the junta that ruled with an iron fist for twenty-three years. Indeed, it is remarkably surprising to hear key Burmese officials of the post-2011 administration, most of whom held high-ranking positions under the SLORC-SPDC, evoke a defunct "Tatmadaw government" when referring to the *ancien régime* of 1988–2011.[3] In so doing, these senior officials have unmistakably sought to clearly distinguish the "new", "different" post-military administration that emerged after 2011, although many of these "new" leaders were already prominent actors of the "old" nomenclature. But, Naypyitaw's new state leadership seemingly professes, *urbi et orbi*, that the old days of direct military rule are over. In that respect, it has had to publicly embrace—and effectively implement—new policies, in order to break with past behaviors and assert itself as an essential driver of change.

While the military junta had long constrained criticism and seldom tolerated any public dissent,[4] Thein Sein's government skillfully opted for resolutely progressive policy measures after 2011. The first to be agreed upon were those aimed at liberalizing the public sphere and allowing expansion of public debate. For instance, control over the Internet soon slackened after Thein Sein took power. From late 2011, the once dreaded firewall that forced the occasional foreign visitor to look for proxy websites allowing a bypassed access to Hotmail, *Le Monde*, *The New York Times* or the BBC News web services began to be lowered. By mid-2012, access to the World Wide Web was almost guaranteed, nationwide. Myanmar's youngsters could start enjoying access, without much restriction, to Gmail and Facebook, while Burmese exile and immigrant communities around the world rejoiced at the almost unrestricted use of Skype, Gtalk and later on Viber.[5] Many uprooted Burmese families were, in a sense, re-connected through the web. Activist websites previously denounced by SPDC propaganda as mere "destructive elements" releasing a "skyful of lies", such as Voice of America, Radio Free Asia, The Irrawaddy Magazine or Mizzima, an India-based Burmese news agency, rapidly became available.[6] Even Human Rights Watch and Amnesty International reports could be accessed and easily downloaded from within Myanmar—in contrast with China and Singapore.

In 2014, two global telecom companies, Qatar's Ooredoo and Norway's Telenor, were allowed to start rolling out modern equipment to wire up the country, wherever authorized.[7] Wifi is now even developing with no form of prior control in the country's major urban and tourist centers. In early 2015, it was estimated that 4.5 million Burmese had opened a Facebook account.[8] Only on a few occasions, such as when localized communal riots erupted in June 2012 and March and July 2013, have the central authorities opted for a complete shutdown of Internet services, rather than a more complex filtered monitoring. Firewall configurations and techniques are apparently still far from being mastered by Myanmar's surveillance apparatus. Rather than limited access to the Net, it seems, ironically, that the major problem Myanmar faces today—and it is a major one for the population, foreign investors and occasional tourists alike—remains the erratic supply of electrical current throughout the country.

Furthermore, the state censorship board was officially dissolved in September 2012. A year later, the government started issuing licenses to private dailies. Authors, whether journalists, writers, or children's book publishers, were thereafter no longer required to submit page proofs in advance to the censorship board, long called the Press Scrutiny and Registration Division.[9] Private media has since been burgeoning, despite the persistence of some sort of self-censorship among journalists, particularly local ones; occasional crackdowns by the military intelligence (still discreetly active); and a serious lack of skills due to many years of inadequate training. Exiled opposition publications have been authorized, and several outspoken Burmese journalists and other former dissidents have returned to Yangon. The Mizzima News group founded by Soe Myint, a student activist who hijacked a plane to Calcutta in 1990 and remained a refugee in India for two decades, now puts out a weekly magazine. *The Myanmar Times*, long criticized by transnational activists for being too loyal to General Khin Nyunt's former military intelligence services (which actually have long owned the paper),[10] has become a spearhead of this new-found assurance in local media. Vitriolic editorials (especially in the English-language version), portraits of historic opposition figures, investigations into cases of corruption and nepotism and reports on sensitive issues now fill its columns each week.[11]

Still, old habits die hard. When a *Myanmar Times* cartoonist depicts the Tatmadaw in rather an unpleasant manner; when two editors at the *Myanmar Post* mock a military-appointed legislator's allegedly low level of educational achievement; when peace activists joke about the Tatmadaw commander-in-chief; when a Burmese freelancer posts a satirical Facebook message openly criticizing the military past of President Thein Sein, the judiciary—or rather, the military itself—strikes quickly, and often pitilessly.[12] A series of lawsuits against journalists initiated in 2014 has given the world, and the local crowd of reporters, the impression that a new wave of media restriction is emerging after only a couple of years of bold optimism.[13] Also, the rapid post-2011 liberalization has raised new questions about the independence of local media and the radio scene. Many of Myanmar's emerging magazines and private dailies, but also local FM radio stations, have increasingly appeared to fall under the financial control of only a handful of Burmese individuals or conglomerates—many allegedly linked to the powers that be, as recent reports have underlined.[14]

Yet, freedom of speech no longer seemed an empty word after years of blunt censorship. In just four years (2011–14), Myanmar has jumped from 174 to 145 in the rank of the Reporters Without Borders World Press Freedom Index.[15] Long-time observers with whom I have discussed Burmese affairs, such as Robert Taylor, Andrew Selth or David Steinberg, have all noticed that open political discussions have once again become the norm—in particular in urban areas in the center of the country. Street teashop afficionados can now sit and publicly pronounce the names of their state leaders, including that of "The Lady", with far less caution than before—at least, in my experience since I first set foot in Myanmar in the early 2000s. Beyond street talk, the Internet and social media have also become crucial instruments for journalists, politicians and engaged citizens alike. Even the Tatmadaw—a first since Khin Nyunt's era in the 1990s—has appointed three high-ranking army and navy officers to act as spokespersons in charge of liaising with the media and the wider civilian scene, locally and internationally: Major-General Aung Ye Win, Commodore Aung Thaw and Brigadier-General Soe Naing Oo.[16] Commodore Aung Thaw, a high-ranking navy officer (equivalent to a one-star general), had already been appointed spokesman for the ministry of defense a year earlier.[17]

Moreover, in October 2011, the newly formed Union parliament authorized the formation of trade unions, long outlawed, and legalized the right to strike. In December of the same year, a bill was passed establishing regulations for street protests and public rallies.[18] Civil society and the political class scarcely delayed in testing the new authorities' threshold of tolerance. Throughout 2012, a number of public demonstrations were held, often without prior permission from the authorities (despite this being an essential criterion for legality).[19] At first spontaneous, these demonstrations have gradually become better organized, especially those denouncing the ongoing spoliation of farmland by the armed forces or the large conglomerates in its nexus. Many public expressions of anger, frustration and determination have lambasted damages from mineral exploitation in the country's northern and peripheral areas, unregulated labor in state-owned or even private factories, and the unreliability of the public electrical grid, in ways previously unthinkable, especially since the crackdown on the Sangha insurgency of late 2007. The Letpadaung mining project near the city of Monywa (to the west of Mandalay), the Chinese-funded Myitsone dam in northern Kachin State or the multi-billion-dollar deep water port development project in Dawei, close to the Thai border in the south, have all offered new political opportunities for Burmese citizens, transnational actors and local civil society groups to coalesce and openly mobilize.[20]

In 2012 and 2013, few of these street demonstrations were brutally repressed by the police or anti-riot forces, in contrast with the norm in the not-so-distant past—during the "Saffron Revolution" of September 2007, for instance. This doesn't mean that Myanmar's security apparatus now systematically handles all street protests and riots with restraint, calm and conciliation—far from it. The shocking photographs of beaten students and the well-documented violence observed during the crackdown on popular demonstrations in Yangon and Letpadan in March 2015 have illustrated how the

Myanmar Police Forces and their civilian "auxiliaries" have still proved ready to use the full extent of their monopoly of violence.[21] But, as Andrew Selth has underlined, the post-2011 reform movement nonetheless seems to have affected the state security forces.[22]

While the media, youngsters, rising civil society associations and avid social media users seem to have grown bolder since 2011, the domestic political class has not been eclipsed either, even if some historic opponents to the successive military regimes are still having trouble adapting fully to the new rules of the post-junta game. Although the new administration has yet to grant a blanket retroactive pardon, most political prisoners arrested during the SLORC-SPDC era have been released in several waves of amnesty since 2011—confirming in that respect the broadening and liberalization of the political space. In May 2011, a handful of prisoners of conscience—as they have also been euphemistically known in the country—were freed in the midst of a massive governmental clemency program targeting almost 15,000 prisoners.[23] Common practice for the Buddhist-dominated authorities—seeking atonement—this release was followed by another notable presidential pardon in October 2011. President Thein Sein then announced the release of about 200 well-known political prisoners, including the comedian Zarganar and Su Su Nway, a woman activist close to the NLD.[24]

The speaker of the lower house, ex-general Thura Shwe Mann, soon stated that more amnesties were to be expected.[25] The newly crafted parliament, unwilling to let Thein Sein's government take the sole lead in the initial steps of 2011's post-junta *glasnost*, also started to discuss the release of prisoners during the second plenary session of the Union legislature, held in August 2011. It was a civilian legislator then with the National Democratic Force (NDF), Thein Nyunt, who first drafted a proposal to enact a "general amnesty order", on 26 August 2011.[26] Astonishingly, the proposal was widely approved by a majority of legislators, including the military-appointed parliamentarians who represent a quarter of both chambers in the Union parliament.[27] The release of political prisoners has long been a major hobbyhorse for the international community, especially Europe and the United States. The topic was systematically discussed by Western dignitaries visiting Myanmar in the 1990s and 2000s. Not only a key element in the reconciliation of Burmese elites, the release of prisoners of conscience has also long been considered an essential policy move if Burmese rulers wanted the international community to prove more accommodating. Thus it was a major theme of Hillary Clinton's landmark visit in 2011.[28]

A month later, in January 2012, the most charismatic of the political prisoners still behind bars were, in turn, granted amnesty by the presidential office. Among them were the monk Ashin Gambira, one of the leaders of the 2007 "Saffron Revolution", the blogger Nay Phone Latt, and champions of the 1988 student uprising such as Ko Ko Gyi, Nilar Thein, Htay Kywe and Min Ko Naing. Also freed was Shan leader Hkun Htun Oo, whose political party was among the winning forces of the 1990 (and later the November 2015) elections.[29] While Ashin Gambira left the monkhood and went into exile in Thailand after his release,[30] the generation of former 1988 student leaders—now mostly in their late forties and early fifties—has embarked on a series of social and political initiatives since 2012.[31] Most have targeted the grassroots levels of society, organizing public speeches and protest campaigns. Interestingly, several prominent members of this informal network of like-minded Burmese activists have developed robust anti-elite—and even anti-NLD—discourses.[32]

In August 2012, the president's office published a former blacklist of 2,000 Burmese and foreign personalities henceforth permitted again to enter Myanmar. This enabled the return of several charismatic Burmese exiles, some of whom have since become indispensable advisors to an executive eager to enact reform.[33] In May 2013, the Assistance Association for Political Prisoners (AAPP), the main Burmese political prisoner organization, based in Mae Sot, Thailand, stated that only 160 prisoners of conscience remained in custody in Myanmar, compared with 2,200 hardly three years previously.[34] December 2013 saw another round of releases.[35] In October 2014, Thein Sein's government acknowledged in a surprising statement that thirty political prisoners were still languishing in the country's jails—but announced that twenty-seven of them had committed serious crimes unrelated to their political activities.[36] Soon after the general elections held in November 2015, the AAPP revised its list of political prisoners: it still numbered 127 Burmese individuals of various profiles.[37]

Perhaps more importantly, the post-SPDC regime soon pardoned its own stray sheep. In addition to the several historical civilian junta opponents freed between 2010 and 2012, Khin Nyunt, the powerful military intelligence chief until his removal from office in October 2004, also regained his freedom in January 2012. He and several of his associates in the military intelligence services had spent more than seven years either under house arrest or in jail.[38] Officially indicted for corruption, Khin Nyunt and his entourage of sophisticated—and feared—intelligence officers had unexpectedly fallen from grace in 2004, soon after Khin Nyunt's appointment as SPDC prime minister. Senior-General Than Shwe had ordered him sacked, and the whole intelligence apparatus he had headed since his anointment by General Ne Win in 1984 was purged. With the official retirement of Than Shwe in 2011, under-the-radar loyalty networks were reactivated, and several high-ranking regime officials—including within the armed forces—pressed new president Thein Sein to pardon Khin Nyunt and his close entourage. This was done gradually, again following a Buddhist tradition of "mutual forgiveness". It also underlined the importance of patronage politics in contemporary Myanmar.[39] Another wave of releases for expunged intelligence officers took place in October 2014, notably for ex-general Thein Swe, former head of the international relations section in Khin Nyunt's office.[40]

However, the release of ex-intelligence officers is still hotly debated, inside and outside Myanmar. Domestic and transnational social media are filled with complaints and discontent about the newfound freedom of erstwhile powerful military spooks. Indeed, activist groups have seldom included imprisoned ex-army and -intelligence personnel on the extensive list of "political prisoners"—unless they were publicly sentenced under laws specifically designed to curtail basic individual liberties.[41] In December 2013, a proposal drafted by Thein Nyunt, the elected legislator who had in August 2011 initiated the parliamentary debate in Naypyitaw on political prisoners, was rebuffed. The Political Prisoners Scrutiny Committee, formed by Thein Sein's administration earlier in 2013, had indeed refused to add ex-intelligence officials to their updated list, prompting Thein Nyunt to revise his proposal. He thereafter asked the committee rather to consider such ex-officials' release on "humanitarian grounds".[42] Most army and intelligence officers still imprisoned have been sentenced according to the long-standing and much dreaded Emergency Provisions Act of 1950—which was only revoked in April 2016.

Likewise, in November 2013, three grandsons of the former military ruler Ne Win and their father (one of Ne Win's sons-in-law) were released under an amnesty order enacted by the president's office. They had been charged in 2002 with attempting a coup—quite a preposterous accusation, as not even the local regional military command in Yangon had been mobilized for their arrest—and spent eleven years behind bars.[43] Ne Win's clan had also been the victim of military infighting with other rival patronage networks in the early 2000s, and was expunged as early as March 2002, a few months before Ne Win himself passed away.[44] A more reasonable justification for the four men's arrest can be found in the fierce financial competition between Ne Win's clan on one side and, on the other, the SPDC's ruling elite and the cronies in its nexus.[45] However, after their release in 2013, Ne Win's grandchildren did not seem poised to join politics. As Aye Ne Win said, laughing, during an interview held in his office, where a two meter-high portrait of his grandfather stands, they have other businesses to look after and a family legacy to (re) polish.[46]

Opposition and Multipartism (Re)legalized

Even more significantly, the post-junta reformist moment has enabled the re-emergence of multiparty politics. Political parties are the bedrock of a lively parliamentary democracy and an essential part of the institutional machinery of a modern state. They are key elements in the policymaking process, and the extent of their independence, organizational strength and policy input reflects the quality of the political system they shape.[47] Democratization needs strong and multiple (at least two) competing parties. In Myanmar, with such a legacy of either one-party rule (1964–88) or a "no-party-at-all" landscape (between the nullified 1990 elections and the 2010 polls), the consolidation and institutionalization of political parties has historically proved more than weak, yet will be crucial in years to come. However, again, if history is any guide in Myanmar, there are serious reasons to be quite pessimistic about the re-emerging multiparty scene's capacity to move beyond fragmentation, clientelism and the personification of power. Out of the ninety-two political parties allowed to contest the 2015 legislative elections, only thirteen managed to gain a single seat in the Union parliament. The latter morphed from a body utterly dominated by the USDP in 2010 (78.8 per cent of contested seats) to one seemingly conquered by the NLD in 2015 (79.4 per cent). Yet political parties will be necessary forces, tasked with accompanying the ongoing transitional process currently led by high-profile personalities and state institutions such as the armed forces or an NLD government. They will be needed to act as the robust, long-term institutional foundations of Myanmar's parliamentary democracy-in-the-making (as we will see in detail in Chapter Six).

As early as 2009, a handful of Burmese veteran politicians, civil society groups and think-tanks started to position themselves to take part in the electoral process scheduled by the SPDC's seven-step roadmap to a "discipline-flourishing democracy". The decision to join an electoral contest certain to be entirely controlled by the then-ruling military administration was fervently debated, both inside and outside the country.[48] For a few social and politically engaged domestic forces, such as the regime-backed Union Solidarity and Development Association (USDA, formed in 1993), participation in the elections was all but evident. For others, though, tough questions and quandaries abounded.

The most illustrative cases of internal dilemmas generated among prominent political movements by the planned elections occurred within the ranks of the three parties that had largely won the 1990 elections: Aung San Suu Kyi's NLD, Hkun Htun Oo's Shan Nationalities League for Democracy (SNLD) and the Arakan League for Democracy (ALD). With their leaders behind bars in 2009, when such internal debates emerged, the second-tier officials of these parties ripped each other apart. This led to the formation of new parties: the NDF, which broke with the mainstream NLD in a bitter clash of competing egos,[49] and the Shan Nationalities Democratic Party (SNDP), which departed from the SNLD's decision, like the NLD, to boycott the upcoming polls, and supported its long-term value of staunch opposition to the ruling elite.[50] Similar divisions were observed in the Rakhine political landscape, with the ALD, aligned with the NLD in 1990, refusing to join hands with the Rakhine Nationalities Development Party (RNDP), which successfully ran for national and provincial seats in 2010.[51]

The 2010 Elections

In August 2010, the regime-controlled Union Election Commission (UEC, an eighteen-member body nominated by the SPDC that March) announced the first nationwide polls since 1990, scheduled for 7 November.[52] Earlier in March, the UEC had enacted the Political Parties Registration Law (No. 2/2010), which (re)legalized the formation of political parties—provided that the latter respect a handful of highly restrictive basic principles. In total, forty-seven political forces applied for registration, forty-two of which were accepted, and thirty-seven were allowed to run in the planned elections. Five years later, ninety-two parties were registered for the polls held on 8 November 2015. Prominent among them in 2010 were the USDP, based on the USDA's structures, finances and loyalty networks. Senior-General Than Shwe himself has long been the latter's patron. The National Unity Party (NUP), the successor of Ne Win's sole legitimate party (Lanzin), which was crushed in the 1990 elections, also announced its (re)formation in 2009 and its willingness to follow the "incremental process of transition from a Tatmadaw government to a people's government".[53]

Another legatee of Myanmar's early postcolonial years was the Democratic Party-Myanmar (DP-M). The DP-M was registered in May 2010 by its octogenarian chairman, Thu Wai, assistant in the 1950s to Deputy Prime Minister Kyaw Nyein. Reviving its 1990 election platform, created in 1988, in 2010 the DP-M gathered scions of numerous prominent politicians of the various governments led by the Anti-Fascist People's Freedom League (AFPFL) between 1948 and 1962. Kyaw Nyein's daughter, Cho Cho Kyaw Nyein, joined the DP-M as general secretary, returning to a role she was asked to fill twenty years before by Thu Wai, for the 1990 polls.[54] Nay Yee Ba Swe, daughter of former Prime Minister Ba Swe (1956–7), joined, along with her brother Nay Phoo Ba Swe.[55] So did Than Than Nu, daughter of ex-Prime Minister U Nu, who was deposed twice by General Ne Win, in 1958 and 1962.[56] The "three daughters" of these still-renowned political veterans, now gathered under the DP-M umbrella, were soon to be labelled the "three princesses" by the international and domestic media.[57]

While the government-controlled UEC allowed most parties to register, a few were nonetheless barred from contesting the 2010 elections. Unmistakable red lines were then drawn by the military regime, and any suspected connection with either the outside world or one or more of the armed insurgent forces—mostly ethnic-based—would result in denial of official registration. The Kachin and Rohingya minorities were particularly targeted—each according to different rationales. Manam Tu Ja, a former high-ranking officer of the Kachin Independence Organization (KIO), declared his intention to run in 2010 in Kachin State early on. He then formed the Kachin State Progressive Party (KSPP), but his alleged continued links with the KIO leadership gave the UEC the perfect justification for banning a rising and popular political force in the northern Kachin territories.[58] Manam Tu Ja's participation in the 2010 polls was thus proscribed. Nevertheless, rising political interest could be observed among the urbanized Kachin community of Yangon and Myitkyina.[59] To respond to it, a handful of other prominent Kachin leaders chose to enter the electoral race, and were allowed to do so by the UEC. Those who founded the Unity and Democracy Party of the Kachin State (UDPKS), for instance, were able to win two seats in the Union parliament in 2010. One of the two UDPKS legislators was even elected chairman of the upper house on the day its first session was convened.[60] Five years later, Manam Tu Ja was in a position to lead a new political formation, the Kachin State Democracy Party (KSDP), whose registration had eventually been accepted in by the UEC in 2013. The KSDP fielded fifty-five candidates in the 2015 elections, but took only four seats.[61]

For its part, the Rohingya community has long been considered "foreign" to Myanmar's polity. The Burmese state does not recognise the Rohingyas as members of the national community—or as belonging to any of the 135 "national races". This Muslim minority comprises more than a million individuals scattered throughout the country; but most live segregated in three remote districts of Myanmar's Rakhine State, bordering Bangladesh.[62] As foreigners cannot, by law, participate in domestic politics, their political aspirants and most ambitious personalities have long had to be declared ethnically "Bamar", and to join existing political parties or form parties without identifiable "Rohingya" identity markers. Shwe Maung, for instance, decided early on to join the USDP in order to run in Buthidaung, his native constituency in northwestern Rakhine State. He would subsequently be elected to the lower house in 2010.[63] His opponents, of the same ethno-religious background, chose to gather in low-key political parties whose name did not refer to any "Rohingya" identity. None were elected in 2010.[64] In the run up to the 2015 polls, the UEC developed a far more restrictive policy, provoking an international outcry. For the first time in decades, the vast majority of Rohingya voters found themselves disenfranchised, while most Rohingya candidates were denied registration by the UEC.[65] The decision was even backed by the Union parliament and the constitutional tribunal. Shwe Maung, after five years as a Union-level parliamentarian in Naypyitaw, was thus prevented from standing for re-election.[66]

Having opted for a general boycott of the polls, Aung San Suu Kyi's NLD failed to register with the UEC in 2010. The majority of exiled dissidents (and MPs elected in the annulled 1990 elections) being NLD members, the party insisted on the regime's eventual recognition of the 1990 results. It was therefore not allowed to compete in the 2010 polls, and officially became "illegal" as early as May 2010, as did Hkun Htun Oo's SNLD. With the by-elections organized a year-and-a-half after the 2010 polls, the NLD was soon offered an opportunity to re-register and "return to the legal fold".[67] Despite their newfound legality, however, most political parties have continued to face a difficult legal and political environment during the electoral campaigns of late 2010 and September–November 2015. Unwritten constraints still linger, and the scope of parties' activities is considerably limited by the UEC's requirements of fiscal accountability, as well as various fundraising restrictions. Their relations to external organizations—potential donors or groups providing capacity building or training—are also closely monitored by the UEC.[68] They must not, for instance, receive any funding from foreign organizations or governments, nor from any religious-based associations, under Article 407 of the 2008 constitution.

Table 1: Seat composition of the Union parliament and fourteen regional and state *hluttaws* after the 2010 general election

Political Parties	*Pyithu Hluttaw (lower house)*	*Amyotha Hluttaw (upper house)*	*State and Region Hluttaws*	*Total*
USDP	259	129	495	883
Tatmadaw	110	56	222	388
NUP	12	5	46	63
SNDP	18	3	36	57
RNDP	9	7	19	35
AMRDP	3	4	9	16
NDF	8	4	4	16
CPP	2	4	6	12
PNO	3	1	6	10
CNP	2	2	5	9
PSDP	2	3	4	9
KPP	1	1	4	6
WDP	2	1	3	6
TPNP	1	1	4	6
INDP	1		4	5
UDPKS	1	1	2	4
DP-M			3	3
NDPD			2	2
KNP			2	2
KSDDP	0	1	1	2
88 Youths			1	1
Lahu NDP			1	1
Independent	1	1	4	6
Vacant	5			5
Total	440	224	883	1547

Source: author's compilation.

Echoing the last "free and fair" national polls, held in February 1960 under the supervision of Ne Win's caretaker military administration, general elections were held on 7 November 2010 under the full control of the SPDC. This was the fifth step of Khin Nyunt's seven-step roadmap towards a "discipline-flourishing democracy", unveiled in 2003.[69] Many irregularities were denounced during the electoral campaign and several frauds signaled on voting day.[70] The results were widely condemned as a sham, at home and abroad.[71] The USDP, a political platform gathering retired technocrats, ex-army officers, local leaders and a few enigmatic business cronies, won a comfortable majority. It took more than three quarters of all seats contested, at both Union and provincial level (see Table 1). Because of this utter dominance, observers even argued that a new form of electoral authoritarianism had emerged in the country.[72] The NUP came a distant second with 5.4 per cent of the seats at Union level. Then followed the SNDP with 4.9 per cent of the seats, the RNDP with 3 per cent, the All Mon Regions Democracy Party (AMRDP) and the NDF, each with 1.4 per cent, and the CPP with 1 per cent.

Towards Free and Fair Polls? The 2012 By-elections and 2015 Elections

At the turn of the 2010s, Myanmar has thus experienced a revival of pluralism and a renaissance of political and inter-party debates. This has become even more manifest since the NLD eventually decided to field candidates in the 2012 by-elections. To everyone's surprise, these polls bore no resemblance whatsoever to those held two years before.[73] Both the ballot and the electoral campaign, during which Aung San Suu Kyi toured the central plains for several weeks to a triumphant reception, were considered the freest since the 1960 elections. Addressing the parliament in Naypyitaw on 30 April 2012, United Nations Secretary-General Ban Ki-moon even congratulated the Burmese state leadership, in a historic speech calling for the lifting of sanctions.[74] The NLD won hands down, taking forty-three of the forty-five contested seats. Aung San Suu Kyi herself was elected to the Pyithu Hluttaw (lower house) for the rural constituency of Kawhmu, a few miles south of Yangon.[75] The party best embodying resistance to military rule since 1988 was thus propelled to become the third parliamentary force in Naypyitaw, after the USDP and the military bloc (see Table 2).

The run-up to the 2015 polls further illustrated the tremendous development of the party scene in Myanmar, even if, among the ninety-two political formations authorized to compete, only a few resisted the thundering landslide victory of the NLD and gained a parliamentary seat.[76] The general election held on 8 November 2015, exactly five years after the electoral controversies of November 2010, was the freest Myanmar has known in decades. The huge, well-financed rallies that the NLD has been allowed to hold throughout the country—from Yangon's eastern outskirts to Rakhine State and the conflict-ridden Kachin areas in the north—clearly indicated the openness of the electoral campaign, which started in early September. The NLD's unexpected landslide in 1990 has led many observers to forget that Myanmar was then under martial law, that the junta imposed systematic restrictions on canvassing, public gatherings and candidates' media appearances, and that Aung San Suu Kyi herself was under house arrest, and so not even standing. Twenty years later, the representativeness and fairness of the 2010 polls were no less questionable. Aung San Suu Kyi was still incommunicado, along with about 2,200 other political prisoners.

Table 2: Seat composition of the Union parliament after the 2012 by-elections

Political Parties	*Pyithu Hluttaw*	*Amyotha Hluttaw*	*Total*
USDP	222	123	346
Tatmadaw	110	56	166
NLD	37	4	41
SNDP	18	4	22
NUP	12	5	17
RNDP	8	7	16
NDF	8	4	12
AMRDP	3	4	7
CPP	2	4	6
PSDP	2	3	5
CNP	2	2	4
PNO	3	1	4
WDP	2	1	3
UDPKS	1	1	2
TPNP	1	1	2
Independent	1	1	2
KPP	1	1	2
INDP	1		1
KSDDP	0	1	1
Vacant	6	1	5
Total	440	224	664

Source: author's compilation.[77]

In stark contrast, the 2015 campaign proved startlingly free and competitive, and the Burmese people eager to cast a vote.[78] A few cases of pre-electoral violence were reported, such as the odd sword assault of an NLD candidate in Yangon or the shooting of two ethnic Shan Ni (or Red Shan) members of the Tai'Leng Nationalities Development Party (TNDP) in the jade mining areas of Hpakant, Kachin State—a remote Burmese version of the Wild West. Though the civil war was still raging in many areas of Myanmar's northern peripheries, violence and turmoil directly linked to the elections were minimal. Aung San Suu Kyi has campaigned all over the country, as she has never before been allowed to. The ninety-two political parties' candidates have been authorized to hold meetings, gather troops of sympathizers, and use conventional, state and social media for their own political purposes.[79]

True, the 2015 vote was known to be unfair from the beginning. The landslide victory of the NLD, reaffirming the annuled triumph of 1990, should not overshadow the fact that, on this occasion, a significant proportion of potential voters were deliberately disfranchised long before election day. 2015 saw the cancellation of the Temporary Registration Cards (or 'white cards') belonging to hundreds of thousands of Rohingyas in Rakhine State, but also to various minority groups of Indian, Gurkha, Chinese, and Kokang origins residing in Myanmar's northern peripheries. Besides, only about a few dozen thousand, or less than 1 per cent, of the 3 to 5 million-strong Burmese population living abroad were able to cast an advance vote. The 150,000 refugees sheltered in UNHCR-run camps in Bangladesh and Thailand did not vote either. Within the country, conflict in Kachin State has produced about 100,000 Internally Displaced Persons (IDPs) since June 2011. Almost none voted on 8 November 2015. Their villages had been emptied and polls cancelled well in advance by the UEC in more than 600 village-tracts (compared with 418 in 2010) and seven full constituencies (there were five in 2010, and seven in 1990).

The 2015 polls were nonetheless received far more positively than expected by the international community, but more importantly by the Burmese themselves. Some 8,000 to 10,000 Burmese and international observers were allowed to closely monitor the process in more than 40,000 polling stations.[80] International media and freelance foreign reporters flocked into Yangon from late October 2015. Eventually, Aung San Suu Kyi's NLD won a thundering victory: almost 80 per cent of the contested Union-level seats (see Table 3).[81] This even surpassed the predictions of party headquarters.[82] The incumbent USDP was crushed, including most of its heavyweights: Thura Shwe Mann, the outgoing speaker of the lower house, Wai Lwin and Hla Min, two former defense ministers, and Htay Oo, the party chief, all faced humiliating defeats. Fewer than thirty retired military officers won a seat, leaving the new legislatures almost free of soldiers-turned-politicians, a first for post-SPDC Myanmar.[83] Hla Htay Win, the recently retired joint chief of staff, will be the only four-star general sitting in the new Union parliament. Three former navy chiefs of staff also managed to grab a seat: Soe Thane, a former minister in the presidential office, took a seat in the upper house (as an independent), as did Thura Thet Swe for the Coco Islands constituency and Nyan Tun, one of the Union's two outgoing vice-presidents.

Table 3: Seat composition of the Union parliament and fourteen state and regional *hluttaws* after the 2015 general elections

Political Parties	*Pyithu Hluttaw*	*Amyotha Hluttaw*	*State and Region Hluttaws*	*Total*
NLD	255	135	496	886
Tatmadaw	110	56	225	391
USDP	30	11	76	117
ANP/RNP	12	10	24	46
SNLD	12	3	26	41
TPNP	3	2	7	12
PNO	3	1	6	10
ZCD	2	2	2	6
Lisu NDP	2		3	5
KSDP	1		3	4
Independents	1	2	1	4
MNP		1	2	3
WDP	1		2	3
TNDP			2	2
Lahu NDP			2	2
NUP		1		1
AMRDP			1	1
KPP			1	1
KDUP	1			1
Akha NDP			1	1
SNDP			1	1
DP-M			1	1
UDPKS			1	1
WNUP			1	1
Vacant	7		14	21
Total	440	224	898	1562

Source: Union Electoral Commission and ICG (2015, pp. 15–16).

Only thirteen parties out of ninety-two fielding candidates secured a place in the new Union parliament. Those political forces that chose to play the SPDC's constitutional game in 2010 were wiped out five years later: Khin

Maung Swe's NDF, Thu Wai's DP-M and several ethnic parties such as the SNDP, the AMRDP and both Chin movements, the CPP and CNDP. Vote splitting took its toll in most ethnic-dominated areas, which voted—though not massively—in favor of Aung San Suu Kyi's party.[84] The latter was certainly perceived as a more capable force than the myriad of other smaller political groups, even those founded by charismatic ethnic leaders. More importantly, the vote was free, unlike in 2008 and 2010, for instance. The credibility of the electoral process has been asserted,[85] and this was far from a done deal before the polls, according to the most critical observers.[86]

Civil Society Expands

A present and dynamic "civil society"—the sociopolitical forces residing between the state, the private sector and the family—has long been construed as a key element needed to help democracy broadly advance.[87] Yet, the relationship between democratic change and civil society is extraordinarily complex. Despite an impressive body of scholarship addressing the democratizing potential of what forms a "civil society", there is no specific conceptual framework that allows us to convincingly evaluate the impact on democratization—diffuse, diverse, multiple—of the organizations, associations and intermediate groups that commonly shape a civil society.[88] The argument that civil society is a primary agent of democratization is thus often misdirected. Since Alexis de Tocqueville, we have known that it takes a lot of time for a civil society to nurture a democratic culture, instill pluralistic mores, modify political behaviors and change mindsets. Besides, sometimes a civil society can hardly resist the emergence of antidemocratic tendencies within its own ranks, such as the rise of religious extremism or the co-optation and manipulation of some of its actors by authoritarian ruling elites. Among others, Muthiah Alagappa has shown that the role of community-based organizations (CBOs) in advancing openness and positive change is not as straightforward as claimed by these CBOs themselves.[89]

For Larry Diamond, though a robust and lively civil society is key to building and consolidating democracy, its role cannot be construed as decisive in the initial years of a transitional process.[90] Other authors too have considered the influence of civil society actors on the first stages of a democratization process to be indispensable, but rather indirect, if not "soft".[91] Rather, it is commonly argued, a civil society serves to accompany the initial phases of change; it will prove a far more important determinant at a later stage of transition, to expand the scope of political change in a post-authoritarian society, and consolidate democratic practices. Its impact also much depends on the legacy and duration of the preceding authoritarianism. Using European post-communist societies as case studies, Bernhard and Karakoç have demonstrated that, in the early stages of the transition, the longer the totalitarian or dictatorial rule, the weaker the democratic achievements of a civil society are.[92] This is a significant caveat for post-junta Myanmar.

Nonetheless, political openings produce new forms of mobilization and popular action. As the authoritarian regime relaxes its grip and allows for liberalization of the sociopolitical realm, the politicization of the people increases, and activism grows. In transitional moments, an often dormant or stifled civil society commonly re-emerges. It starts to provide new policy input, and to act as a substitute for a failed state in various sectors and areas where the state is normally expected to perform well. This is O'Donnell and Schmitter's "resurrection" of the civil society, after years under authoritarian state control.[93] Yet, as they go on to caution, the renaissance of a civil society is often met with a highly explosive environment. Hidden grievances resurface quickly, demands long repressed rematerialize, and new forms of protest develop.[94] Confusion can subsequently emerge and potentially derail the initial path of the transition (especially if top-down and "pacted") and thus either push democratic change further forward, or on the contrary bring back the authoritarians, even prompt a military coup—as Myanmar experienced in the aftermath of the 1988 upheavals, for instance.

Myanmar's civil society has been the object of increasing interest over the past fifteen years. In the 1990s, in the midst of the "third wave" of democratization observed elsewhere in the world, scholars of Myanmar were rather unequivocal about Burmese civil society's insignificance. Since the 1988 military coup, the very few organizations or community-based associations allowed by the SLORC were far from forming a credible "civil society". The "intermediary groups" supposedly beyond the scope of both the family and the military-run state either had been stifled or were kept under strict government control during Ne Win's era and into the 1990s.[95]

Gradually, though, a handful of segments of that "dormant" indigenous civil society started to emerge, and grew more influential during the 2000s. Many local non-governmental organizations (NGOs) and community-based movements were progressively allowed to operate throughout the country, provided that they kept a low profile, did not engage in contentious politics and, most importantly, provided initiatives and dispensed activities that the ruling administration was unable, or unwilling, to deliver.[96] Burmese academic Kyaw Yin Hlaing has for instance insisted on the relentless contributions of religious associations—within the Buddhist, but also Christian, Hindu and Muslim fabric—and of informal social and business actors. Myanmar's "associational life", was thus not as void as it then seemed.[97] Many local agencies and informal social gatherings therefore started to flourish on the basis of the developmental, educational and humanitarian programs they could offer.

This was particularly noticeable in Myanmar's ethnic-dominated borderlands. Acute feelings of deprivation and even segregation since independence have prompted various ethnic-minority communities, throughout the country and beyond its official borders, to craft local and transnational networks of solidarity. Ashley South, among others, detailed early on the rising dynamism of ethnic-based civil society actors.[98] Karen, Shan, Kachin, Chin and Mon groups have dramatically expanded their social and humanitarian activities since the mid-1990s, with strong support from a wide range of foreign donors. From 1989 to 1995, the series of ceasefire agreements negotiated between ethnic armed groups and Khin Nyunt enabled a flurry of local NGOs with links to the signatory groups to operate in territories still controlled by the latter after the deal with the SLORC. These local and community-based Karen, Shan, Kachin or Mon organizations, founded by local elites and educated leaders, started to flourish in the border areas. They astutely benefited from the support, training and assistance they could find on the other side of the border, in Thailand, India and beyond.[99] Among others, Reverend Saboi Jum and his daughter Ja Nan Lahtaw, as well as Seng Raw, who number among the best-known Kachin activists in the country, were founding members of the Metta Foundation, an NGO.[100] Other individuals such as Alan Saw U, a senior Karen civil leader, Harn Yawnghwe, descended from Shan princes (*sawbwas*), and Lian H. Sakhong, a high-profile Chin figure, are further examples of senior ethnic leaders involved since the 1990s in local or transnational capacity-building and developmental projects, but also increasingly in policy-oriented movements. All, however, have been heavily criticized for their engagement with the local authorities over the years.

A series of reports and master's and doctoral dissertations, prepared over the course of the 2000s by Burmese and foreign students who have carried out fieldwork along the Thai-Myanmar border or in India, have quite thoroughly documented the growing influence of these civil society groups, both pan-Burmese and ethnic-based.[101] In the course of my own doctoral research in the mid-2000s, I also benefited greatly from my interactions with Chin NGOs operating out of New Delhi; with Rakhine women's associations based in Dhaka, Bangladesh; with Rohingya activist groups residing in Kuala Lumpur, Malaysia; with Kachin associations based along China's Yunnan borders; and with Shan and Karen organizations in the Thai cities of Mae Hong Song and Chiang Mai.

As Kyaw Yin Hlaing showed in the early 2000s, beyond their initial focus on the welfare of local communities and the need to improve livelihoods, rising civil society actors inside and outside Myanmar have incrementally distilled new policy ideas and campaigned on a number of key political issues under the SPDC regime.[102] In the course of the 2000s, prominent and well-respected Burmese individuals with a large clientele and highly valued moral capital—such as intellectuals and university professors, veteran politicians, retired army officers and dissidents in exile—gradually gained the ear of a few elements of the junta leadership and the armed forces, even after (or thanks to) the ousting of Khin Nyunt and the dismantling of his military intelligence services in 2004. New policy discourses began to be developed and encouraged, civil society actors started to pinpoint state deficiencies and state representatives' lack of responsibility, and to encourage a "third way" to approach developmental, but also political, problems in the country—neither a fully-fledged continuation of military-defined policies nor a sudden instauration of a hypothetical, NLD-led democracy.[103] Many local actors, however, continued limiting themselves to humanitarian, environmental and socioeconomic development until the late 2000s, to avoid too visible a politicization.[104]

From the mid-2000s, however, there has emerged a staunch discussion and questioning, inside and outside Myanmar, of the (in)effectiveness and value of transnational support to various Burmese local agencies, as well as the involvement of international NGOs and donors in the country.[105] Since the 1988 coup, Myanmar has been the subject of an array of international diplomatic and commercial sanctions, and their impact on foreign aid and transnational assistance to local Burmese agencies has been hotly debated since the late 1990s.[106] For instance, among the foreign actors operating inside the country, David Tegenfeldt of Hope International has long argued that foreign aid was needed,[107] despite the inappropriateness of having to deal with an authoritarian and military-led regime that was the object of international opprobrium.[108] Thus, over time, renowned scholars, policy practitioners and the local and international crowd of NGO workers and leaders have offered comparative reflections on the value of foreign aid to a society under authoritarian rule, to better contextualize the Burmese case in the 2000s.[109]

The passage of Cyclone Nargis in early May 2008 considerably heightened the Burmese people's sociopolitical awareness, and highlighted the need to bypass the role—and rules—of the military-led Burmese state.[110] In the wake of the tragedy, a formidable wave of solidarity emerged across the country. Burmese personalities, singers, movie actors, teachers, journalists, and civil servants started to mobilize and drive supplies to affected areas beyond Yangon, into the Irrawaddy delta. Wealthy Burmese businessmen contributed to relief efforts. Religious orders collected donations and supervised their distribution to local communities in despair.[111] In the northern and eastern parts of the country, the Shan, the Kachin and the Mon joined the rescue efforts southward in a rather unprecedented upsurge of inter-ethnic solidarity. The military authorities reacted ambiguously to this new form of domestic mobilization, on the one hand arresting many prominent members of this newfound local solidarity movement (such as the comedian Zarganar), while on the other hand attempting to manage relief efforts through completely unprepared military troops. Indeed, the public relations exercise launched by the armed forces after Nargis[112] failed miserably. The passage of the cyclone in 2008 is now recalled by the substantial majority of the Burmese people, as well as the international community, as a moment of extreme xenophobia, inward-looking policy reaction and failed relief intervention on the part of the military authorities.

As in many other cases where natural disasters have struck unprepared societies, Cyclone Nargis appeared to have served as a catalyst for societal and political change. An increasingly politicized collective identity has emerged in Myanmar since 2008—in the midst of the constitutional referendum held that May—with civil servants, Burmese NGO workers and members of the intelligentsia and the arts world gradually realizing the potential of a mass mobilization around humanitarian, developmental and environmental issues. Cyclone Nargis neither wiped out an entire rebellion (as in Aceh after the 2004 Tsunami), nor gave birth to massive political unrest (as in East Pakistan after the passage of Cyclone Bhola in 1970), nor toppled the authoritarian military regime in place, far away in Naypyitaw and spared the cyclone's devastation. But Nargis has considerably raised awareness among a new generation of Burmese people. Domestic civil society groups have led the mobilization and filled the gaps opened by an incapable—or unwilling—state, as in Turkey after the Marmara earthquake in 1999, for instance.

After Nargis, the emerging civil society players seemed ready for a dramatic move beyond the mere "management of needs" and into the realm of political engagement. Elliott Prasse-Freeman has noted that years of authoritarian legacies and a habit of fear have long tended to restrict the scope of civil society action in Myanmar. But when a catalyst for change pops up, as Nargis did in 2008, civil society actors are presented with an opportunity to strengthen civic engagement, "magnify political demands" and challenge the political status quo.[113] Along with Nargis, the campaign for the constitutional referendum in 2008, but even more so that preceding the 2010 general election, has strongly re-politicized several segments of this rising civil society, notably extending beyond the already active borderlands in Thailand, for instance, to include domestic elements. The new legislation on political parties adopted in 2010 was thus construed as an opportunity for various politically engaged groups inside the country to re-emerge as officially recognized political movements and therefore contest the polls scheduled for late 2010.[114]

As underlined by Michael Lidauer, among others, an "elections-related" civil society strengthened its presence throughout 2010 by broadening its activities before and during the November polls.[115] Particularly active—since the NLD opted to boycott the elections and was subsequently stamped as illegal—was the heterogeneous so-called "Third Force". Separate both from the historic opposition embodied by Aung San Suu Kyi (under house arrest until a week after the elections) and from the military regime and its political clientele, the "Third Force" gathered political parties and militant associations that were allowed to operate and were very much willing to join the 2010 electoral contest, educate voters and instill civic values and responsibility among the general public.[116] The "Third Force" has emerged as an incontrovertible player in the country's post-Nargis reconstruction, but even more significantly in the broadening of political space at the turn of the 2010s—even if the initiative has still long been with the upper strata of the Burmese intelligentsia and foreign-trained experts.[117]

The Myitsone hydroelectric dam episode was a further foundational moment in this regard. In 2006, a contract was signed between the SPDC and the China Power Investment Corporation (CPI), a Chinese state-owned enterprise, to build a massive dam. The site chosen was in Myitsone, a township in the northern Kachin State, near the Chinese border. It was to be one of China's many pharaonic projects (this one for about US$3.6 billion) undertaken in Myanmar. As it turned out, in addition to the many evictions and relocations of Kachin villagers living on the land where the dam was to be built,[118] and the direct environmental threats to a region treasured in Burmese culture—the Myitsone site being located at the source of the Irrawaddy River, which symbolically and economically nourishes the country—most of the electricity to be generated by the dam power plant was to supply the western Chinese provinces (first among them Yunnan), but not Myanmar, with cheap electricity. Various Kachin organizations started to mobilize in the late 2000s.[119]

They were joined, over the years, by many other groups from all spheres of Myanmar's emerging civil society. Even the Yangon-based political elites began to take position, particularly Aung San Suu Kyi. On 11 August 2011, she made a public statement describing the Irrawaddy River as "under threat" and urging the Burmese and Chinese governments to "reassess the scheme".[120] A month later, to everyone's surprise and despite Beijing's ire, President Thein Sein announced that since the government was "elected by the people", it had therefore to "respect the people's will."[121] Construction was henceforth suspended for the duration of Thein Sein's mandate. It should, however, be pointed out that generally speaking, and in the Myitsone dam case in particular, Naypyitaw's decision to suspend the project was also crucially influenced by concerns about Myanmar's overdependence on China, which has mobilized many segments of the military and governmental elites since the early 1990s. In fact, for some observers, the Chinese factor is one of the main reasons for the entire acceleration of the transition process since 2011.[122]

Two years later, in 2013, the copper mines of Letpadaung focused the attention of Burmese civil society. The Chinese state company Wanbao Mining Corporation had invested nearly US$1 billion in this development located northwest of Mandalay, near the city of Monywa.[123] Local farmers first staged demonstrations there early in 2012 to denounce the site's excessive pollution, forced evictions and the inadequate compensation offered by the local authorities and the Chinese firm. Politicians, activists in Yangon and elected Union parliamentarians soon bandwagoned.[124] Violent clashes took place between farmers and the police in November 2012.[125] A parliamentary commission symbolically chaired by Aung San Suu Kyi was thereafter formed to evaluate the project, and gather complaints. In the report it submitted in March 2013, the commission recommended maintaining the Chinese company on site, but that the latter should improve working conditions, better compensate the farmers driven off their land and ensure compliance with international environmental standards.[126] Two years on, large-scale demonstrations and violent acts by individual local militants—openly hostile to Aung San Suu Kyi's stance—continued to prompt extremely brutal reactions from local police forces, as well as the country's judicial system. Several key demonstrators were given harsh prison sentences, generating strong international criticism and doubt about sociopolitical progress since Thein Sein was sworn in as president in 2011.[127]

Yet, in the mid-2010s, Myanmar's civil society was far more dynamic, though diffuse and fragile, than at any point since the 1950s. Its most prominent representatives have become powerful actors, in a position to influence policy discourse around major issues and provide tentative, if contested, solutions to the major challenges facing Myanmar. What is more, from the late 2000s, many of the Myanmar-focused civil society groups operating from abroad have started to move deeper into the country, partly to establish an official presence. Dominant international NGOs and potential donors have similarly extended their influence in the wake of the post-SPDC transitional opening. Thus, in the first half of the 2010s, Yangon has promptly replaced Chiang Mai or Bangkok as the main center of Myanmar-focused NGO activism. Since 2011, domestic civil society groups have regularly offered input to both the new government and the newly elected parliamentarians in Naypyitaw. Though not always taken into consideration by the MPs and government—far from it—the voice of Myanmar's rising civil society is getting louder.[128]

With the 2011 transitional opening and, in particular, the easing of state censorship, a greater space for advocacy and political debate has thus taken form.[129] Many Burmese NGOs, as well as the local media, the wide networks of religious organizations, political parties and even the private business sector, today have enough room to maneuver to be able to pinpoint the failings of the still military-dominated government system, the oligarchic national economy and the opaque methods of political and bureaucratic decision-making, including at local level. As regards foreign investment or social and environmental threats, Myanmar's expanding civil society has proved to be particularly active, and all the more effective since the development of the Internet and social networks in the mid-2010s.

This has come at a price, however. New challenges have emerged with the opening up of Myanmar's sociopolitical space, including expanding religious extremism. Under a less oppressive political environment and with the skyrocketing development of the Internet and the social media since 2012, ethnoreligious-based violence has blossomed (as will be developed in Chapter Five). Yet many other new social and political elements have surfaced. On the one hand, these new elements may well prove positive, as they can foster new debates and extend pluralism in the country beyond the 2010s. They may consolidate some sort of democratic practice by making the country's ruling bureaucratic and political elites more responsive to public demand, more accountable. Civil society may well help strengthen a burgeoning debate on the definition of common goods and of ideas on which to build a peaceful and cohesive Myanmar. In so doing, the various agencies of civil society would certainly impose themselves as key agents in the country's potential democratization, and thus enlarge the narrow circle of Burmese elites that chiefly negotiated the transitional process in the first half of the 2010s. On the other hand, new social conflicts and challenges may well drag the country into further misunderstandings, political gridlock and outbreaks of violence that could further slow down the search for a broader "social pact" in the near future.

3

RESTORING PARLIAMENTARY DEMOCRACY

Democratically elected parliaments are the bedrock of representative democracy. They are supposed to represent the will and wishes of the people that freely, fairly and regularly chooses their members. Elected parliaments perform core tasks essential to the basic functioning of a democratic system: oversight of other state institutions and branches of powers, lawmaking, representation, and constituency services, among others.[1] Legislatures are particularly critical institutions in emerging democracies. Scholars of comparative legislature have differentiated three main types of parliaments, according to the political and electoral system under which they are shaped, their legislative and oversight performance, and their broader impact over constituents: 1) "policymaking" assemblies, as observed in mature democracies such as the United States, Japan and Western European states, where strong and autonomous parliaments have a decisive impact on the way legislation is drafted and governmental policy checked; 2) "policy-influencing" parliaments, which influence policies, but with less decisive sway over the various executive powers; and finally 3) "rubber-stamp" parliaments under non-democratic regimes.[2] As Michael Mezey put it, legislatures can move up and down a scale of legislative performance and effectiveness and thus be more or less active, reactive, vulnerable, marginal and, for the most feeble policy actors, minimal.[3]

Only recently, however, has the body of scholarship on democratization—in Asia in particular—focused on the influence of parliaments over political change. Social scientists and comparativists have now started to examine how legislatures in a wide range of different political systems have meaningfully exercised oversight procedures, determined new policy and legislative agendas, and subsequently consolidated post-authoritarian transitions and fostered democratization processes… or not.[4] Recent comparative studies have specifically questioned the democratizing impact, professionalization and institutionalization of parliaments in post-communist Europe and Russia,[5] Latin America,[6] Africa and the Middle East,[7] and, more recently, Asia.[8] In particular, Olson and Norton have focused on legislatures still in a formative stage—or "parliaments in adolescence", by their definition.[9] They claim that newly formed legislatures are characterized in the first years of their existence by fragility and limited capacity, if not conflict. Their future success and performance much depends on their institutionalization potential, their capacity to increase their degree of professionalization and their ability to move away from the influence of the executive power or any other competitive force unwilling to play by the legislative (and democratic) rules—a military institution, for instance.

Myanmar's new parliament falls into this category of an adolescent, or infant, legislature. Since it first convened in January 2011 after a twenty-three-year hiatus, it has rapidly, and surprisingly, engaged in avid legislative activity.[10] The first post-junta legislature crafted after the 2010 general elections (and the subsequent 2012 by-elections) has quickly gained heightened political status, obviously attempting to play a leading role in reform activity, as recent studies have shown.[11] A new parliamentary class of Burmese politicians has since emerged.[12] Burmese legislators—whether elected or appointed by the commander-in-chief of the Tatmadaw—seem to have gradually, and surprisingly, contributed to the development of Myanmar's revived legislative branch.[13] Still in its infancy however, the new legislature remains vulnerable. This chapter proposes to shed light on the complexities of the re-emergence of parliamentary politics between 2010 and 2015. I will first look at the patterns of the parliament's renaissance as a state institution. I will then attempt to evaluate its initial performance and functions, and identify its most obvious weaknesses and constraints, which will continue to weigh upon future legislatures.

The Resurgence of the Legislatures

Myanmar's post-independence legislative politics as observed between 1947 and 1962 have never been the object of in-depth research.[14] Besides, recent studies have only focused on periods lacking a democratically elected legislature, examining post-colonial factional politics prior to the 1962 military coup,[15] or the composition and functions of the unicameral parliament crafted under Ne Win's 1974–88 one-party regime.[16] The reconvening of the legislature in 2011 therefore offers a unique opportunity to look at the restoration of a parliamentary system in contemporary Myanmar.

The first democratically elected assembly of postcolonial Myanmar was convened in June 1947 and tasked with drafting the country's first constitution.[17] Subsequently, three national legislative bodies were formed, after national polls held in 1951,[18] 1956 and 1960.

However, after General Ne Win's military coup in 1962, parliamentary debates and all other meaningful legislative mechanisms were suspended; the national parliament itself was dissolved at noon on 3 March 1962. After twelve years without any representative body, the second constitutional text of the country, adopted in 1974, established a unicameral "People's Assembly", or Pyithu Hluttaw. It convened for regular, short-lived sessions between 1974 and 1988, but proved the model example of a rubber-stamp parliament. All its members (MPs) belonged to the sole recognised party, the Burma Socialist Program Party (BSPP, or Lanzin), and many were still active-duty military officers. They offered only cosmetic commitments to conventional legislative activities and public debate.

The last assembly under the Lanzin regime, elected in October 1985, was officially dissolved during General Saw Maung's coup d'état on 18 September 1988. As promised by the new ruling junta, nationwide elections were subsequently held on 27 May 1990. But the new regime refused to hand over power to the 485 elected members until a new constitution was drafted. Thus, discounting the two National Conventions formed in 1993–6 and 2004–7 to draft this new constitution,[19] the formation of a bicameral legislature and fourteen provincial assemblies following the 2010 general election was the first sign of democratizing progress for twenty years—a major affair for the country.

According to the constitution ratified in 2008, the Union Parliament (or Pyidaungsu Hluttaw) in Naypyitaw is composed of a lower house of representatives (Pyithu Hluttaw, 440 seats) and an upper house of nationalities (Amyotha Hluttaw, 224 seats). Following the example of the US Senate and House of Representatives, the two houses seem to have relatively equal powers.[20] Often, though, the lower house tends to be the most influential, if only by the number of its members, which gives it a clear advantage whenever there is a decisive vote of the two houses combined. Only three-quarters of seats are elected by universal suffrage. Under the constitution, the remaining quarter of seats in each of the two houses of the Union Parliament—a maximum ("not more than" or ma po thaw) of 110 seats for the lower house (Article 109b) and of fifty-six seats for the upper house (Article 141b)—are reserved for the Tatmadaw. The assemblies of the seven states (Pyinae Hluttaws) and of the seven regions (Tine Dae Tha Gyi Hluttaws) follow the same pattern. 75 per cent of the seats are chosen by the electorate, while the number of military representatives appointed in each of the fourteen provincial assemblies must correspond to a third of the total number of elected civilian legislators—or mathematically speaking, about a quarter of the seats in each assembly (Article 161b). In 2011, 222 military representatives were appointed in these fourteen provincial parliaments; in January 2016, they numbered 220.[21]

Convened on 31 January 2011, three months after the 2010 elections, the first session of the new Pyidaungsu Hluttaw, scheduled while the SPDC still held the reins of power, prompted strong criticism. One of the exiled Burmese opposition media even labelled it the "15-minute parliament".[22] Debate sessions indeed appeared exceedingly brief, and the topics of discussion scarcely developed. Two elements in particular were denounced, both by outside analysts and by those rare legislators from the democratic or ethnic opposition bold enough to voice their criticism.[23] Firstly, the conspicuous presence of unelected representatives from the Tatmadaw, all sitting in uniform in both the national and provincial parliaments, showed that the armed forces were still far from fully retreating from civilian affairs and that the transition from military rule was far from complete. Secondly, the legislature was utterly dominated by the USDP, a true composite of interests and prominent personalities reputed to have been more or less close to the junta and the Tatmadaw, but with no established ideology or political program for the post-transition era.

One year later, however, a major event greatly enhanced the prestige of the legislative institution: the entrance into parliament of the NLD and, above all, of its iconic figurehead, Aung San Suu Kyi. By-elections were held on 1 April 2012 with the aim of replacing the forty-odd USDP legislators who had joined a ministerial cabinet in Naypyitaw, or were nominated by President Thein Sein as chief ministers of one of the fourteen provincial governments. After years of electoral boycotts, the NLD under Aung San Suu Kyi ultimately chose to enter the electoral race proposed by the authorities. This met with strong internal resistance, however.[24] Several historic party leaders, such as the late Win Tin, an opponent from the early days and a political prisoner for nineteen years until his release in 2008, fiercely opposed the idea of the party breaking with its traditional position.[25] Another NLD veteran told me that "a semi-democratic system is not democracy; this is not what the people want", so why play that game?[26] Nevertheless, the party's central committee decided to enter the "semi-democratic" system and work from within. In order to participate, the NLD registered with the Union Election Commission in November 2011, and thereafter fielded candidates for all seats contested.[27]

In this respect, the NLD's entrance into parliamentary politics and its return to the legal forefront considerably raised expectations about its upcoming role as the leading legislative opposition.[28] Not wishing to enter government merely through nomination to a ministerial post, however prestigious, Aung San Suu Kyi had succeeded in compelling her party to engage in a democratic electoral exercise ensuring the legitimacy of its comeback and that Aung San Suu Kyi truly be "chosen by the people". Under house arrest in Yangon during the 1990 elections, the democracy icon had never before been an electoral candidate, and it was not until 2012 that she could claim a personal electoral victory. Along with forty of her colleagues, she joined the ranks of the Union parliament at the end of the third session in May 2012.[29] For its part, the post-junta leadership led by President Thein Sein saw the political consecration of "The Lady" as a chance to restore its image in the eyes of the international community. Indeed, after the vote, Western powers started to dismantle the various sanctions regimes they had imposed on Myanmar since the 1990s.

The individuals who became Union MPs in 2010 and 2012—whether appointed by the armed forces or chosen by the electorate—have since been the object of increasing interest, both inside and outside the country. One can expect this trend to continue with the second post-SPDC—and NLD-led—legislature, elected on 8 November 2015. As the literature on post-authoritarian South Korea, Taiwan and Brazil has shown, in polities experiencing a transition from authoritarian to semi-democratic rule, legislators can often act as "democratizing elites". It matters, therefore, who enters parliament in times of transition, as the profile and past experiences of a policymaker commonly and often strongly influence his or her political behavior and ideology. Parliamentarians are expected to sway the legislative agenda according to their own set of values and ideas, as well as their personal backgrounds and profiles.

Earlier studies of Myanmar's post-independence politics have long emphasized the sheer dominance of Bamar, Buddhist and military-trained male policymakers. Some have even quantified this dominance, including Yoshihiro Nakanishi in his thorough analysis of power in the Ne Winian era (1962–88).[30] As a matter of fact, the USDP's parliamentary supremacy after the 2010 elections gave a general impression that the country's highest legislative body was once again utterly controlled by former senior army officers and retired junta bureaucrats, who had simply traded their uniform for the traditional *longyis* of Bamar Buddhist politicians. Yet, a closer look at at the first post-junta Union parliament's social composition, in both houses, reveals some unexpected features. In contrast with the homogeneity of the executive leadership, the USDP-led legislature, particularly after the 2012 election of forty-one NLD members (including twelve women), exhibited a certain degree of diversity.

Drawing on Hanna Pitkin's concept of political representation,[31] I intend to show here that Myanmar's inaugural post-junta legislature has not been a "mirror image" of the country's current population, or even electorate. A single document compiling the short biographies of 492 elected Union legislators and 166 Union military representatives was released in Burmese in 2012, and translated into English a year after.[32] How this document was compiled, and why it was approved for public release at that time, remains a mystery.[33] Even officials from the Ministry of Defense seemed not to know why the Tatmadaw hierarchy even agreed to divulge the profile of the military parliamentarians appointed in 2012.[34] As my findings on the analysis of the 658 Union legislators have suggested elsewhere,[35] the typical Burmese MP sitting in the first post-junta legislature closely mirrors the conventional archetype of the Burmese postcolonial leader: a man, in his mid-fifties, ethnically Bamar and Buddhist, holding a Myanmar university degree (BA or equivalent), engaged chiefly in business activities or in the public sector, particularly education.

In mid-2012, when the biographical information was first released, the average age of the 658 Union parliamentarians was 53.5. The average age was higher for elected civilian legislators: 56.9 in the Pyithu Hluttaw, and 58.1 in the Amyotha Hluttaw. The 166 military appointees in both chambers of the Union parliament appeared far younger: as professionals, they are constrained by a strictly enforced retirement age, which the Tatmadaw fixes at sixty. In mid-2012, the average military representative was thus 42.5 years old in the Pyithu Hluttaw and 43.5 years old in the Amyotha Hluttaw. Women were sorely underrepresented in the first post-SPDC legislature. Only eighteen female candidates were elected in 2010, while twelve more, all under the NLD banner, entered parliament after 2012. In January 2014, two female lieutenant-colonels were appointed military representatives (out of 166). At the legislature's dissolution at the end of 2015, women MPs formed less than 5 per cent of the assembly. Furthermore, of the 658 MPs registered in 2012, a substantial majority were ethnically Bamar: 71.7 per cent of the Pyithu Hluttaw, and 64.5 per cent of the Amyotha Hluttaw. This appears to reflect the general consensus that Myanmar's total population consists of a two-thirds majority of ethnic Bamars.[36]

In 2012, 405 of 435 elected and appointed legislators in the Pyithu Hluttaw (93.1 per cent), and 197 of 223 (88 per cent) in the Amyotha Hluttaw, have listed Buddhism as their personal faith—Myanmar identifies itself as a Buddhist country, so it is not surprising to find a large majority of MPs claiming to be Buddhist. More notable is the fact that every single one of the 166 military representatives was Buddhist. This seems to validate the scholarship on the Tatmadaw, which has long emphasized that despite absolute Bamar dominance of the senior ranks, ethnic background has been less of an obstacle to promotion than religious background. Thus Rakhine, Mon and Shan army officers could reach the ranks of colonel and above, as long as they could prove that they were Buddhist, well-educated and married to similarly educated spouses.[37] By comparison, there were only twenty-seven Christian MPs in the lower house and twenty-five in the upper house. The whole legislature elected in 2010 numbered only three Muslims.

In the post-2012 Pyithu Hluttaw, 359 elected and appointed MPs (82.5 per cent) were university graduates and held at least a bachelor's degree in arts, law or science, a medical graduate degree (MBBS) or the equivalent. Similarly, 184 parliamentarians (82.5 per cent) in the Amyotha Hluttaw were educated to BA (equivalent) or above. If we leave aside the military appointees—who are army professionals—one of the most interesting features of the socio-professional profiles declared by the 492 elected legislators in 2012 is that, contrary to the widely held stereotype, only a minority of those who entered parliament in 2010 boasted a military background. Many observers of Burmese politics would have expected the first post-junta legislature to be riddled with ex-military officers and former SPDC leaders, yet the latter formed less than 9 per cent of the total legislature.[38] Rather, the substantial majority of civilian representatives in both houses of the Union parliament were involved in trade, business, banking and other commercial activities. A total of 141 elected MPs (21.4 per cent) indicated careers as shopkeepers, merchants, traders, property owners and company managers. This group was followed by professionals from the education sector: teachers, school headmasters, university lecturers, and private tutors (83 MPs, or 12.6 per cent) and then by other civil servants (81 MPs, or 12.3 per cent).

Robert Putnam once considered the social background of elites to be a key indication of where power lies in a society.[39] A longitudinal examination of successive legislatures' social composition can therefore provide "insights into changes in the foundation of social power" in a polity, especially in the context of free and regular elections.[40] Changes in the social composition of leaders, at all levels of leadership, are thus to be considered indicators of the degree of democratization, modernization and professionalization achieved by a society in transition. Consequently, comparative analyses of the composition of Myanmar's present and future legislatures may indicate any fundamental changes in the structure of social power, and whether this change (or lack thereof) has had an impact on the country's legislative professionalization, and ultimately its modernization and democratization. This requires investigation of the differences and similarities in the social composition of Myanmar's first "post-SPDC" legislatures (2010–2015, 2015–2020, and beyond). The same comparative work may also be conducted using Myanmar's fourteen provincial parliaments as case studies, whenever data becomes available. As this monograph went to press, the full biographical details of the 491 legislators elected in November 2015 (including 390 from the NLD) were still not fully investigated.[41]

When it convened on 31 January 2011, the first plenary session—tasked with electing top parliamentary officials and the first post-SPDC presidential team—conveyed the impression that a rubber-stamp assembly was in the making in Naypyitaw.[42] However, the second parliamentary session, convened in August 2011, opened in a more optimistic atmosphere. This time, foreign and Burmese journalists were allowed to follow internal workings and interview legislators at the end of each day. As a matter of fact, news coverage of legislative activities has increased substantially since recording of debates in both chambers of the Union assembly has been permitted.[43] Daily summaries of parliamentary debates have thus been included in evening news broadcasts on state-owned television, and since 2015 even the state-run *Global New Light of Myanmar* devotes its page 2 to legislative happenings. Since the third session (January–May 2012), all subsequent regular sessions—and the sole emergency session, called in May 2013 after a series of communal riots across the central plains—have proved to be equally active, with public debates recorded (see Table 4).

In its five years of existence (January 2011 to January 2016), the Union parliament enacted 232 pieces of legislation—whether new, revised or amended.[44] The lower house in particular has, between 2011 and 2014, introduced twenty-six laws, revoked fourteen others, substituted twenty-seven laws and amended fifty-five.[45] Session after session, a sense of bold optimism was evident among elected legislators. Questions began to be raised on topics once deemed too sensitive to address, including abuses of power by local military authorities and the fate of political prisoners. Lawmakers started to openly challenge most proposals for new legislation put forward by the executive. Drafts prepared by cabinet ministers and the presidential entourage have been rebuffed more and more often; clarifications have increasingly been requested.[46] Legislators, including those from smaller parties, have also proved audacious enough to expose publicly cases from their own constituencies of alleged corruption and land-grabbing by the armed forces.[47]

Table 4: Schedule of the plenary and emergency sessions of the first post-SPDC Union legislature (2010–2015)

Sessions	*Dates*
First plenary session	31 January–30 March 2011
Second plenary session	22 August–25 November 2011
Third plenary session	26 January–2 May 2012
Fourth plenary session	4 July–7 September 2012
Fifth plenary session	18 October–22 November 2012
Sixth plenary session	9 January–21 March 2013
Emergency session	*20–21 May 2013*
Seventh plenary session	25 June–30 August 2013
Eighth plenary session	1 October–15 November 2013
Ninth plenary session	13 January–26 March 2014
Tenth plenary session	28 May–31 July 2014
Eleventh plenary session	11 September–28 November 2014
Twelfth plenary session	19 January–28 August 2015
Thirteenth plenary session	16 November–29 January 2016

Source: *Global New Light of Myanmar*.

The 2008 constitution has enshrined a presidential system. This institutional arrangement logically confers on the executive power a lead role in state policymaking. It consequently leaves the legislative branch with a potentially strong oversight (or "check and balance") function, but a weaker law-making role. The president cannot dissolve the parliament, but the parliament can—provided that several legal conditions are met—impeach the president. In practice, therefore, institutional arrangements intended to limit the role of the legislative branch can be countered by political factors. Bold behavior and extensive legislative activity by parliamentarians—first among them the speakers (or presidents) of the houses—can strengthen elected assemblies vis-à-vis governmental structures. In the face of executive power embodied by President Thein Sein and his proactive entourage of experts and policy advisors—some of whom, after 2011, came from the returning exiled diaspora—the Union parliament started to assert itself from the third session in 2012.[48]

As speaker of the lower house and a charismatic former Tatmadaw joint chief-of-staff, Thura Shwe Mann has proved reluctant to leave management of the reformist agenda to the presidency alone.[49] According to a number of elected representatives—including from the opposition—he has gradually "imposed his style" on the lower house.[50] Speakers are key parliamentary players. They guide debates, can decide the pace and content of legislative agendas, create new parliamentary committees and select their members. They can summon legislators from all parties to discuss the importance of a vote before it is held, shape and reshape coalitions, and act as the principal channel for dialogue with the executive.[51] Since he was elected speaker of the Pyithu Hluttaw—a post he was not tipped to take before the transition, as many observers had predicted he would become president in 2011—Thura Shwe Mann has painstakingly attempted to regulate and control the legislative process. This was even more discernible after 31 July 2013, when the Pyidaungsu Hluttaw leadership was constitutionally bestowed upon him halfway throughout the legislature.[52] From then on, Shwe Mann used the combined houses of the Union parliament as a powerful political instrument and strategic public arena to assert himself as a key actor in the first years of the post-SPDC transition.[53]

For his part, Khin Aung Myint, a former two-star general elected speaker of Amyotha Hluttaw in January 2011, has proved a far more unassuming figure. His leadership did not prevent the upper house from taking part in the resurgence of parliamentary affairs. The Amyotha Hluttaw introduced as many bills as the lower house, and even took bolder and swifter initiatives.[54] For instance, in August 2012, a group of Amyotha Hluttaw legislators started an impeachment procedure against the constitutional tribunal, rejecting the latter's earlier decision denying parliamentary committees the status of Union-level bodies.[55] It was also the upper house that first discussed, and voted in favor of, electoral reform.[56] An NDF upper house representative brought a motion for introduction of proportional representation,[57] something the lower house—including its speaker—has been less inclined to dwell on, voting down the upper house proposal and thus preserving first-past-the-post.[58] Though given far less publicity than debates in the Pyithu Hluttaw—an assembly peppered with charismatic politicians and well-known public figures such as Aung San Suu Kyi, Htay Oo (a senior member of the USDP) and Thura Shwe Mann—those in the House of Nationalities have become surprisingly "lively," according to most of the elected representatives whom I met early on.[59]

Session after session, the legislative branch has shown that it is not merely a rubber-stamper for the executive that succeeded the junta in 2011. Within both chambers, the most dynamic representatives have emerged as unexpected opponents of Union-level governmental bodies, debating presidential decisions and sometimes directly opposing ministerial proposals.[60] Even the sacrosanct armed forces budget has been openly contested by civilian representatives, to the point of being officially reduced from 19 per cent of the national budget in the 2011–12 fiscal year to 12 per cent in 2014–15.[61] Although with much approximation and many shortcomings, parliamentary practices and the complex mechanisms of the legislative process have thus been revisited since 2011.

The parliamentary committee structure, among others, is essential to the work of any legislative body. Committees are made of a restricted number of legislators who enjoy a certain degree of delegated authority to discuss the content of past and new legislation.[62] The 2008 constitution provides for only four standing committees in each house of the Union parliament.[63] All other committees have to be framed *ad hoc*, according to the needs of the moment and, more significantly, the will and whims of both speakers. Forty-one standing parliamentary committees were formed between 2011 and 2015.[64] They were tasked with focusing on issues that both speakers wanted to probe, such as Bank and Monetary Development, Judicial and Legal Affairs, National Races Affairs, or Farmers, Workers and Youth Affairs. Aung San Suu Kyi was asked in August 2012 to chair the newly formed Rule of Law, Peace and Tranquility Committee.[65] Committees have regularly gathered to discuss draft bills, including when parliament is not in session. Legislators—including military delegates—discuss drafts, ask questions, and argue about articles and amendments.[66] A new parliamentary life and working style has thus resurfaced in a country where public, multiparty legislative debate has been absent since the dissolution of the multiparty parliament in March 1962.

Legislative Travails and Weaknesses

The resurgence of parliament was not flawless, however. It is already possible to identify a substantial number of weaknesses and constraints that Myanmar's new legislative branch has been facing—and will continue to face in the coming years. After all, five years after its resurrection, the parliamentary system is still only, as Olson and Norton put it, in its "adolescence".[67] These challenges, from a lack of basic capacity to institutional limitations, Myanmar's traditionally weak and volatile party system, the entrenchment of personalized politics and a growing gap in working efficiency between the central and provincial assemblies may hinder the consolidation of legislative work in future parliaments. As I claimed earlier,[68] odds are that most weaknesses already observed between 2010 and 2015 may well be exacerbated from 2016 under the second post-SPDC legislature—just as dominated by the NLD (80 per cent of elected seats since November 2015) as the first was by the USDP (79 per cent).

Legislative performance is usually secured when parliamentary bodies have adequate capacity and expertise to carry out the various functions they are meant to perform. Perceptibly, the great majority of Burmese individuals who entered parliament in January 2011—as well as in 2016—lacked proper knowledge about the very idea of legislative work. Most legislators I have interviewed, from as early as 2013—including those from the USDP—all underlined this basic lack of capacity. Besides, after decades without legislative activity, the parliaments as institutions did not enjoy the relevant human, financial and organizational resources to fulfill their functions when they were "resurrected" in 2011.

But presiding officers were all aware of these daunting challenges.[69] As a consequence, external assistance was sought. The United Nations Development Program joined with the Inter-Parliamentary Union and various Scandinavian states to set up capacity-building projects to strengthen the internal functioning of the Union parliament. Australia, France, and Poland have sent capacity-building missions. The US-based National Democratic Institute (NDI) set up a Parliamentary Resource Center in Naypyitaw. Its office and staff, funded by the US Agency for International Development, welcome Burmese MPs for training and research, regardless of their party affiliation.[70] The European Union has also organized monitoring workshops for MPs and parliamentary staff.[71] Delegations of Burmese MPs have in turn been invited to visit other parliaments throughout the world: in Berlin, Seoul, Jakarta, New Delhi and Washington, D.C., among others. The bureaucracy assigned to the parliament has progressively been expanded.[72]

In successive sessions, then, elected and appointed legislators have had to learn the legislative ropes. In a sense, the very fact that, within just five years of its existence, the Union legislature has succeeded in regularly and thoroughly discussing ministerial budgets, drafting new bills, scrutinizing policy papers, debating within committees, setting up proper question-and-answer sessions and so on has been most commendable. Most memory of parliamentary affairs during Myanmar's first postcolonial decade has been lost. So far, there have been no scholarly studies, including in Burmese, on how the legislative process technically worked back in the 1950s that might offer a workable background for the new MPs of today.[73] Legislators, and state civil servants seconded to the legislature as parliamentary staff, had to literally reinvent parliamentary life in the early 2010s. And, somehow, it worked.

There is still a long road ahead, though, particularly in light of the 2015 election results; only 13 per cent of incumbent civilian MPs were re-elected.[74] The newcomers will have to learn the ropes in turn. During the first post-SPDC legislature, national and provincial parliamentarians did not benefit from personal offices in their parliament buildings, and had to work wherever they were put up. Very few could boast well-trained assistants or secretaries. Most stood alone to perform their legislative duties, waiting for input from their respective party headquarters or leader in parliament—when they had one. Some employed sons or nephews as personal secretaries or translators.[75] The monthly salaries of Union MPs were more than tripled in a majority vote held in January 2015, from 300,000 kyats to 1 million kyats.[76] Yet, it has remained challenging for MPs representing remote constituencies to travel back and forth during a plenary session.[77] Furthermore, interpreters have long been lacking. All parliamentary discussions and writings, including at provincial level, are conducted in Burmese. Though most major non-Bamar populations do speak the language, a handful of ethnic MPs speaking Chinese or marginal dialects have difficulty following debates. This prevents them from playing a more active role in the legislature.[78]

As underlined by an ICG report, external influences have also been strongly felt in the Union parliament.[79] While lobbying is part of all democratic parliamentary games, the shadowy influence of crony businessmen with vested economic interests and the rise of radical religious movements, some outlining strong anti-Muslim agendas, have pervaded deliberations in the assemblies without any form of check or balance.

Furthermore, the literature on legislatures and democratic change shows that after a noticeable—even euphoric—emergence during the transition period, "adolescent" assemblies often return to the failings of paternalist and factional politics that prevailed under previous regimes—after one or two acclaimed parliaments, post-authoritarian legislatures are commonly drawn back into old-fashioned clientelistic politics. Patrimonial political culture and corruption tend to resurface and to dominate electoral competition and legislative politics. This was observed, for instance, in post-communist Ukraine and Russia in the 1990s,[80] in post-military Thailand and the Philippines at the turn of the century,[81] and in Indonesia in the early 2000s.[82] The shortcomings of Burmese parliamentarianism in the 1950s—internecine conflicts and self-destructive factionalism—could once again undermine the country's legislative life today. The National Democratic Force (NDF) has been a good illustration of such traditional factional infighting.[83] Formed by NLD dissidents who wanted to take part in the 2010 elections boycotted by the head office and Aung San Suu Kyi, this party in turn suffered a split as early as August 2011, when several of its elected MPs created the New National Democracy Party (NNDP), and in 2012, when two others tried to get back in the good graces of Aung San Suu Kyi in order to be reinstated in the NLD.[84] Three years on, the NDF was all but wiped out as it fails to win a single seat in the Union parliament renewed in November 2015. All this strongly echoed the parliamentary shenanigans of the 1950s.

Internal divisions did not only affect Bamar-majority parties. The ethnic parties are equally centrifugal—and many of them paid the price of such division in November 2015 when they too failed to win seats against the NLD. For instance, Shan leaders clashed early on over participation in the electoral process codified by the 2008 constitution. In the 1990 elections, the Shan Nationalities League for Democracy (SNLD) stood among the victors, thanks to a strategic alliance with the NLD. The party has, however, been wavering over entering the electoral game proposed by the 2008 constitution.[85] Its historic leader, Hkun Htun Oo, who was released in January 2012, has long been loath to disown the decades of struggle he has led against successive military regimes—which spurned his party's success in 1990.[86] Like the NLD, therefore, the SNLD opted to boycott the 2010 elections. This prompted several of its leaders to defect and form the Shan Nationalities Democratic Party (SNDP). The SNDP chose to run in 2010; it took some twenty-two seats in the Union parliament and thirty-six in provincial assemblies. Five years later, in the run-up to the November 2015 polls, the SNDP and SNLD looked as if they were irreconcilable.[87] Yet this time, the SNLD entered the electoral race, again in alliance with the NLD. It subsequently won fifteen seats in the Union parliament, while the SNDP was crushed.

The Karen have also been divided between those eager to participate in the post-2010 constitutional order and those who still consider the 2008 constitution illegitimate.[88] In late 2014, the two Chin parties boasting lawmakers at the Union level also succumbed to factionalism. A third Chin-based political force was then formed by members of the now defunct Chin National Party.[89] The inter-party turmoil considerably weakened the incumbent Chin MPs, all of whom lost their seats in November 2015 to the NLD or the Zomi Congress for Democracy (ZCD), save one who had re-joined the NLD in March 2015.[90] The Rakhine, long seen as unified under strong nationalist agendas defended by the Rakhine Nationalities Development Party (RNDP), have also had to deal with gradually rising infighting. The January 2014 merger between the RNDP and the Arakan League for Democracy (ALD) has not proved as successful as expected and the cadres of the newly formed party, the Rakhine/Arakan National Party (RNP/ANP), have appeared increasingly at odds in the build-up to, and aftermath of, the 2015 polls.[91] Thus, after the NLD's November 2015 landslide, and with a highly volatile party system based on loosely institutionalized political parties unable to survive internal crises, the prospects for a healthy and stable multiparty parliamentary system appear quite bleak.[92]

Lastly, there is a deepening gap between the Union parliament and the fourteen provincial assemblies, in terms of both influence and jurisdiction.[93] So far, only five or six of the provincial assemblies appear to have been moderately active and to have adopted significant legislation on local social, economic and technical matters. The most dynamic has certainly been the *hluttaw* of Yangon, the former capital.[94] The regional assemblies of Mandalay, Bago and Ayeyarwaddy have also regularly convened to discuss socioeconomic and technical issues—provincial *hluttaws* are not entitled to vote on key political matters, which reside with the Union parliament. For their part, the Chin and Rakhine state *hluttaws* have conducted surveys plans on poverty reduction.[95] The Mon state *hluttaw* has discussed the use of vernacular languages on official signboards.[96] Others, including the Kachin state *hluttaw*—which has since 2011 proved unable to seriously address the ongoing armed conflict between the central government and armed forces and the Kachin Independence Organization—have remained relatively passive.[97] Too often, the state *hluttaws* fall under the sole authority of the provincial executive power, headed by a chief minister constitutionally appointed by the Union president—regardless of provincial election results. Until some constitutional reform is adopted by the parliament, habits of political and administrative centralization will remain the norm.[98] Besides, many state and regional ministers have kept their parliamentary seats between 2010 and 2015, consequently exercising both executive powers and legislative functions simultaneously. Unlike Indonesia in the immediate post-Suharto era, when decentralized elected bodies had a decisive democratizing impact,[99] Myanmar still seems far from ready to implement sweeping decentralization measures, despite progress.

More empirical research, therefore, is needed to measure the impact the parliament has had since it reconvened in 2011 over both the transitional process and, more broadly, the process of change at work in post-junta Myanmar. Criticism abounds in Yangon's political and media circles.[100] Yet the renewal of parliamentary activism in the country is good news. Raising the performance and strengthening the institutionalization of the new legislative branch will be essential to consolidate the political process.[101] The 2015–20 performance of the second post-junta legislature, overwhelmingly led by the NLD, will give key indications of the resilience, autonomy and value of the resurrected legislative branch. As late 1990s Indonesia has shown, the affirmation and empowerment of parliamentary institutions is a crucial element in consolidating the first steps of a transition.[102] In Myanmar, the executive branch—the armed forces, as a matter of fact, but potentially a government under the full control of one iconic leader—traditionally tends to concentrate power and influence in its own hands. An autonomous legislative apparatus is therefore needed, in order to develop the capacity to counter the authoritarian temptations of newly empowered elected politicians and bureaucrats—or the armed forces. Otherwise, the newly formed legislative power may remain bogged down either in staunch opposition to the powerful presidential office, or in a rubber-stamp role without the capacity to move up the scale of legislative influence and transform into a real policymaking body.

4

PATTERNS OF PERSISTENT PRAETORIAN BEHAVIORS

Despite the broadening of the political space and the resurgence of multipartism in the "post-SPDC" landscape of the 2010s, the Burmese military intends to remain a key political actor. Of that there is no doubt. The senior military officials who succeeded Senior-General Than Shwe and his associates in 2011 have made it clear: the armed forces are to remain politically involved, in order to "support" any kind of political process at work in a country that they perceive as still under constant internal and external threat of disintegration.[1] The Tatmadaw continues to construe itself as the "caretaker" of the political process. Its historic roots in Myanmar's independence struggle and postcolonial society are such that it would be hard for its hierarchy to conceive of a political arena in which soldiers had no acknowledged policy role. Since the 1950s, the Tatmadaw has developed an integrated sense of self that makes its presence felt in the country's social, cultural, economic and, of course, political realms of power. Driven by enduring multidimensional perceptions of threats and a powerful coercive apparatus, its overall clout has reached every corner of Burmese society.[2]

Reversing that historical trend promises to be particularly arduous, if not quixotic, in the foreseeable future.[3] As long as the country is prey to continual political violence and potential fragmentation, as long as the ethnic issue persists and social and communal conflicts are not resolved, the de-politicization of this interventionist military institution will remain utopian.[4] As much as their predecessors since the 1960s, the current Tatmadaw elite still consider themselves "obliged" to participate, beyond the mere defense of the country against external threats—the traditional role of any military apparatus—in Myanmar's governmental affairs, if only to ensure national cohesion.[5] The Deputy Commander-in-Chief, for instance, said as much before his promotion.[6] His direct superior, Senior-General Min Aung Hlaing, who took over from Than Shwe as supreme commander in March 2011, has also recalled this point regularly in major addresses to the nation. The armed forces' exclusive function remains that of leading the country on the path of development, reform and democracy, while safeguarding the unity and integrity of both the nation and its new constitution, ratified in 2008.[7]

Therefore, the establishment of a Western type of army professionalization, grounded on sound civilian control of the armed forces and the latter's complete disengagement from politics, still appears impractical; so has argued Maung Aung Myoe, an authority on Burmese military affairs who regularly teaches at the National Defence College in Naypyitaw.[8] Just a few years after the transition was initiated in 2011, the Tatmadaw looked as if it had now perfected its "praetorian" and resolutely interventionist role. Its position on the scale of intervention clearly illustrates Nordlinger's "guardian" type of military institution or Mutiah Alagappa's "participant-ruler" type.[9] The current generation of Burmese senior officers appears to have construed the fact that the military's sovereign function of restoring order and "tranquility" (*htee-ngyein aye-chan-yeh*), which began in 1988 with the SLORC coup, was effectively accomplished and confirmed by the disbanding of direct military rule in 2011.[10] Henceforth, as Chapter One clarified earlier, the armed forces have been striving to defend a more indirect policy function, as "guardians" of political institutions and potentially, in the long run, to transform themselves into "arbitrators" or "moderators" of Myanmar's civilian political scene—provided the latter proved pacified and cohesive.

Apparently, then, the Tatmadaw officer corps of the 2010s is far from contemplating complete subordination to any type of civilian power.[11] Put in Machiavellian terms, why indeed would armed men obey unarmed ones? Patterns of praetorian behaviors have been routinely observed in the country since the early 2010s, as this chapter emphasizes. The armed forces, either directly or through more subtle means including various legislative tools and their shadowy control over the judiciary, still intrude into national and—more crucially—local politics. Odds are that these praetorian tendencies will continue to linger in the foreseeable future, unless large-scale, cohesive and credible civilian alternatives emerge to balance the political clout of the armed forces, and thus offer civilian—rather than military and coercive—responses to all kinds of political, social and economic problems and challenges facing Myanmar in the short and long term.

Who Is In Charge?

The scope of military intervention in Burmese contemporary society seems unique, even compared with other Asian postcolonial societies that have experienced deeply entrenched military rule, such as Thailand, Pakistan or Indonesia. As observed during the 1970s when General Ne Win embarked his regime on a gradual civilianization process, the Tatmadaw's underlying grip on all levels of power, even after it initiated another partial withdrawal in 2011, should not be overlooked. The Burmese armed forces, as an institution, still maintain significant control over the country's main avenues to power, influence and wealth, built over five decades of military dominance.[12] The gradual and official disengagement from day-to-day politics, exciting much comment at home and abroad since 2011, does not, therefore, indicate a complete exit from the political, social and economic realms. As David Steinberg has argued, despite hopes for the creation of new non-military avenues for social mobility, the civilian sphere in post-junta Myanmar is still far from able to fully and independently oversee state policymaking.[13]

This has led to a certain degree of confusion, even among long-standing experts of Burmese affairs. Who is in charge now, in the mid-2010s? How has the decision-making process been reshaped since the disbanding of the junta in 2011? Who controls what? Who decides what, and when? For twenty-three years, the junta, or SLORC-SPDC, effectively ran the country from above as a high military command, with first General Saw Maung (1988–1992) and then Senior-General Than Shwe (1992–2011) as its uncontested supremo. By contrast, the first post-junta administration, as observed between 2010 and 2015, could no longer be assimilated as a pure military high command with a clear pyramidal and hierarchical structure, under the sole authority of a small unit of generals and, ultimately, one supreme commander.[14] Since the transfer of power to a semi-civilian government and legislature in early 2011, power and decision-making has become more diffuse than it was under naked military rule. This has confused even local political actors, baffled by the muddled policy structures and chain of command. I recall a discussion I had with an NLD veteran about two years after the transition started. He was still constantly mixing up the acronyms SPDC and USDP, implicitly conveying the idea that the SPDC had simply mutated into the USDP in 2011, and that the channels of power and policy decisions had not evolved one iota since the alleged "transfer of power" following the 2010 elections.[15]

It is true that the armed forces remain involved in all major state institutions. Under the 2008 constitution, the Tatmadaw retains three Union-level ministries (home, defense and border affairs) and one provincial-level ministry in the fourteen decentralized states and regions. It also reserves a quarter of parliamentary seats in all national and provincial legislative bodies. The state bureaucracy and police forces, which both fall under the scope of the military-controlled ministry of home affairs, can still largely be construed as proxy instruments of military control.[16] The country's corrupt and inept judiciary is yet to become a defiant and assertive branch of government inclined to prosecute military personnel and force the Tatmadaw into greater accountability, in contrast, for instance, with the Pakistani judicial system.[17] The Tatmadaw appears to have grown even more independent since 2011, moving away from the tentative efforts at transparency and answerability promoted by the new state legislative and executive branches under the aegis of former generals such as Thein Sein, Khin Aung Myint and Thura Shwe Mann.

On the other hand, the Tatmadaw top brass is no longer in full control of all these state institutions. Discordant and plural voices are now heard in Naypyitaw, and since 2011 policy decisions have routinely been made without the full consent of the military leadership. In an increasingly diversified political landscape, under a more open and even globalizing society, the Tatmadaw simply cannot keep a direct eye on everything. It has neither the capacity, nor the ability, not even—as now seems evident—the will to continue to micromanage the country and its economy as it did before 2011.[18] As a matter of fact, despite including three ministers still in full uniform and being two-thirds dominated by retired senior army or navy officers, Thein Sein's government has successfully adopted policies of its own since it was sworn in. Since it first convened in January 2011, the first post-SPDC Union parliament has likewise discussed and adopted bills or motions that the armed forces openly opposed. Only in constitutional matters does the Tatmadaw have an effective veto in parliament. Yet as far as the regular legislative process is concerned, the 2008 constitution does not provide the military with sufficient instruments to impose its will regarding any policy decision made by the executive or legislature, as the speaker of the upper house proudly emphasized during our discussion in one of the thirty-odd parliament buildings.[19] This will become even more pronouncd under the second post-SPDC legislature, led by the NLD. New centers for policy discussion have thus emerged since 2011, to be consolidated after 2015. All have struggled, but continue with relative success to move gradually away from the nexus of the active armed forces.

Certain events have confirmed, intentionally or otherwise, the impression of a muddled chain of decision-making in Naypyitaw. Take, for instance, the resumption of the Kachin civil war in June 2011. Rejecting the Border Guard Forces scheme unveiled by the SPDC in 2009, the Kachin Independence Organization (KIO) was subsequently unable to reach a political compromise with SPDC representatives during the 2010 electoral campaign. Its leadership thus opted for the reopening of the insurgent front against the Tatmadaw after a seventeen-year ceasefire. The new government of President Thein Sein, having embarked on a new round of peace talks with a dozen ethnic armed groups in late 2011, has repeatedly proved incapable of halting the military offensives launched by the Burmese armed forces throughout Kachin State and in the northern parts of Shan State, where the KIA (the KIO's armed branch) has secured strategic strongholds. Unlike in a mature democracy, where civilian control of the military is guaranteed, Myanmar's president is not the supreme head of the armed forces—the commander-in-chief holds this position, and neither can impeach the other. In December 2011, Thein Sein publicly ordered the Tatmadaw to stop its incursions into KIA-controlled areas. Nevertheless, several army battalions, out of touch with their respective military headquarters, continued the fighting against the Kachin rebels for weeks.[20] Three months later, Thein Sein overhauled the composition of the governmental negotiating team commissioned to dialogue with the Kachins, placing at its head a loyal advisor, ex-general Aung Min. But the latter failed to convince the KIO leadership that Naypyitaw had made great efforts in late 2012 to pressure the Tatmadaw top brass to withdraw from the vicinity of the KIO's headquarters in Laiza, near the Chinese border.[21] In January 2013, the Union parliament passed a resolution calling for a halt to the conflict. The Tatmadaw responded in a statement that it would not launch direct offensives against the Kachins, but rather act in self-defense whenever needed, implicitly dismissing the legislature's orders.[22]

Some local observers have argued that a classic good cop/bad cop approach has thus been at play in the north of Kachin State since the early 2010s.[23] The quasi-civilian administration in Naypyitaw has attempted to publicly de-escalate the conflict since it resumed in 2011, at the same time as local Burmese military commanders—seemingly with the blessing of the army top brass—have basically continued arguing for the use of broader coercive measures against the KIA. Other analysts have tended to oversimplify the complex situation as a mere illustration of the army hierarchy's retention since 2011 of absolute control over decision-making. In other words, the Tatmadaw gives little weight to the voice of civilian branches of the government, even when these are led by retired top military officials. "We knew that the Burmese army was full of tricks", a KIO official told a correspondent of *Time* magazine.[24]

Between 2011 and 2015, the state's failure to provide a coherent and unified response to Myanmar's social and ethnic conflicts has thus conveyed, voluntarily or not, the idea that the post-SPDC leadership actually represents a manifold group of very diverse and muddled institutional identities, strategic interests and policy actors, of whom only the armed forces has clearly distinguished itself. In terms of civil-military relations, this had led to even more confusion, notably with regard to the positioning of the defense ministry, the president's office and the commanding heights of the Tatmadaw.[25] How, in the post-junta context, should we understand the interactions between the commander-in-chief and Myanmar's elected head of state (the Union president), who is constitutionally *not* the head of the military? And what are the relations between the minister of defense (a military man, under the 2008 constitution), his direct superior (the commander-in-chief) and the Union president, under whom he is nonetheless supposed to perform his ministerial functions?

Often, when talking about the authorities, Burmese ordinary citizens routinely refer to "they", "up there", nodding towards the north or above—towards Naypyitaw or, when Yangon was still the capital, towards the Tatmadaw's original headquarters in the northern outskirts—just as if a powerful and relatively identifiable force in military garb, distant and obscure yet never far off, stubbornly remained the ultimate decision-maker in the country. Recurrent crises and moments of tension observed in the post-junta period may indeed have vindicated this local conventional wisdom. As conflicts emerge, as threats escalate, as local contentious politics grow seemingly uncontrollable in the post-2011 semi-civilian context, the size of the basic decision-making unit seems to have shrunk to a few powerfully-connected military men. When student and radical protestors from all over the country initiated a protest march from Mandalay to Yangon in March 2015, it was the minister for security and border affairs of the Bago region—a serving military officer under the 2008 constitution—with whom they had to negotiate. The decision to release or detain them was not in the hands of the (civilian) chief minister, a former army general and SPDC foreign minister, nor of the local mayors.[26]

Likewise, when political tensions mount in the peripheries and ethnic-dominated regions, more often than not it is military representatives that step in to diffuse—in military fashion—the crises. Between 2012 and 2014, the western state of Rakhine was rocked by inter-ethnic and communal violence. Its chief minister, himself a former army colonel, was subsequently sacked—or rather "allowed to retire"—by the presidency in June 2014. Naypyitaw then sent to Sittwe (the state capital) a successor directly drawn from the army, Major General Maung Maung Ohn. The newly appointed chief minister was previously (albeit briefly) a Union-level deputy minister for border affairs—one of the ministerial portfolios under full control of the Tatmadaw. Putting a serving member of the military in this specific position has further indicated the military leadership's continued assumption that soldiers are better equipped to restore order and tackle the problems of a state persistently marred by communal violence.[27] Interestingly, although all elected MPs from the Rakhine National Party sitting in Sittwe's provincial parliament opposed the major general's appointment, many other Rakhine politicians viewed rather favorably the nomination of a military man to the state's top policy position, given their anxiety at seeing their home region allegedly falling under threat from Rohingya and other Muslim groups.[28]

Similarly, keeping a tight control over the various populations of the country, beyond war zones and areas under the full control of rebel militas, is still a significant armed forces objective. This control, though far from fully effective, is not only exercised through physical force. It is also made possible through the regular use of authoritarian legislation and regularly updated bureaucratic constraints that aim, with more or less acuity, to monitor the whereabouts and movements of Burmese citizens. The Tatmadaw's perspective in the matter, a transnational activist group has recently claimed, has not much evolved since the transfer of power in 2011.[29] In August of that year, the newly-appointed Union minister of home affairs, Lieutenant-General Ko Ko, introduced a draft bill in parliament that purported to revamp the legislation on guest registration that has prevailed in the country since the colonial era. The new Ward or Village Administration Law was debated in both houses in September–October 2011, and eventually adopted by the Union legislative branch in February 2012.[30] It intended to repeal a series of laws adopted as early as 1907. Yet the spirit of the new bill did not much differ from that of the previous legislation: every single Burmese individual is requested to register each household guest s/he receives in her/his home with the local authority. This new law confers broad enforcement powers on public officers at the ward and village levels—both under the command of the home ministry's General Administration Department, and therefore the military.[31] Since 2014, these have increasingly been used to prevent the free movement of potential activists and public demonstrators throughout the country.[32]

Many analysts have argued that, after a few quiet post-transition years, the Tatmadaw has reverted to its old authoritarian habits and become increasingly assertive in 2014 and 2015. As the country prepared for a new round of general elections five years after the first phase of the planned transition in 2010, the armed forces have appeared less tolerant of criticism and dissent, obviously no longer accepting blame as in the early months of the transitional process.[33] Despite the considerable easing of censorship since 2012, each time local journalists have bluntly criticized the army, as an institution or targeting only one of its members, the reporters, bloggers and photographers were hunted down and brought to court. In October 2014, when a former close aide to Aung San Suu Kyi turned reporter died in army custody deep down in Mon State, the local military authorities tried to cover up the event, which only became public three weeks after the death of the journalist occurred. The local police were overtly reluctant to investigate the case.[34] Public demonstrations were held in front of Yangon's city hall and some forty civil society groups released a public statement condemning the lack of transparency, if not immunity, displayed by military officials.[35]

An impression of military and police impunity undeniably lingers in the collective mind of the Burmese people and many other observers of Myanmar's civil-military relations. For many of its critics, the Tatmadaw remains a power machine basically seeking only rent, control and profit, and this throughout the country. It has developed such an extensive network of patronage and control over land and people in postcolonial Myanmar that it would be practically impossible to effectively dismantle such a Leviathan overnight.[36] The Tatmadaw has, moreover, long implicitly encouraged a hierarchical, highly corrupt and authoritarian approach to law enforcement, as Nick Cheesman has emphasized in thorough research work.[37] Underlining the legacies of impunity that all Burmese men in uniform have enjoyed since the colonial period, Cheesman has shown how the Tatmadaw has frequently used civilian courts to prosecute any Burmese citizen criticizing the army or undermining its morale.

As early as the 1950s, particularly during Ne Win's 1958–60 caretaker administration, the army leadership systematically and rigorously tried every single Burmese parliamentarian, journalist or community leader that had disparaged the Tatmadaw.[38] In January 2015, two Kachin girls were raped and murdered in the northern borderlands of the country; their fate provoked a strong emotional response in social and traditional media alike. Believed by many to be the culprit, the Tatmadaw promptly released a statement warning that it would prosecute anyone arguing that Burmese soldiers were responsible under Article 211 of Myanmar's Penal Code, which deals with "false charges" created for a case.[39] Robert Taylor has even argued that through the SLORC and SPDC years, when it was routinely accused of all kinds of crimes, the Tatmadaw has become even more efficient in dealing with its opponents' accusatory initiatives.[40] The Tatmadaw also favors the use of martial—not civilian—courts to take action against its own black sheep. This is one of the key judiciary prerogatives of the armed forces, as stipulated by Article 319 of the 2008 constitution.

Nonetheless, modest yet positive steps have deliberately been taken in recent years, by the leadership itself, towards reducing the political clout of the military and improving its relations with civilians.[41] On a few recent occasions the Tatmadaw has handed over the prosecution of soldiers—usually rank-and-files—to civilian courts. This has particularly been the case when individual soldiers have been accused of rape or murder while not on active duty.[42] In the northernmost Kachin territories, militarization is rife and violence observed on a daily basis; a Union MP representing one of the most remote constituencies there has long denounced the "Wild Wild West" scenes constantly played out in those areas. He rejoiced at recent investigations carried out by the Tatmadaw into a series of murders perpetrated by local soldiers. For these to happen, he had to liaise with military-appointed MPs in the Union parliament, so that they could refer the matter to their hierarchy.[43] The latter then sent a letter to the elected MP to notify him—and his constituents—of the arrest, sentencing and demotion of the soldiers involved in homicides. The MP in question has reflected that, when carried out discreetly, pressure on the military seems to pay off.

Lastly, the Burmese armed forces continue to enjoy an extensive foothold in the country's formal and informal economy. The scholarship on civil-military relations suggests that business and financial activities controlled by a military institution, and the personal stakes of military personnel, are often construed as key drivers of the praetorian armed forces' political ambitions.[44] Although their financial clout has been visibly reduced since the economic liberalization launched by Thein Sein's administration in 2011,[45] two military-owned conglomerates have maintained a high level of commercial activity throughout Myanmar and still own considerable areas of agricultural land, natural forest and urban space. The Myanmar Economic Corporation (MEC) and the Union of Myanmar Economic Holdings Limited (UMEHL) have continued to develop and invest in many types of commercial activity and industry in the country, with impressive rates of growth in the 1990s and 2000s at a time when the junta secured them *de facto* state monopolies.[46] Since 2011, President Thein Sein's cabinet has taken steps to abolish a substantial number of these monopolies, seeking at the same time to diminish the Tatmadaw's hold over both the UMEHL and the MEC, whose secretive bureaucracies have remained solidly dominated by retired and active military officers. But, many analysts insist,[47] the country's decades-old patronage-driven system, over which the military holds considerable sway, is still powerfully grounded, and will thus hardly be shaken in the coming years. One unwelcome consequence—especially for the post-2015 NLD leadership—is that the state-owned and military-controlled financial and economic "behemoths" will most probably remain a drag on the country's economic progress and development.

The Military in Legislative Affairs

One particularly innovative channel through which the Burmese military continues to hold sway over post-junta policymaking process is to be found in the legislative arena.[48] As the national and provincial ministries are reserved for the Tatmadaw, the presence of men in uniform in all of Myanmar's legislative assemblies also remains highly controversial. In the country's newly-formed legislative branch, the armed forces have constitutionally secured one quarter of all parliamentary seats. With such a presence, the Tatmadaw can continue to claim a major legislative role, and therefore extend its clout over the post-SPDC lawmaking process, as well as any potential constitutional reform aiming to challenge the order established after the completion of the 2003 roadmap. This was illustrated in June 2015, when the military MPs vetoed the major points of the first amendment bill ever submitted to the Pyidaungsu Hluttaw (Union Parliament).[49]

Under the 2008 constitution (Chapter XII), "more than" 75 per cent of all Union parliamentarians, gathered in an exceptional joint meeting of both houses, are needed to pass a constitutional amendment. The Tatmadaw thus essentially has a veto. The fact that the 166 military-reserved seats—unlike the civilian seats—have been continuously filled between 2011 and 2015 demonstrates how significant the issue has remained for the military top brass.[50] This constitutional veto can be construed as an (undemocratic) means for the armed forces to guard against amendments and other undesired interventions not only from the civilian opposition, but also from any party gaining absolute domination of the Union legislature. In the first post-SPDC legislature, the USDP ultimately proved far less loyal to military interests than many observers had speculated.[51] As Khin Aung Myint, speaker of the upper house (Amyotha Hluttaw), stated when I first interviewed him in August 2013:

> "Both houses of the parliament have twenty-five percent of unelected armed forces representatives. The reason for that was that there was a fear that there would be a one-party dictatorship inside the parliament. So, soldiers, who are not involved in party politics [but rather only in 'national' politics], were added to balance [the parliamentary debates]".[52]

The distinctive use of the terms "party politics" (*pati naing-ngan-yeh*) and "national politics" (*amyotha naing-ngan-yeh*) must be underlined. It is certainly more than just a semantic difference endorsed by a few Tatmadaw ideologues. It has been constantly stressed by, and in, the military's official discourse since the early 1990s.[53] The Tatmadaw has unremittingly viewed itself as the embodiment of the Myanmar state (*Myanma naing-ngan-daw*), and therefore feels it ought to be engaged in "national" politics (construed as noble) and anything potentially affecting the security of the state (*naing-ngan-daw loun-kyoun-yeh*). But, at the same time, the armed forces should not indulge in "party politics", which are perceived by the military psyche as parochial, divisive and at the roots of the instability that propelled the Tatmadaw to power in the late 1950s.[54] Therefore, both seat reservation in legislative bodies, and military-controlled ministries in the Union and provincial governments, have been construed as the best institutional tools to enable the Tatmadaw to remain a policymaking actor, without having to form a specific political party shaped for and by soldiers—which, despite its closeness with the armed forces, the USDP was not. The post-junta Tatmadaw aims to maintain a direct policy influence, without having to rely on a political proxy and indulge in potentially disruptive party politics.

Reserved parliamentary seats for the military are a relatively rare institutional arrangement, however. This original instrument of legislative influence, which embodies Mutiah Alagappa's "participant-ruler" type of politically engaged armed forces,[55] is still found today in China and a few African countries. Between 1932 and 2000, the Thai legislature has been systematically influenced, if not fully dominated, by the Royal Thai Army.[56] Under General

Soeharto's administration (1965–98), Indonesian army officers were also appointed to legislative bodies as well as to the civilian bureaucracy, following the official doctrine of *dwifungsi*, or dual function, which legitimized the mixture of military and political roles of the Indonesian armed forces. Between 1977 and 1997, 20 per cent of seats in the national assembly in Jakarta were reserved for senior army officers. Only in 2004 were the latter fully withdrawn, in the midst of the country's democratic consolidation.[57] The presence of non-elected legislators in parliament is not necessarily a characteristic of authoritarian regimes—as the House of Lords in the United Kingdom illustrates. Yet, the Burmese case, whereby representatives of a state institution—the armed forces—act as a fully independent and unaccountable policy actor, is problematic. The 25 per cent parliamentary seat reservation for Tatmadaw officials is indeed repeatedly denounced, at home and abroad.[58] Appointed men in uniform seldom share common views with elected civilian legislators who are first and foremost supposed to be responsible to and for their immediate constituents.

Since 2011, however, the role and significance of the military representatives has evolved, at least in the Union legislature. While remaining very discreet, they do not seem to be mere bit players. Among the 166 military legislators first appointed on 20 January 2011 by former junta chief Senior General Than Shwe, there were very few high ranking officers: three colonels in the Pyithu Hluttaw, two in the Amyotha Hluttaw. Likewise, only one colonel was appointed to the head of the military delegation of each of the fourteen provincial parliaments, except for the Kayah state assembly, in which the highest ranking officer was a brigadier general (he was then appointed chief minister of this state). All the others were lower ranking officers. The Tatmadaw's revaluation of its role in parliament became apparent in April 2012. Vice Senior-General Min Aung Hlaing substituted fifty-nine low-ranking army officers in both houses of the Union parliament with higher-ranking senior officers, including four brigadier generals in each chamber.[59] With this move, Min Aung Hlaing apparently wished to reaffirm that the Burmese military, as an institution, was bound to remain explicitly engaged in broader non-military policy and legislative matters.[60] In that respect, Tatmadaw officers ought to be ready to devote a few years of their soldiering career to non-combat and administrative functions, including as legislators. The image of responsible officers devoted to public affairs, occupying a bureaucratic office for the good of the nation, has long been a key element in the rhetoric of upper Burmese military circles.[61] Courses in political science and comparative parliamentarianism have, moreover, been added to military academy curricula in such institutions as the prestigious Defense Services Academy (DSA) based in Pyin U-Lwin, near Mandalay.[62]

Military appointees have been regularly replaced with no civilian oversight. They do not retire or resign from their army position. Essentially, they are seconded to legislative bodies for each parliamentary session by their hierarchy.[63] They therefore keep their salaries as employees of the armed forces—unlike civilian MPs, who are paid a monthly allowance during their entire tenure[64]—and are nonetheless granted the daily stipend that civilian MPs receive when parliament is in session. Being seconded to the parliament also seemingly does not prevent or slow down internal promotion. For instance, Brigadier General Thet Tun Aung was an army colonel when he was appointed to the Union parliament in April 2012; he was later made a one-star general whilst still a parliamentary representative of the armed forces.[65]

Initial assessments of the military representatives' behavior in parliament (2010–15) have highlighted several patterns.[66] Far from being a silent, immobile and obstructive force in parliament, military legislators interact and work alongside their civilian colleagues, especially within the forty-odd parliamentary committees that have been set up in both houses.[67] The first observation to be made is that the military appointees have not, since the inaugural session held in 2011, favored systematic obstructionist tactics. Obstruction and disruption of legislative debates are an active parliamentary policy routinely used by opposition or minority groups, as legislatures in Taiwan, India, Ukraine or South Korea have frequently illustrated.[68] The Tatmadaw parliamentary group has stated that it would staunchly oppose any substantial change only on constitutional matters and a few select issues, such as Article 59(f), which bars Burmese citizens with foreign relatives (including Aung San Suu Kyi) from presidential nomination. In November 2014, for instance, a spokesman for the Tatmadaw, Colonel Htay Naing, publicly declared that the army was resolutely against a swift constitutional revision.[69] On 25 June 2015, he was proved right when the military parliamentary bloc uniformly opposed five of the six constitutional amendment proposals put forward in parliament—including on Article 59(f).[70]

Yet, constitutional amendments apart, military appointees cannot impose a decisive veto on any other legislative activities. This was, for instance, observed during the impeachment of the Constitutional Tribunal, initiated by the parliament in August 2012. Civilian legislators from both the USDP and the NLD had objected to a decision of the tribunal denying parliamentary committees the status of Union-level bodies. A majority of elected representatives from the

Amyotha Hluttaw then voted to impeach the Tribunal; all military MPs present in the upper house opposed the bill.[71] The same scenario was reproduced in the Pyithu Hluttaw a week later: all elected legislators voted in favor of impeachment, whilst 101 military MPs opposed.[72] This was a case of all civilian MPs—USDP, NLD, and those from ethnic parties—working in concert, while the military MPs could not put forward sufficient legislative instruments to effectively veto this move.[73] Thus, if Tatmadaw parliamentary delegates retain a critical right to veto most alterations to the 2008 constitution, they cannot boast any decisive veto on other basic legislative procedures.

Interestingly, on various issues, including discussions related to the annual defense budget, military legislators have sometimes voted against proposals put forward by cabinet ministers, or even the USDP parliamentary group, which had a supermajority in both houses of the Union parliament between 2010 and 2015—even though both houses include many former senior army officers.[74] The military MPs have also regularly abstained on, or even sometimes approved, certain bills drafted by opposition representatives, including NLD members after they entered parliament in April 2012. Military representatives also publicly discuss in the assemblies subjects that were previously taboo. For instance, as early as September 2011, the speaker of the lower house, Thura Shwe Mann, proposed a motion to release political prisoners still in custody. The motion was adopted thanks to the unanticipated support of the military MPs.[75]

As most interviews I've carried out in parliament have revealed, a form of cordial dialogue has gradually been established between civil and military representatives in the corridors and offices of the parliament. As an illustration, during the 2013 debate on the annual defense budget, military appointees approached civilian representatives from various opposition parties behind closed doors, in order to convince them not to vote against the budget prepared for the 2013–14 fiscal year by the Ministry of Defense. They asserted that the budget for the armed forces was one of the lowest in Southeast Asia and that too great a reduction would hurt the country's "national security." As a result, only sixty civilian MPs voted for a reduction during the vote.[76] A handful of parliamentarians from various ethnic parties have also outlined how they have progressively attempted to establish some sort of friendly discussion with their military colleagues, especially the mid-ranking officers.[77] No close relationship seems to have been established yet, however; senior military officers remain an isolated elite in Myanmar.[78] USDP legislators have only had slightly more success, however. Smiling at me, one retired air force officer sitting as a Yangon representative in the upper house laughed: "We [active and retired officers] come from the same boat".[79] But a retired infantry lieutenant-colonel, also a USDP legislator in the Amyotha Hluttaw, sighed that secrecy remains the norm, and that the less contact Tatmadaw soldiers have with civilians—including retired officers—the better.[80]

It is also worth noting that military representatives do not always stand together when they vote. Unquestionably, each time a drafted bill appeared to interfere with the Tatmadaw's corporatist interests—or violate constitutional principles—they have showed that they are capable of expressing themselves as one. However, on a number of occasions, their hierarchy seems to have granted them greater flexibility. This has been noticeable mostly on civilian and non-strategic issues, at both Union and provincial level. This is in line with the image that the Tatmadaw wants to project: of the responsible, poised and sophisticated officer, well informed about the problems of his country and able to respond on his own initiative.[81] For instance, during an early 2013 session of the Yangon regional parliament, Dr Nyo Nyo Thinn, an elected MP, tabled a draft bill to regulate the granting of trishaw (three-wheel bicycle taxi) licenses. The speaker of the assembly then requested a public, non-secret vote. Four Tatmadaw majors rose to approve the draft, whereas the rest of the military parliamentary group all abstained.[82]

Furthermore, military appointees have directly submitted only a handful of draft bills since 2011. Most proposals dealing with military matters and security issues are formulated entirely by the executive branch, the ministry of defense and the ministry of home affairs in particular, rather than by Tatmadaw delegates in assemblies.[83] Neither the Pyithu Hluttaw nor the Amyotha Hluttaw has convened the defense and security parliamentary committees which can, under Articles 115b and 147b of the 2008 constitution, be formed in both houses. Of the very rare draft bills drawn up by military representatives, some appear quite trivial compared with the usual national security affairs that have long concerned the Tatmadaw. They do, however, often, reflect the deep seated nationalism of the armed forces. For instance, in September 2011, Major Soe Hein Naung submitted a proposal urging the government to "supervise the orthography of Myanmar language in local media" during the second session of the Pyithu Hluttaw.[84] Two weeks later, Colonel Htay Naing submitted a similar proposal, to "use the word Myanmar in works of writing, compiling and publishing with the aim of promoting the national prestige (...) and prohibit use of the word in unsuitable place and usage, including use of the word as a brand."[85] As soldiers, military MPs tend to obey and look to their superiors for advice and guidance. Thus it remains quite difficult for a mid-ranking officer, such as an army captain or major, to take overt individual initiative in parliament, especially in the presence of a direct superior. Only the few senior army officers seem to have more room for maneuver.[86]

Military legislators have, therefore, hardly become significant "lawmakers". The level of the Tatmadaw's legislative activity has obviously remained low during the first post-SPDC legislature (January 2011–January 2016). The Tatmadaw parliamentarians have instead opted to remain mere "arbitrators" or "law checkers," and might not move beyond this basic function, which, as a matter of fact, has proved a relatively quiet one since 2011. Far from proving an active lawmaking force in parliament, the military appointees have perhaps simply been under instructions to fulfill their traditional "tutelary" function, as protectors of the 2008 constitution (Article 20f). As for the fourteen provincial *hluttaws*, the role of military appointees remains unclear, although the same patterns may be observed.

Yet, Myanmar's parliamentary landscape will evolve dramatically under the impetus of the supermajority held by the NLD since November 2015. The second post-SPDC legislature will prove very different from the first one. Clearly, in the new Union parliament formed in January 2016, the military parliamentarians are the most evident opposition bloc to the dominant NLD. Indeed, they enjoy 25 per cent of the seats, while the USDP is a distant third bloc with only 8 per cent of seats in the two chambers. The military MPs, then, may intervene more openly in upcoming legislative debates than before 2016. They might become directly involved in the preparation of new laws to better suit the interests of the Tatmadaw, as an interventionist institution. They may also work to counter legislations prepared by political parties openly hostile to military interference in civilian and legislative affairs (that is, the NLD), or even act as an obstructive force to a future executive branch daring enough to begin dismantling the military's preserved political and economic domains.

The fact that three major generals have been appointed to the two chambers of the Union parliament in January 2016 points to a greater capacity for decision-making by the military parliamentary bloc in the second post-junta legislature. It also suggests that, even if it had hoped to encourage a few military Tatmadaw to "cross-floor" and join forces with Aung San Suu Kyi's bloc, the NLD will in reality hardly be in a position to provoke divisions within military ranks.

Military MPs, especially at the Union level, may indeed change their legislative behavior and strategy in parliament to become stalwart lawmakers in coming years. They may, for example, make systematic use of petition to the constitutional tribunal to delay the legislative process. This will, however, depend on the authority, charisma and power of future Tatmadaw commanders. As very few long-standing observers of Myanmar appear optimistic enough to envisage the post-2015 emergence of a serene and pacified parliamentary scene, a prompt military disengagement from the country's legislatures therefore remains bleakly distant.

5

THE SALIENCE OF ETHNIC AND RELIGIOUS CLEAVAGES

All future scenarios for the democratization and stability of Myanmar will require thorough addressing of the country's long-standing ethnoreligious question. A wide body of research on Burmese postcolonial politics has relentlessly emphasized the salience of the country's ethnic conundrum, largely inherited from the British colonial era.[1] Successive postcolonial governments, whether democratically elected or military-led, have failed to devise state policies that meaningfully bridge the social, economic and political gaps between Myanmar's various ethnic and religious communities,[2] a matter that has inspired violent conflict without resolution since independence was won in 1948.

Most minority groups have often considered the historical legacies of an anti-colonial struggle led by the (majority) ethnic Bamars (especially the *Thakins*, or "masters", such as Aung San, U Nu), of post-1948 nation-building and the need for a national language and Buddhism's prevalence in the country's heartland to be key features of a long-standing Bamar hegemony.[3]

Evolving ethnic identities and continuing internal migration—whether forced or voluntary—have further complexified the country's ethnic landscape in recent decades. Already a composite social, cultural and ethno-linguistic patchwork in the late colonial era, Myanmar's post-independence multiethnic society has, with the passing of generations, become even more complicated. In the late 1990s, anthropologist Ananda Rajah highlighted the quasi-absence of "rationality" underlying the country's multiple ethnicities defining their belonging to a specific identity.[4] Besides bewildering name changes by ethnically mixed individuals (Shan-Bamar, Mon-Karen, Shan-Palaung, Bamar-Dawei and so on), anthropologist Maxime Boutry argues that political contradictions and far-flung "Burmanization" processes imposed by the central state, far from unifying ethnic minorities in a common front against the Bamar-dominated center, have instead fractionalized ethnic groups into legions of politicized sub-communities.[5]

Burma's ethno-political landscape has become a multifaceted web of inter-ethnic and intra-ethnic tensions; this has diminished the threat that ethnic separatism posed to the central authorities in the early postcolonial days. Apart from a few marginal tribes dwelling on the fringes of Myanmar's polity, most minority communities continue to maintain a highly complex symbiotic relationship with the ethnic Bamar majority. Claims for outright secession from the Union of Myanmar are now clearly in decline in the early twenty-first century, but demands for greater political autonomy, self-government, resource-sharing and the respect of non-Buddhist and non-Bamar social and cultural rights still stand very high on the agenda of the country's minority elites, such as the Kachin, Rakhine, Mon, Shan or Karen. To echo Donald Horowitz's argument, ethnic affairs in twenty-first-century Myanmar have gradually metamorphosed from forthright "secessionism" in the early postcolonial state to more conventional (yet still confrontational) "ethnic politics" within the delineation of the contemporary "Union" of Myanmar.[6] However, many authors have claimed that, unless they are depoliticized, ethnic and religious identities in contemporary Myanmar will continue to be at the core of multiple power plays and conflicts in the decades to come.[7]

Ceasefire Politics and the Transition

The most troubling political burden weighing on post-junta Myanmar is the protraction, if not aggravation, of inter-ethnic conflicts. Between 1989 and 1995, various Kachin, Shan, Wa, Pa'O, and even Karen armed outfits chose to normalize their relations with the junta that emerged from the 1988 coup. Lt. Gen. Khin Nyunt, then military intelligence chief, was the new brain behind this round of "gentlemen agreements" with ethnic insurgents. Echoing a policy periodically tested by General Ne Win between the 1960s and 1980s, fragile but guaranteed deals enabled various armed groups opposed to the central government to control economic flows and local administrations on their peripheral territories, while effectively ditching their long-standing secessionist struggle against the Burmese authorities in the course of the 1990s and 2000s. Around 40 to 50,000 rebels entered a form of truce with the SLORC in the early 1990s, and benefited from the country's gradual opening up, especially towards a booming China or Thailand.[8] The Tatmadaw was then able to refocus its counterinsurgency campaigns against the remaining Karen, Karenni, Shan or Naga insurgents, driven back to the Thai and Indian borders. But ceasefires were only meant to be an "entry point" to a further, more substantive political dialogue between the various ethnic political leaderships and the Bamar-dominated central government. Apart from periodical meetings, for instance between the Kachin Independence Organization (KIO) and Khin Nyunt's offices in the late 1990s and early 2000s,[9] the expected political dialogue was put back indefinitely by the ruling establishment—even more so after Khin Nyunt and his entourage were purged by the SPDC top brass in 2004.

Ethnic tensions re-emerged with the adoption of the 2008 constitution, which envisioned a form of decentralization in the creation of fourteen provincial governments and legislative bodies, but remained fundamentally Jacobin in spirit. In April 2009, the SPDC unveiled a Border Guard Force (BGF) plan, which anticipated bringing all "armed forces" under the sole command of the Tatmadaw. This implied demobilizing all the ethnic militias still armed so as to unify all of the country's military troops, as stipulated by Article 338 of the 2008 constitution. The BGF policy thus purported to reduce these local armed groups to mere border policing forces, and was therefore promptly lambasted by the most powerful of these ethnic-based rebel outfits.[10] The Mandarin-speaking Kokang minority and the Shan State Army-North (SSA-N), both of which had negotiated ceasefires with Khin Nyunt as early as 1989, soon expressed strong opposition to Article 338. The KIO, whose last and only ceasefire agreement was signed in 1993, has also long refused to see its soldiers come under the control of the Burmese central authorities.[11]

Only a few small ethnic militias which were already acting as *de facto* border police forces, such as the Kachin National Democratic Army (NDA-K) along the borders with Yunnan or the Democratic Karen Buddhist Army (DKBA) near Thailand, initially accepted the BGF plan.[12] Most others staunchly opposed it. In the run-up to the 2010 elections–when the SPDC still held power–armed conflict resumed between Tatmadaw troops and several ethnic rebel outfits. Whereas only one ceasefire had been broken throughout the 1990s,[13] the first cracks in the system appeared in August 2009 when the Kokang militia, the Myanmar National Democratic Alliance Army (MNDAA) was suddenly crushed by the Tatmadaw. Under the aegis of a notorious drug lord, Phone Kyar Shin (or Peng Jiascheng in Chinese), the MNDAA was rather reviled by the Burmese military commanders for its communist roots and close links with China. The Burmese offensive against it was supervised by Lieutenant-General Min Aung Hlaing, then chief of the Bureau of Special Operations No. 2, based in Lashio.[14] The Burmese state—the SPDC—had chosen, for the first time in years, to use violence to deal with one of the weakest ceasefire groups.

But it was after the disbanding of the SPDC, in the midst of the 2011 transition, that the seventeen-year-old ceasefire between Myanmar's central authorities and the KIO was eventually broken. On 9 June 2011, the KIO's armed wing, the Kachin Independence Army (KIA), resumed a low-intensity insurgency in many parts of Kachin State where Kachin, Bamar, Shan and other communities (including Chinese ones) have long competed over resources and land, as well as in the north of Shan State, near the Yunnan borders. A real thorn in the side of Thein Sein's new government from 2011, the Kachin political elites (mostly Christians) have since recovered their unity and the admiration of the Kachin people, whose support they had lost after signing the 1993 ceasefire.[15] Various Kachin political parties saw their registration refused by the SPDC-controlled Union Election Commission in early 2010. As a direct consequence, the most prominent Kachin leaders were barred from joining the 2010 general elections. The maneuver frustrated many of those who had wanted to participate in the polls—and somehow give a nod to the much-debated roadmap to "discipline-flourishing democracy"—throughout the Kachin State.[16]

The armed conflict, which spread out across the north of Shan State, was still at a stalemate in early 2016 despite a vast deployment of military might. It has highlighted growing distance between the armed forces top brass and Thein Sein's administration in Naypyitaw. There have most probably been hundreds of deaths in the ranks of the Tatmadaw and the KIA since 2011,[17] although neither side has issued any precise information on the subject. The conflict has also generated more than 140,000 refugees and displaced persons along the Sino-Burmese borders since 2011.[18] At the same time, this once again awakened the neighbouring "Chinese dragon", anxious at the growing instability on its periphery and mounting anti-Chinese feeling observed on Burmese social media. In particular, Beijing has not forgotten President Thein Sein's suspension of the Myitsone dam construction, also in Kachin State, in September 2011. In 2013, however, unlike during the Kokang troubles of 2009, the Chinese authorities publicly offered to mediate between the KIA and the Burmese government, straightforwardly discarding their usual rhetoric of non-interference in the domestic affairs of China's neighbors. Several rounds of peace negotiations between the Tatmadaw and the KIA leadership were held in the Chinese border town of Ruili, Yunnan province.[19] The area is too vital to China's economic and strategic interests, particularly in Yunnan, for Beijing to let political instability spread.[20]

While the Kachins took up arms once again in 2011, other ethnic nationalities have, on the contrary, chosen to negotiate with the post-SPDC government in Naypyitaw. In the new atmosphere of optimism and reform, they saw a fairly good opportunity to negotiate something new with the post-junta authorities. This was a time to be on board for a negotiated pact, when key political and military leaders of groups long at odds with the Bamar elite met the latter around the negotiating table. Among them were the leaders of the Karen National Union (KNU), which has waged one of the world's longest-running civil wars since 1947, as well as the Palaungs, the Chins and the main Shan rebel group operating near the Thai border. In November 2011, President Thein Sein charged one of his key advisors, ex-major general Aung Min, with conducting negotiations with those ethnic minorities that had never signed a truce with the Burmese state.[21] Two other prominent retired army officers, Thein Zaw and the late Aung Thaung (both elected Union MPs in 2010), were more specifically charged with negotiations with armed militias considered tougher to deal with, such as the Wa and the Kachin in the north of Shan State.

A momentous policy realignment—albeit led by men drawn from the erstwhile junta—was thus ushered in by the post-SPDC regime, one that soon prompted positive domestic and international responses. As with Khin Nyunt's strategies in this regard between 1989 and 1993, these new initiatives met with rapid success. Military truces were easily reached in late 2011 and early 2012, and talks about the revival of a nationwide, government-inspired peace process soon gained greater credibility. Most of the ceasefire agreements already in effect—including that signed in 1989 between the SLORC and the powerful and untamed United Wa State Army (UWSA)—were renewed. A former military intelligence officer, Aung Min also secured the signature of historic agreements with General Yawd Serk's Shan State Army-South (SSA-S) in December 2011, then the KNU's dominant armed faction, the Karen National Liberation Army (KNLA), and the Chin National Front (CNF) in January 2012. In February 2012, the New Mon State Party (NMSP) also resigned itself to a peace accord; the Karenni National Progressive Party

(KNPP) agreed to a ceasefire a month later and the Arakan Liberation Army (ALA) in April. Efforts continued in 2013, with the signing of an agreement between the All Burma Students' Democratic Front (ABSDF), an armed group formed by primarily Bamar students along the Thai border area just after the 1988 uprising. In March 2015, a total of sixteen armed groups were signatories to the draft of a nationwide ceasefire agreement proposed by Thein Sein and Aung Min.[22] To supervise the various processes of inter-ethnic peace talks and further advise the president's office in the matter, the Myanmar Peace Center (MPC) was established in Yangon in late 2012.[23] It has been supported with European, Japanese and UN funds. Under its aegis, hundreds of peace negotiations, bringing together an increasing number of formal and informal representatives of ethnic political and social forces, the Tatmadaw and the central government, have been sponsored in various places, including on foreign soil, in Thailand and Yunnan.[24]

After decades of warfare, the building of trust among Myanmar's ethnic and Bamar leaders was always bound to be an extremely arduous, if not herculean, task. One acclaimed aspect of the peace parleys initiated by Thein Sein's administration since 2011 has been the involvement of a large number of civil society groups. The inter-ethnic dialogue has not been left solely to the Tatmadaw or a handful of commanding political elites in their ivory towers. Political parties, ethnic or faith-based NGOs, international consultants and the local media were involved in, and summoned to, the talks from the early stages. The Kayin People's Party (KPP), which had been allowed to register as a political party and run in the 2010 elections, quickly stood as a key mediator between Aung Min and the KNU.[25] The NLD itself has regularly sent representatives to the peace parleys, including Win Htein, lower-house MP for the constituency of Meiktila for three years (2012–15). Myanmar Egress, an NGO and think-tank already influential under its founder Nay Win Maung (d. 2012), has also been present in most negotiations, as has the Shalom Foundation, mediating with and within Kachin groups.[26]

After four years of parley, peace negotiators of all stripes pushed for the signature of a draft nationwide ceasefire accord before the end of President Thein Sein's tenure, in late 2015. They argued that addressing the underlying causes of Myanmar's endless civil war head on and to finding political, non-military solutions to the quagmire was impossible without first reaching a nationwide peace—a first since independence.[27] This assumption was also based on the promise that a Nation-wide Ceasefire Agreement (or NCA in the local jargon) would lead, at last, to substantive "political talks" between all the major ethnic and Bamar leaderships. Yet this was left for the second phase of the post-SPDC transition, after a new government and legislature would have been formed in early 2016. How will the NLD, whose legitimacy was enhanced by electoral victory in November 2015 (including in ethnic areas), attempt to restore a form of in-depth, perceptive and farsighted political dialogue among all ethnic groups so as to envision a workable "Union" of Myanmar? To give one example, Aung Min, who lost his parliamentary seat to an NLD candidate in 2015, promised as early as 2012 the organization of a national conference, along the lines of the 1947 Panglong Agreement, signed by Aung San himself.[28]

There remains much to accomplish at the local level to pacify areas in conflict for so many decades. Most ethnic representatives still seem to want to work with the Bamar majority on a political agreement of the same national resonance as the Panglong Agreement.[29] But skirmishes between Tatmadaw battalions and various Shan, Ta'ang (Palaung) and Karen militias that still have not been disarmed have been more than frequent in the jungles bordering Thailand and China.[30] The Kokang rebels, wiped out by the Tatmadaw in 2009, attempted a comeback six years later, in the territories it formerly controlled in northern Shan State.[31] The KIO and several other armed groups still refuse to recognize the 2008 constitution, which they would like to see either dramatically amended or simply abrogated.[32] As Article 20(f) states that the Tatmadaw is ultimately responsible for safeguarding the constitution, the gridlock is all but obvious. Even the Wa and their militia of over 20,000 heavily armed men have laid down new conditions for any future political negotiation with Naypyitaw.[33]

The Union parliament has also begun objecting to its sidelining by the government team since 2011.[34] Thura Shwe Mann, speaker of the lower house between 2011 and 2016, and his own loyalty networks among army ranks and the civilian administration, seem similarly upset at being left out of a process first dominated by two ageing USDP parliamentarians, the late Aung Thaung and Thein Zaw, a retired brigadier and former minister in the SPDC junta. Elected ethnic representatives—whether Lisu, Shan or Kachin—have increasingly voiced the same complaint.[35] A Kachin legislator from the upper house who has regularly visited Laiza, KIA's headquarters on the Chinese border, has lamented the fact that third parties are seldom invited to peace talks between the government and the armed groups. "The KIA and the Tatmadaw can fight on for decades", he bluntly claims, if there is no third party to help untie the Gordian knot.[36]

Criticism of the peace process has also come from below, from several domestic and international civil society organizations. The peace process since late 2011 has in particular focused on several territorial economic concessions and local humanitarian or development programs in areas more or less controlled by ethnic armed groups—as an incentive for peace, before Union-level political negotiation can even start.[37] A popular narrative developed by some ethnic elites and civil society groups over the past twenty years has cynically denounced the "hidden agenda" of the ceasefire strategies already extensively tested by previous Burmese regimes—including that of General Ne Win in the 1960s and 1970s. Often, military truces offered by the Tatmadaw are construed as mere ploys to reduce armed conflict so that Bamar-dominated companies or central government institutions can expand their influence and exploit territories that have long eluded Myanmar's Leviathan state-building. This point has frequently been argued by Kim Jolliffe, a consultant with expertise in, and on, the Thai-Myanmar borderlands.[38] Since 2012, the international community—especially the Scandinavian countries, the United Nations and Japan—has attempted to assist the ongoing process logistically and financially, particularly in the conflict-ridden Kayin State.

Occasionally, however, foreign aid simply consolidates the power of the dominant political and military forces on the ground, while excluding other elements from the peace process. As Wright and Winters have suggested using pan-national data, foreign assistance from democratic countries to states under authoritarian rule can sometimes reward political contestation but not necessarily political inclusiveness.[39] Indeed, many Burmese local associations and transnational groups not party to the ongoing parleys have voiced increasing concern, especially as the prospect of a nationwide agreement loomed closer. In October 2015, forty-one Karen civil society organizations signed a petition denouncing the KNU leadership's acceptance of the national ceasefire agreement proposed by Thein Sein's government.[40] The Women's League of Burma (WLB), a pan-Burmese women's organization based in Thailand, has similarly criticized the full peace process for its lack of concern about female ethnic voices. High-ranking peace negotiators have, indeed, been almost exclusively Bamar male.[41] Ethnic activists equally lament that the misfortunes of the tens of thousands of internally displaced Kachin, Shan and Karen have not been properly addressed during negotiations.[42] More significantly, while "talking peace", the Tatmadaw has never halted its military offensives against the Kachin, Palaung or Kokaung rebels in the northern and most remote parts of the country.

Nevertheless, after some 300 meetings of various sizes over a period of four years, a National Ceasefire Agreement (NCA) ceremony was finally held on 15 October 2015.[43] However, of the sixteen original armed groups that signed the first draft in March 2015, only eight agreed to put their name to the seventeen-page final document. These groups, including the KNU, the CNF, the SSA-S and the PNLO, have since been taken off the government list of illegal organizations (under the Unlawful Associations Act). Other armed groups, including the KIO and UWSA, have proved reluctant to sign a deal from which certain outfits, such as the Kokang militia, were deliberately excluded by the government and the Tatmadaw.[44] The NCA document was eventually approved in December 2015 by the outgoing Union parliament, during its last plenary session.[45]

This attests to the challenges facing the second post-SPDC legislature and executive (from 2016) in dealing with the ethnic conundrum. Beyond the mere signature of a "peace of the brave"—which echoes past experiments by Khin Nyunt and Ne Win—what does a "political dialogue" mean? How, Burmese academic Min Zin has asked, could further steps be taken towards a meaningful inter-ethnic "negotiated pact"?[46] Safeguarding the 2008 constitution is a key objective assigned to the Tatmadaw. If and when peace is relatively within reach, how can antithetic constitutional views be reconciled? Despite the opportunities for minority participation guaranteed by the first constitution (1947), and the creation of seven ethnic-based administrative states under the 1974 constitution, on paper it is the 2008 constitution that has seemingly attempted to establish the most meaningfully "federal" system. The "dead tiger of federalism", which is anathema to past and present Burmese military rulers, has long been construed by them as a mere synonym of secession.[47] Officially, the 2008 constitution delineates greater rights for Myanmar's ethnic minorities. The Union has the duty to develop the languages, arts and culture of the "national races" (Article 22a) and to promote inter-ethnic solidarity and mutual assistance (Articles 22b and 22c). The 2008 constitution has also allowed the right to a federal type of elective decentralization, through fourteen provincial governments and fourteen (partially) elected legislative bodies.[48] The latter were first formed after the 2010 general elections, and renewed after the 2015 polls.

But the ruling elites in Naypyitaw, as well as the National League for Democracy political elite, are still grappling with the idea of federalism and the functioning of proper state decentralization. Myanmar's administrative elites have yet to define a more palpable division of political jurisdiction between the dominating center—Naypyitaw—and its distant peripheries. In the seven states and seven regions (formerly divisions), the separation of powers between the new executive and legislative bodies is seldom guaranteed.[49] Under the 2008 constitution, provincial governments are led by a chief minister, appointed by the Union president, not by the elected state and regional assemblies or the winning parties. A tentative constitutional reform bending this rule was vetoed by the military parliamentarians in June 2015.

Since 2011, the fourteen regional and state *hluttaws* have met with much less regularity than the Union parliament, and their sessions have been far shorter. They have often only dealt with local public grievances.[50] Of the fourteen provincial assemblies, only those in the Yangon, Mandalay, Bago, and Irrawaddy (Ayeyarwady in Burmese) regions have convened fairly regularly.[51] The workings of most *hluttaws* depend on the whims of their respective speakers or the political clout the latter can boast over the state chief minister or the regional military commander.[52] Even the speaker of Yangon's regional parliament (2010–15), ex-army colonel Sein Tin Win, has proudly reported that a few of his counterparts chairing other state or regional assemblies have travelled down to the former capital seeking legislative advice on how to nurture a more productive parliament.[53] Yet, if the provincial legislative bodies could function more regularly, their legitimacy would most probably be enhanced in future legislatures, especially under proactive speakerships. On paper, as in post-Suharto Indonesia, the provincial *hluttaws* could become one of the pillars of an effective decentralization program, a vital condition for democratization, and for greater stability between the Bamar majority and the ethnic minorities.[54] But this would require all ethnic political leaders, the armed forces and the NLD to work on a thorough revision of the 2008 constitution.

Buddhist Revivalism in a Transitional Context

Religion has been a recurrent source of social and political conflict in postcolonial Myanmar, a Buddhist-dominated yet "plural" society. The country presents a mosaic of ethnic and religious identities. The dominant ethnic Bamar are almost exclusively Buddhist, as are the majority of the Mon, Rakhine, Shan and Karen communities dwelling in the peripheries of the country. Ethnic Chin and Kachin minorities, as well as a few Karen and Karenni populations, were Christianized in the nineteenth century. British colonization also brought Hindus, Sikhs and Muslims from the Indian subcontinent, and fostered the migration of Chinese Muslim and Confucian traders, mostly in urban areas. Aside from contested inter-ethnic issues and power struggles, Myanmar has also been beset by social conflicts involving religious matters.

The reformist liberalization initiated by President Thein Sein in 2011 rekindled hope for many citizens in Myanmar. The lifting of censorship and the broadening of public space allowed new forms of expression. Echoing debates of the late colonial era, religion, moral values and the place and influence of "outsiders" in Myanmar's society resurfaced as major themes of public debate, along with punctual and localized communal violence. Buddhist organizations started to regain a political voice in the early 2010s and ignited new discussions on the involvement of the state in religious affairs that would not have been possible a decade ago. When elements of the Burmese Sangha demonstrated in the streets of Yangon and a few other urban centers in September 2007 during the misnamed "Saffron Revolution", the Buddhist-inspired protest movement was swiftly crushed by the SPDC and intense repression followed.[55]

In the early 2010s, however, religious organizations re-emerged as powerful actors seeking to shape public values and influence policymakers. One narrative popular among international observers has argued that this rising tide of inter-religious violence and the political mobilization of Buddhist monks could potentially derail the transition and democratization processes at work since 2010.[56] But the monastic community of ordained nuns and monks (the Sangha) has always been highly decentralized in Myanmar. Only a few Burmese monks have developed enough clout to reach out to a nationwide clientele. Chief among other movements emerging in the early 2010s was the "969" force[57]—named after the holy attributes of the Sangha, the Buddha and his sacred teachings—which notably mobilized communities around anti-Muslim campaigns. Its leaders have articulated a strong discourse presenting Islam as a fundamental threat to Buddhist identity and traditional Bamar values. The movement even launched a sort of "buy Buddhist, boycott Muslim" public campaign, aimed at protecting both the Sangha and the Buddhist religion itself (*sāsana*).[58]

Concomitantly, several riots broke out in 2012 between Muslim and Buddhist mobs in the western territories bordering Bangladesh, and eventually in the urban commercial hubs of Myanmar's central plains. Communal violence was at first chiefly localized in the town of Sittwe and along the coastlines of Rakhine State. It erupted between the majority Buddhist ethnic group and the 1 million-strong Muslim minority of Rakhine, known since the 1950s as Rohingya.[59] The violence then spread eastwards to the country's interior and affected other Muslim communities, including those of Chinese origin.[60] Entire Muslim neighborhoods in the town of Meiktila (north of Naypyitaw), for instance, and then in Lashio, along the historic "Burma Road" towards the Chinese border, were razed and wiped off the map in March and May 2013 respectively.[61] Mandalay, Myanmar's second largest city, was affected by another round of serious communal riots in early July 2014.[62]

Except for the 'Mujahid' revolts of the 1940s and early 1950s in Rakhine State (formerly Arakan), Burmese Muslims have never launched any credible armed rebellions on Burmese soil.[63] Yet since the colonial period Burmese society, primarily Buddhist, and ruling authorities of all ilks have discriminated against the very diverse Muslim communities in numerous ways.[64] Sectarian violence in the country has often been cyclical, depending on the degree of (non-)involvement on the part of central and local state authorities, the Tatmadaw in particular. The British colonial authorities had already recorded anti-Indian and anti-Muslim pogroms throughout the largest cities of the Burmese province in the 1930s. Massive forced migrations of Arakani Muslims[65] took place during the Second World War, in 1978 and in 1991.[66] Outbreaks of anti-Muslim unrest were reported in Yangon as early as 1961, in Mandalay in 1997 and in Sittwe and Toungoo in 2001.[67]

Citizenship remains a thorny question in Myanmar, as does the issue of religious minorities' loss of universal rights and liberties.[68] With the relaxing of censorship in 2012 and the development of the Internet, social networks and new technologies have routinely been used to propagate discourses of racial hatred and incitement to violence. Religious intolerance is not new to the Burmese polity, but with the endless opportunities for engaging the public offered by growing social media and the weaknesses of Myanmar's modern surveillance networks (or the basic absence of any Internet firewall since 2012), Islamophobic discourses have proved rampant.[69] The Rohingya minority is the most specifically targeted. Comprising more than a million individuals in Myanmar, most of whom live in makeshift villages apart from the rest of the Rakhine State population, they are almost systematically considered "Bengali" by all other Burmese communities.[70] Most understand them to be mere foreigners who illegally migrated in recent decades from Bangladesh (or East Pakistan before 1971), which most Rohingya leaders deny.[71] Total segregation and coercive population control policies, like a new form of apartheid, are particularly favored by the Rakhine ethnic group whose members—almost exclusively Buddhist—feel threatened in their very existence by the substantial growth of the Muslim populations in their home region.[72]

The post-junta central authorities' relative passivity and their predicament since 2011—wishing to break with old despotic habits and swift and brutal crackdown strategies, in order to make a good impression on the international community—have perhaps contributed to the most recent conflagrations. What is more, neither the Thein Sein government nor the NLD has shown itself to favor a reasoned assimilation of the Rohingya populations.[73] President Thein Sein himself was once allegedly quoted in favor of the Rohingyas' resettlement outside Myanmar by the United Nations.[74] Aung San Suu Kyi declared just before the 2015 elections that the issue should not be "exaggerated".[75] A government-appointed commission of experts was nevertheless tasked with shedding light on the reasons for the violence and assigning responsibility for the 2012 riots in Rakhine State.[76] Despite an attempt at objectivity, some of its recommendations have since been severely criticized, including by Muslim representatives of the then-ruling party, the USDP.[77]

A highly visible segment of Burmese society has increasingly demonstrated that it is not yet prepared to play along with national reconciliation, considering moreover that the Rohingya—and other Burmese Muslims—are not even part of the core Myanmar nation. A few Buddhist monks have openly led radical popular movements denouncing the "invasion" of Myanmar by Muslim communities. Elites in Yangon and the international community have become very wary of the Islamophobic violence unashamedly advocated by one Buddhist leader in particular, the monk Ashin Wirathu.[78] This *pongyi* (political monk) hailing from Mandalay is highly representative of the new form of quasi-unchecked radicalism that has recently emerged within Myanmar's civil society. Strikingly, he spent eight years (2003–11) in jail during the SPDC's heyday for inciting racial violence. Since his release, he has spearheaded the 969 and, more recently, the Organization for the Protection of Race and Religion (MaBaTha, in its Burmese acronym), drawing strong criticism from international and local communities. In July 2013, the US-based *TIME* magazine labeled him the "Face of Buddhist Terror".[79]

Following a ban on public use of the "969" logo, around 2014 the MaBaTha movement emerged. For Walton and Hayward, the very name of the organization illustrates how intimately racial and national identities are tied up with Buddhism in Myanmar.[80] Wirathu and Sitagu Sayadaw, another prominent 969-allied monk, have served as the most outspoken, yet ambivalent, MaBaTha figures. Among the mobilized monks' many topics of focus in the early 2010s was a series of controversial bills—adopted in 2015—purported to defend the "race and religion" of Myanmar's dominant community, the

Bamar Buddhists.[81] MaBaTha leaders started to curry favor with public intellectuals, politicians and elected parliamentarians, especially in the Mandalay region, the heart of Myanmar's Buddhist and royal culture. A few Union MPs, including a couple from the National Democratic Force (NDF), began to appear in public with the monk Wirathu. Daw Tin New Oo and Daw Khin Waing Gyi, two women MPs elected in 2010, helped the monastic organization to articulate its demands. A draft bill was submitted to President Thein Sein's office in July 2013.

Eventually, President Thein sent a message to the Union parliament in March 2014, encouraging it to establish an *ad hoc* commission to draft a new law addressing two issues: religious conversion and demographic control of certain populations.[82] Two other issues championed by MaBaTha were to be discussed—monogamy and interfaith marriage—but directly through consultation with Myanmar's Supreme Court and the Attorney General's office, not through the new parliamentary commission. After six months of opaque debates, four draft bills were eventually tabled for parliamentary discussion in November 2014.[83] The Religious Conversion Bill and the Population Bill were submitted by the ministry of religious affairs and the ministry of immigration respectively. The Interfaith Marriage and Monogamy Bills were submitted by the Union Attorney General's office. The parliamentary debate began in January 2015, when the twelfth plenary session first convened.

The four bills have been roundly criticized by rights groups, at home and abroad, as discriminatory on religious and ethnic grounds. 180 domestic civil society groups signed a petition warning against them,[84] and the international community has started to raise concerns.[85] But there has also been a certain degree of support towards these four laws within Burmese society.[86] The monogamy law appears to be quite popular among Christian communities—mostly Kachin, Karen and Chin.[87] The bills were supported by most ministers in President Thein Sein's cabinet and a substantial majority of the Union legislators elected in 2010, from across the political spectrum.[88] A few cases have already been reported of these new laws being used in tribunals. In a remote town in the Irrawaddy delta, for example, the police charged a married Muslim man, under the monogamy law, for living with a Buddhist woman who was not his legal spouse.[89]

Interfaith peace-building efforts will, however, necessitate years of patience and steady commitment from all local and international actors involved in the shaping of pacified Buddhist-Muslim relations. The continuing communal tensions and religious-based violence, especially in the run-up to national and local elections, should not divert the Burmese political elites of the moment from pursuing dialogue and encouraging democratic interfaith debates, as many civil society groups are already doing. Violent social and religious movements are sometimes driven by certain elites of a democratic society in order to consolidate existing social cleavages and categories, Amrita Basu (among others) has argued, using the case of aggressive Hindu nationalism in democratic and plural India.[90] Myanmar's policy establishment and the broader Burmese civil society may indeed need to better outline their opposition to radicalism in their own ranks; to combat both sectarianism and the return of a popular xenophobic nationalism that has long proved a regrettably powerful—and successful—policy instrument for successive ruling authorities in the not-so-distant past.

6

ENDURING BURMESE REALITIES

Beside the persistence of praetorian and interventionist behaviors among the still-dominant Burmese military elite, and the salience of ethno-religious conflicts and social cleavages, there are many other issues hampering Myanmar's evolution towards a stable and healthy parliamentary regime with little military intervention. This last chapter focuses on two enduring concerns that the country will continue to face well into the second half of the 2010s, and which may not only slow down the incremental process of military withdrawal from state politics, but also hinder the prospect of rapidly establishing a fully functioning parliamentary democracy.

First, recent post-SPDC reforms seem neither to have altered the clientelistic nature of Burmese society, nor to have toned down ordinary Burmese people's tendency to look to miracle-workers, savior-heroes and great leaders, rather than institutions. With more open electoral competition and the end of censorship rules, these phenomena will probably continue to prosper in Myanmar. The thundering victory of Aung San Suu Kyi's party in November 2015 has further illustrated this tendency. As in other Asian countries, political clientelism and the personification of power remain deeply rooted in Burmese society. These phenomena commonly translate into extensive political fragmentation and divisive fractionalization of the polity along lines drawn by a handful of charismatic individuals, who are perceived as a far better embodiment of leadership than any other institutions. As democratization pundits Przeworski and others have recently summarized the situation, the more fractionalized and segmented a society is, the more difficult it is to govern—whether democratically or not.[1] And in contemporary Myanmar, greater political segmentation routinely translates into greater military intervention in politics.

Second, Myanmar's peculiar geographical position between two contending emergent giants, India and China, at the crossroads of a volatile Southeast Asian region and Indian Ocean where global powers (starting with the United States) vie for strategic influence will certainly continue to take its toll on the country's future domestic policies. Indeed, no other state boasting similar geopolitical stakes, such as Pakistan, has ever proved successful in containing the leadership of its interfering and politically engaged armed forces and intelligence services. Aqil Shah, for instance, has argued that the formative experience of the Pakistani military "under conditions of geopolitical insecurity"—vis-à-vis archenemy India—"has profoundly shaped its political interventions and influence by justifying the authoritarian expansion of its role in state and society".[2] The scholarship on Latin American juntas has also underlined the role of regional security threats as primary drivers of continuing military dominance, as in Brazil or Cuba.[3] With such a geographical setting, Myanmar's military elites will certainly seek to retain control over border and security affairs, but also over broader state policymaking so as to counter—in their eyes—ill-advised strategies that may be developed by future civilian politicians, especially those ostensibly close to one foreign power or the other.

Resilient Clientelism(s) and the Personification of Power

Although many commonalities with other traditional and modern Asian societies can easily be identified, Burmese political thought and social construction of politics present some unique features. As anthropologist Gustaaf Houtman demonstrated in his *Mental Culture in Burmese Crisis Politics*, the way the Burmese broadly view the world and reflect on how best to arrange governance and collective life can sometimes be puzzling to outsiders.[4] Myanmar's complex and highly symbiotic interactions between religion, philosophical thought and politics have long been construed as being largely at the roots of its deeply entrenched social and political conundrums. In particular, although one should avoid perilous oversimplification, clientelism and the personalization of politics have proved remarkably resilient in the Burmese postcolonial context.

Allan Hicken defines "clientelism" in the *Annual Review of Political Science* as a personal interaction based on an "enduring exchange" between a client and a patron at all levels of society.[5] In that sense, clientelism differs from bribery or the broader concept of corruption, both of which imply a one-time (even if recurrent) exchange of goods or favors for political or economic support, not a continuing personal relationship. Conventional wisdom construes patron/client relationships as a powerful impediment placed in the way of a society's path to modernity. Patronage networks are often viewed as symbols of a persistent tradition retarding the consolidation of democratic practices and a society's passage into political and social modernity, especially for its most marginalized citizens.[6] James C. Scott, among others, has long highlighted the impact of political clientelism in 1950s and '60s Southeast Asia, when electoral competition expanded alongside rapid development and growth.[7] In those highly clientelistic Asian societies experiencing a form of postcolonial democratization through competitive elections, the patrons (elected politicians) were increasingly expected to redistribute resources to their clients (voters) in order to stay in office and preserve their legitimacy. As stressed by Scott, this has often made emerging democratic regimes more fragile and vulnerable to demagoguery and populism, and therefore instability. For many other theorists, political clientelism commonly contributes to political fragmentation, and thus makes society and the state more vulnerable to instability.[8]

Yet the relationship between clientelism and democratization is very complex. An emerging body of scholarship has showed that their correlation should not always be understood negatively. Patronage is not always construed as antithetic to the very idea of democracy, as Abente-Brun and Diamond have recently underlined.[9] The waxing and resilience of patron/client relations in a society may not necessarily systematically derail democratic processes. As Tina Hilgers highlighted using the modern Mexican and wider Latin American case, when citizens choose personal exchange and patronage networks over democratic means, they do not necessarily reinforce age-old traditional authoritarian behaviors.[10] Citizens can learn the skills of democratic practice through patron-client interactions, and the latter can even strengthen electoral processes and widen marginal or minority groups' access to power. Using the example of post-independence India, the largest and most diverse democracy in the world, New York University professor Kanchan Chandra has demonstrated that ethnic-based political parties are more likely to emerge and succeed when political competition is dependent on traditional patron-client networks.[11] Several other Southeast Asian polities have also revealed how clientelistic democracies can become entrenched.[12]

Gustaaf Houtman once wrote that the Burmese are "spun into a web of patron-client relationships".[13] Everyone in contemporary Myanmar seems to respect or owe allegiance to a "*saya*"—a master, teacher, even "boss". Whether in the army ranks, in Buddhist monastic schools, at university, in administrative bureaux or at the local level of a hamlet, ordinary Burmese citizens—including those belonging to non-Buddhist communities—appear to selectively recognize the authority (*awza*) of a handful of charismatic individuals to whom they voluntarily owe allegiance while accepting his or her command. However, as the small group of anthropologists and political scientists researching the topic since the 1950s has explained, this allegiance can evolve over time, as the concept of *awza* remains highly subjective. Crude power (*ana*) and the authority to command (*awza*) can constantly be contested and challenged by contentious individuals. But, unless a new body of empirical research emerges to update the arguments proposed by Manning Nash,[14] Melford Spiro[15] and Maung Maung Gyi[16] among others, the issue will remain a black hole in the contemporary political study of Myanmar. What, Robert Taylor has recently asked, are the dynamics of today's local and national Burmese politics, at the birth of the twenty-first century?[17] Besides, since independence there have been too few periods of open political competition to thoroughly research the resilience of political clientelism and its direct impact on contemporary party politics, electoral behaviors and the processes of political leader selection.

Recent studies by Win Min, Mary Callahan and Andrew Selth have shown the significance of loyalty networks, personal entourages of senior officers and intra-military groupings within the ranks of an institution that has long dominated the country's political landscape.[18] Furthermore, several recent interviews with retired Tatmadaw officers elected in 2010 have confirmed the salience of the patron/client dynamics beyond active duty. Such anecdotal data do not, of course, constitute scientific evidence. But many military retirees turned legislators told me that on retirement from the army—and sometimes many years after—their own *saya*—whoever that man was—called on them and asked for their support and continuing service "for the nation". As a former army lieutenant-colonel recounted, one of his *saya* (never named) happened to be the leader of a USDP branch in his home town, in rural Bago region. He strongly encouraged the ex-lieutenant-colonel to compete in the 2010 polls—something a client could not refuse his local patron. The military retiree, an ethnic Bamar, was subsequently elected to the upper house eight years after he had left the infantry.[19] Interestingly, the same phenomenon has also been observed among non-Bamar retired officers, although generalization should be avoided. An ethnic Danu, also a former lieutenant colonel, recalled in an interview that, as a former member of the Tatmadaw, he too was convinced by his *saya* to run for office in his native town in 2010.[20] Having been "forced to retire" (in his own words) from the army in 1994, he was one of the only ex-Tatmadaw officers of Danu origin. He was therefore expected to act as a reliable and faithful mediator between the local authorities (the USDP and the military) and the Danu constituents.

Thus, as the anthropological literature indicates, clientelism and the personalization of power seem to derive from a complex set of interactions between the notions of *awza* and *ana* in Myanmar. Besides, both phenomena have been described by scholars as powerful catalysts in the early postcolonial fragmentation of parliamentary politics. Manning Nash spoke in the 1950s of the "mercurial character of Burmese politics".[21] Highly segmented, explosive and episodic, the volatile politics of Myanmar's first post-independence decade was understood as a direct consequence of personalization and patronage. This has long been presented as the perfect incentive for military intervention in unstable societies. The more fragmented the political landscape, and the more divided and factionalized the crowd of civilian policy-makers and thinkers appears, the more interventionist the military institution proves. Indeed, the Tatmadaw, as its own propaganda has relentlessly asserted, presents itself as the sole cohesive, unified and disciplined state institution capable of assuring stability, and therefore development and democratization.[22] It did, in fact, step in—in 1958, 1962 and 1988—to restore a political order that it perceives as persistently undermined by factionalism, "splitism" and fractionalized politics among the civilians.[23]

Analyzing the major rift in the ranks of U Nu's ruling AFPFL in 1958 (which led to the first Tatmadaw intervention in September of that year), Frank N. Trager interestingly recalled how, even before independence, "Burmese political life in the 1920s and 1930s suffered more than anything else from fragmentation".[24] Dr Maung Maung further described how the AFPFL split in 1958 reached down in every direction and durably fractionalized most other major political and social forces.[25] Looking in the 1970s at Burma's powerful underground communist movements, John Badgley then underscored how "splitism" also considerably affected non-governmental political organizations such as the "Red Flag" and "White Flag" Burmese communist parties.[26] Writing in the early 1990s, Ralf Hoffman noted that the May 1990 elections perfectly illustrated how deeply political fragmentation was embedded in post-Ne Win

Myanmar.[27] A total of 235 political parties had registered for these elections, and ninety-three effectively ran. Ninety-two parties ran in the 2015 polls, yet only thirteen gained any seats in the Union legislature. Many parties were (and still are) mere personal vehicles for local charismatic leaders unwilling—or unable—to join broader and more credible political platforms. Other have simply developed deeply antagonistic political ideologies.

The splintering of political parties in post-independence Myanmar has long been emphasized, including by the Burmese themselves. The joke goes that if two Burmese meet in a teashop, they will form three political parties. Burmese politicians seldom appear to agree to disagree within the institutionalized structure of a political party. If one can neither command, nor blindly follow a venerated leader, then one quits and forms another group. Both brought into the ranks of the newly formed National League for Democracy in 1988, ex-Tatmadaw heavyweights Aung Gyi and Tin Oo soon appeared at odds with each other.[28] Aung Gyi promptly left the NLD. Twenty years later, when Khin Maung Swe and Thein Nyunt, two veteran NLD politicians, favored participation in the 2010 general elections, in disagreement with other NLD patrons, they chose to withdraw and form the National Democratic Force (NDF).[29] A few months after the polls, when Thein Nyunt fell out with Khin Maung Swe and other leaders of the party, he pulled out of the NDF and formed his own platform, the New National Democratic Party (NNDP). Both parties failed to win a single seat in November 2015.

Among Shan politicians, a similar rift occurred in the run-up to the 2010 elections, with the SNDP and SNLD—the two main "pan-Shan" parties—proving irreconcilable purely because of the bitter personal rivalry between their respective leaders.[30] Five years after their split, the two parties were each still busy attempting to co-opt and win back members of the opposite camp. Illustratively, several SNDP Union MPs, obviously willing to remain loyal to the charismatic Hkun Htun Oo, re-joined the ranks of the SNLD in the build-up to the 2015 elections.[31]

The Chin National Party (CNP) and the Chin Progressive Party (CPP), which both won Union and provincial parliamentary seats in 2010, have also proved incapable of keeping their political structures intact for a full legislative term (2010–15). In late 2014, another party, the Chin National Democratic Party (CNDP), was formed by members of both the CNP and the CPP, whilst the two latter parties continued under different leaderships.[32] In February 2015, one of the most prominent CPP legislators in the upper house left the party to join the NLD, still an attractive political force despite the criticism it has generated.[33] It paid off: he was the only incumbent Chin legislator to be re-elected in November 2015. The CPP and the CNDP were crushed by the NLD and its political ally in the north of Chin State, the Zomi Congress for Democracy.[34] The Democratic Party-Myanmar (DP-M), a remnant of the old Anti-Fascist People's Freedom League led by the octogenarian Thu Wai, has also found it increasingly difficult to retain his own flock.[35] In 2012, Nay Yee Ba Swe—one of the "three princesses" of the DP-M on whom the Burmese media romantically focused during the 2010 polls—and her brother Nay Phoo Ba Swe left the DP-M and applied for NLD membership.[36] This was a smart move—in 2015 Nay Phoo Ba Swe was elected on an NLD ticket in Pabedan constituency, downtown Yangon.[37]

In a healthy parliamentary democracy, as a stable and enduring yet evolving institution, it is the political party that stands at the core of the political and electoral processes—not the candidate, nor the charismatic party leader. Thus a process of political personalization based on divisive clientelistic patterns straightforwardly challenges the logic of such systems. Modern liberal democracies, for all their flaws, seem more commonly grounded in the early twenty-first century on a de-personalization process, although charisma still plays a major role in democratic politics. In a Weberian sense, in a stable parliamentary system the rule of "law" and "institutions" is meant to replace the rule of "man" (or woman).[38] As many seasoned scholars have demonstrated at length, power in Myanmar has always been highly personified and therefore remains quite unpredictable.[39] Personalized politics have traditionally been more important than institutional practices. As Burmese scholar Maung Maug Gyi has stressed, authority and power lie in personal attributes, not in institutions or laws, despite the criticism this cultural approach commonly receives.[40]

This dependence on personalities—including within the military—makes it difficult, at least in the near future, for Myanmar to enjoy the rational stability a modern state and its bureaucracy normally desire. Well into the 2010s, most Burmese political parties still appear far from institutionalization. This includes the National League for Democracy, despite its resounding electoral victory in 2015, which was made possible by the uncontested (and sole) charisma of Aung San Suu Kyi. Most political parties seem entirely tied to the fortunes of their founders and are yet to become self-sustaining political forces that can survive regular internal crises and the demise or ill luck of their leaders.[41] Incompatible political ideologies were also were also key causes of "splitism" in the 1950s, and they may well once more need to be taken into consideration when examining future Burmese parliamentary debates. Though a more liberal and tolerant political atmosphere has been created in Yangon and Naypyitaw by the post-SPDC *glasnost*, and with more acuity in the midst of the 2015 electoral moment, there is still a long way to go before Myanmar's political parties can efficiently spearhead its various processes of democratization.

The literature on democratic transitions has further shown that increased competition among political forces and parties, as well as pluralism and greater diversity in political society, commonly strengthens democratization.[42] But can the development of Myanmar's party political scene be sustainable, given the country's legacies of conflict, factionalism and personalized power, and the more recent quasi-mystic prevalence of Aung San Suu Kyi? Can political parties in Myanmar become credible and autonomous actors in the various processes, attempting to challenge the still-dominant military institution and to pave the way for a legitimate parliamentary democracy to emerge?

As Mary Callahan has remarked, long-standing paternalistic behaviors, tendencies to personalize power, institutional weaknesses and a decades-long legacy of blunt authoritarianism do not recommend an optimistic reading of the future role of party politics.[43] Burmese political parties, as institutions and bureaucratic machines, tend to play second fiddle to party leaders. The 2015 elections—an effective plebiscite on Aung San Suu Kyi and her party—have further highlighted the conundrum. Such Burmese party founders are usually charismatic individuals, with a large clientele of followers unready to challenge their authority and institutionalize internal party mechanisms to balance, and move beyond, the leader's control over the party. The recurrent problem in Myanmar's recent political history is that the more segmented and personalized the civilian political and parliamentary scene appears, the less confidence the Tatmadaw has in the broad political process—and the more palpable is its willingness to keep an eye on civilian affairs, and therefore remain involved in politics.

Geopolitics and the Military, or the Burden of Geography

The political geography inherited from the British has certainly presented some formidable challenges for Myanmar's successive governments. The country's particular situation, at the crossroads of Asia, will continue to take its toll on future domestic politics, well into the twenty-first century. Because of its geostrategic position, Myanmar cannot avoid a series of key transnational and international security challenges. The country is directly connected to the Indian Ocean, through which most of the world's seaborne trade in oil transits, and in which all global (and would-be global) powers have strategic stakes. It is sandwiched between the two emerging giants of China and India, in the wider—and volatile—continental context of Southeast Asia. This geographical position may well offer considerable opportunities for future development and growth, as has relentlessly been argued by Thant Myint-U, who has been a key advisor to President Thein Sein since he returned to Yangon in 2011.[44]

But, at the same time, this unique geographical position might also increasingly raise Burmese elites' concerns over global powers and neighboring states seeking to gain sway in a country long openly mythologised as an El Dorado, or the "last frontier" where abundant natural resources and profit can still be found. Another recent monograph by Bertil Lintner, a veteran reporter, has underscored the continuing significance of the country's geopolitical stakes in the 2010s.[45] In addition to a legacy of distrust of the outside world dating back from the 1940s, Myanmar's geography might also prove a commanding obstacle to greater openness and probably, in the long run, to a full and durable disengagement of the military from domestic political affairs.

A state's security, defense, and foreign policies do, understandably, fall within a military institution's wide-ranging interests. As early as the 1970s, Edward Feit described armed forces as natural instruments of their state's foreign policies.[46] As protectors of the state and managers of violence, soldiers are supposedly more preoccupied with their country's security than civilians. Geopolitics and international or regional security matters are therefore likely to propel military men into broader policy roles under the cover of "national security" priorities, as civil-military relations expert Amos Perlmutter has stressed.[47] Interventionist armed forces thus tend to impose on civilian authorities the type of foreign policy that best fits the military's global agenda, not only in terms of security or relations with other states, but also the ideological, financial and vested interests of the armed forces—or its leadership.[48]

But a state under military rule is not necessarily a state at war with its neighbors, or the wider world. Indeed, the late Samuel Huntington was early to demonstrate that praetorian rulers were more inclined than civilian statesmen or "sultans" with militaristic ambitions to downplay inter-state war as a primordial instrument of diplomacy.[49] Interventionist military officers tend to adopt more cautious foreign policy objectives. In order to preserve the military institution's exclusive essence and internal functioning against both domestic challenges (civilian opposition, ethnic groups, civil society, internecine rivalries and so on) and external or transnational threats, armies with praetorian habits tend to favor the conduct of more prudent and disciplined inter-state relations. Yet they surely seek to keep the broader process of foreign policymaking under their watch, as shown by the Pakistani armed forces' enduring influence since 1947 over Pakistan's political interactions with its archenemy, India.[50]

From the late 1940s, the Tatmadaw acquired a key influence in all matters constructed as "national security" (*amyotha loun-kyoun-yeh*). Thorny decolonization processes in a country ravaged by the Second World War, as well as the rise in the 1950s and 1960s of communist and ethnic rebellions more or less linked to the US or to Burma's immediate neighbors, strongly influenced the Tatmadaw's early strategic perceptions. Under the guidance of General Ne Win, it therefore developed an early authority over state foreign policy.[51] Regular military-cum-diplomatic trips, carried out by General Ne Win and all his successors up to Senior-General Min Aung Hlaing in the early 2010s, have consolidated the Tatmadaw's sway over Myanmar's postcolonial foreign affairs.[52] Besides, since the 1950s, high-ranking Tatmadaw officers have frequently been appointed to senior diplomatic posts in most of Myanmar's thirty-odd embassies abroad—a crucial practice for spreading the international leverage of armed forces, according to the literature on civil-military relations.

A closer look at the 2008 constitution also reveals that the Tatmadaw can still control much foreign policy decision-making. All three of the significant ministries left under its sole authority (home, defense and border affairs) are essential to the definition of any type of foreign relations. More importantly, now well into the 2010s, the Tatmadaw leadership continues to insist (and this is a key element of every official speech, statement or pamphlet prepared by the officer corps) on the multifaceted threats to "state security" (*naing-ngan-daw loun-kyoun-yeh*).[53]

There are, therefore, sound indications that the Burmese military establishment will continue more or less strongly to influence foreign and security policymaking in the coming years, and may not fully accept any civilian input. The hyper-nationalist Tatmadaw will most certainly—for a while, at least—continue to resist letting the people decide the country's interactions with the rest of the world, especially its immediate neighbors. However, as long as the political transition continues to unfold—albeit selectively—in the late 2010s, Myanmar is bound to cautiously broaden its international ties.[54] For anyone holding power in Naypyitaw, this will mean taking into account a wide range of old and new strategic stakes, evolving domestic imperatives and the increasing external influence of both the West and—still—China. The Burmese military regime's decision to begin mutating in the early 2010s was little influenced by Western-imposed international sanctions since the 1990s, the overblown Sino-Indian "rivalry" or China's shadowy dominance over Myanmar since 1988.[55] True, the will to restore a more positive international standing and end a humiliating diplomatic exclusion lasting two decades may have played a role, as did the need to re-join the global economy, while moving away from the multidimensional Chinese influence imposed since the early 1990s. But, as many authors have argued,[56] these elements were less determining factors in the process of political change than other, internal considerations.

This is not to say that Myanmar's post-2011 domestic development has not rekindled the country's relations with the outside world and the current ruling elite's strategic perceptions.[57] Although still very much a prominent economic player in Myanmar, especially in the northern territories of Mandalay and Yangon, China has been seen as one of the regional powers that has lost the most influence since 2011.[58] Under the Democrat administration in Washington, D.C. since 2008, the United States, long at odds with the Burmese junta, has launched a multi-faceted rapprochement.[59] Although far from being a done deal, international analysts increasingly draw hasty conclusions about a Sino-American rivalry brewing over Myanmar.[60] Along with Japanese, South Korean, Qatari, Russian and Indian companies, the re-entry of European firms into the Burmese market following the suspension and then, in April 2013, the lifting of EU sanctions has started reshaping and further diversifying Myanmar's economic and developmental landscape.

Future Burmese administrations and diplomatic circles may well continue to maneuver between traditional nationalist and prudent diplomatic attitudes on the one hand, and, on the other, the will to modernize through better, more diverse—yet still quite limited—economic partnerships with the outside world, including the West. Prime Minister U Nu once stated, in front of fellow parliamentarians in 1950s Rangoon, that the Burmese were "hemmed in like a tender gourd among the cactus".[61] This description is still extremely pertinent in the 2010s. In fact, conventional wisdom would say that the diplomatic stance best suited to Myanmar is a tactful neutralism and even handed diplomacy between the two neighboring giants, India and China, as well as the other global powers boasting strategic ambitions in the Southeast Asian region or the Indian Ocean. For years, images of ambitious foreign powers and greedy neighbors, all yearning to exploit the country's vast reservoir of natural resources, have molded the outlook of Burmese military officers, politicians, diplomats and the common people. They will continue to do so, particularly if the broad "gold rush" atmosphere depicting Myanmar as the "last frontier" for foreign investment and Western strategic thrusts endures.

CONCLUSION

GLASNOST WITHOUT *PERESTROIKA*

This book is concerned with the process of political change at work in Myanmar since the controversial general elections of November 2010. Only five years have passed between Aung San Suu Kyi's third release from house arrest—on 13 November 2010, a year and a half after her 2009 trial—and her outstanding victory in the second post-junta elections, held in November 2015. The political transition bracketed by these two events has routinely been praised, by Burmese and foreign observers alike. Arguments have burgeoned that it represents a "Burmese Spring", far more peaceful and less tainted with political convulsion and social breakdown than the various uprisings that have concomitantly spread throughout the Arab world since 2011.

A new sense of optimism emerged among both the Burmese people and foreign observers in August 2011, when Aung San Suu Kyi was invited to meet the newly elected Union president, ex-general Thein Sein, in Naypyitaw. This crucial meeting seemingly unveiled a new political era of liberalization and openness—some sort of *glasnost*, to draw a parallel with the 1980s Soviet policy of transparency. In the space of just a few years, under the impetus of the post-junta government that succeeded the SPDC, renowned political prisoners were released, new legislative bodies were convened, economic and social reforms were introduced, state censorship was eased and ethnic peace talks were revitalized between the central administration and the country's major armed insurgent groups. Almost all aspects of life in Myanmar have been touched, in varying degrees, by the reformist agenda proposed soon after the long-awaited disbanding of the military junta in March 2011.

However, the quasi-euphoric feeling of confidence and hope for the future—best illustrated by the suspension of most international sanctions against Myanmar from April 2012, the endless courtesy calls paid to Aung San Suu Kyi by foreign dignitaries and world leaders, and the portrayal of a "Burmese Spring" unfolding on one of the world's "last frontiers"—has been tinged with extreme caution.[1] In the not so distant past, warn Burmese activists and veteran politicians, hopes have regularly been dashed.[2] If world history is any guide, swift and peaceful transitions to democratic rule seldom occur. Extremism, radical contentious politics and other "dark social forces" have also resurfaced in Myanmar following the easing of state and military control since 2012 and the build-up to the 2015 elections.

Above all, even if a feeling of *glasnost* has obviously been palpable at the very top level of the central administration, there has been no major *perestroika* moment during the first "post-SPDC" presidency and legislature (2010–15). No fundamental restructuring of the Burmese state and society has been proposed, or imposed.[3] Revolution has erupted neither in the streets of Yangon (as during the 1988 uprising), nor in the minds of army leaders—as in 1962, when the Tatmadaw aimed to spearhead a revolutionary path to socialism. Neither has the location of power been essentially challenged during this transitional moment of the early 2010s. Despite the National League for Democracy's unambiguous electoral victory in November 2015, the Burmese armed forces still linger as the most powerful policymaking institution. According to the most recent Tatmadaw literature, its political clout will certainly remain quite untested in the near future.[4]

But a transitional process, full of uncertain developments, was effectively at work between the two landmark electoral moments of 2010 and 2015. Officially outlined in 2003 in the seven-step roadmap to a "discipline-flourishing democracy"—but in fact first thought out in the early 1990s—the long-awaited transition materialized with the convening of a new legislative branch in January 2011 and the selection of a new set of state leaders to succeed the SLORC-SPDC junta, which was dissolved two months later. Despite obvious flaws, the new constitution ratified in 2008 unprecedentedly enshrined new political and decisional echelons: a president, two vice presidents, decentralized regional governments run by a chief minister, and above all one national and fourteen provincial assemblies, (partially) elected by universal suffrage. Beside this more complex and diffuse governmental structure, the new constitutional order also guaranteed the armed forces an essential role in the new legislative and executive branches, and former junta members a high level of immunity. In

March 2011, the last two generals holding onto power twenty-three years after supervising the 1988 coup—Than Shwe and Maung Aye—finally retired, successfully securing a safe exit from government.

As Burmese historian turned policy advisor Thant Myint-U stressed, the easily identifiable era of direct military rule was to be considered over after 2011. For him, Myanmar in the early 2010s offered a "much more fractured system of power than what existed before—with a powerful presidency distinct from the army, as well as a ruling party leadership distinct from both. [...] There is a tension, a system of checks and balances designed into the heart of the new system."[5] The post-junta system was, however, designed to retain a true praetorian hue beyond 2011 and even 2015, although it has installed power sharing between civilians and the military. Above all, the new system was meant to consider itself only a "transit" regime, under which the armed forces agreed to share government business with the civilian leaders before returning full time to their barracks—if that is to happen in the foreseeable future.

Drawing on the literature on civil-military relations and praetorianism, this book has argued that the Tatmadaw leadership, by effectively engaging a transitional opening in the early 2010s, merely opted to move down a notch on the scale of political intervention. This partial disengagement of the armed forces from politics was carefully planned. For anyone who has read and taken at face value the SPDC's seven-point roadmap to democracy of August 2003, there should be no surprise in the way the transition has unfolded. Yet, to pursue that top-down transition beyond 2011, a political "pact" was needed. Consequently, a "pacted transition" was sought between some elements of the old state and military nomenclature (Thein Sein, Thura Shwe Mann, Khin Aung Myint and a few others) and a handful of newly empowered interlocutors from outside the *ancien régime*, including Aung San Suu Kyi herself, who finally agreed to join the parliamentary and constitutional game in April 2012. This allowed the transitional process, full of exciting possibilities, to unfold after 2011 with no major bumps in the road, until the second scheduled electoral exercise—intended to drive the transfer of power further forward—credibly took place in November 2015.

What can be expected hereafter? If the recent body of research on intra-elite pacts and democratization holds up in the case of post-2011 Myanmar, the immediate future of the transition does appear quite bleak. Negotiated transitional processes, fraught with grave risks according to this emerging literature, seldom survive the first powerful challenges they face.[6] "Pacted" transitions prove particularly vulnerable when key players part of the initial settlement are quick to renege on its terms, or when actors excluded from the initial political bargaining grow stronger and articulate competing and increasingly popular agendas for a different type of transition. What the NLD will make of its decisive 2015 victory remains to be seen, although Aung San Suu Kyi has already given indications that she is willing to engage in face-to-face dialogue with the commander-in-chief of the armed forces.

According to the scholarship on democratization, "pacted" and elite-driven transitions are more successfully managed than those initiated by popular revolts, palace coups or the death of a leader. Post-Franco Spain and post-military Brazil, Portugal and South Korea in the 1970s and 1980s serve as good illustrations. When the political agreements discussed among society's political elites are broad and inclusive, and gather all major social forces of the post-authoritarian polity, elite pacts tend to last longer. Transitional processes are more effective when they benefit from already well-anchored and stable domestic institutions, upheld by moderate leaders willing to work on the terms of settlements broadly supported by a popular mobilization.[7] However, none of these conditions seem fully to be met in Myanmar in the mid-2010s.

The 2011 transitional moment raised considerable hope in Myanmar, even euphoria—euphoria largely fueled by Aung San Suu Kyi's startling election to parliament in 2012, reinforced at the national level in November 2015. Too much so, perhaps, as such enthusiasm has overshadowed the ills still plaguing the country, starting with the ethnic conundrum, communal tensions and the rise of radical and contending political ideologies, as well the military's seemingly never-ending tutelage over the country's polity, bureaucracy, and economy. Aung San Suu Kyi herself has started criticizing the way the post-junta reform may have "stalled" in the run-up to the 2015 elections, which she even threatened to boycott.[8] As this book has shown, Myanmar continues to face a number of enduring political, social, economic and strategic challenges well into the 2010s, and beyond. These realities, unless tackled head-on by present and future Burmese leaders, risks not only slowing down the military's incremental withdrawal from state politics after the late 2010s, but also hindering the peaceful establishment of a fully functioning parliamentary democracy in the near future. Countering the flurry of news reports celebrating a "Burmese Spring", many scholars of Burmese affairs have argued from the beginning that the building of transparent, autonomous, efficient and civilian-controlled institutions will take years, if not generations. So too will the entrenchment of democratic rules and practices in its society.

In 2015, Yangon, the former capital and gateway into the country, was putting on airs of Phnom Penh in the early 1990s, rapidly hosting a myriad of international, humanitarian and philanthropic organizations as well as hoards of Western and Asian tourists. Its sudden boom was, however, also reminiscent of Luanda in the 1990s, in the aftermath of the Angolan Civil War. Thousands of businessmen were flocking in, whilst multinational oil companies were prospecting in search of an El Dorado to exploit. As with the restoration of peace in Cambodia in the 1990s, the international community's swift and unbridled penetration into Myanmar might turn out to be a particularly destabilizing factor for the multiple Burmese societies undergoing such social and political metamorphosis since the turn of the twenty-first century.[9]

The bloated Burmese state bureaucracy—including the military—might, in the short term, see its traditional power dwindle against the rising power of local and international NGOs, foreign advisors and consultants, multinational companies and humanitarian agencies, which will inevitably seize those rare members of the Burmese workforce who are well-trained, open to the world and, especially, better paid. This may well be to the detriment of Myanmar's ministries and government agencies, essential for implementing long-term transitional, economic and democratic reforms. Today, young educated Burmese aspire more than anything to work for a development NGO, build a school, open a smartphone shop or become a sports reporter, not to become a civil servant or even join the army. And yet it is bureaucrats who will be called on to implement further reforms and economic liberalization in the years, if not decades, to come.[10] These two faces of Myanmar taking form in the 2010s are likely to perpetuate a brand of hobbling clientelism.

Besides, for many observers, the institutionalization of Burmese state and political structures cannot be accomplished if the new civil structures and agencies remain too dependent on a handful of charismatic figures. As in other Asian countries, the personification of power remains a deeply rooted phenomenon in Burmese society. If this trend were to continue, as Aung San Suu Kyi's electoral successes in 2012 and 2015 indicate, the impetus for reform would be too reliant on the goodwill of the authorities, and especially of a democratic icon who turned seventy in 2015, and whose political succession still remains highly problematic. Aung San Suu Kyi's sympathizers are themselves aware of this. But both Myanmar's civil society and the political class are yet to drop old habits. One need only alert the current authorities in power (the government, the party leader, the bureau director, the company manager, and so on) to an error or failure of the system, and ask them to step in to correct it. When Aung San Suu Kyi orders the people to clean the streets and collect garbage, they finally oblige.[11] As this book has briefly demonstrated, Myanmar still has no room for any institutionalized mechanisms in a field that reproduces paternalism and patrimonial clientelism to such extremes. Bureaucracy, the judiciary, education, business, trade unions, the media—all these institutions, essential to a democracy, though emerging and benefiting from the post-2011 broadening of the sociopolitical space, are still too fragile to take full control of the reform process.

The international community finally appears to have made up its mind to become involved and give assistance such as capacity-building training, beyond mere emergency aid and purely speculative investment. Nevertheless, inevitable structural resistance to change will emerge in the months and years to come. It will not necessarily come from active military personnel, though some analysts fear that they might stage another coup to better protect their interests. The deep generational transformation of the post-Than Shwe Tatmadaw, and the constitutional preserves it has secured, seem to be neutralizing this threat in the medium term.[12] The new generation of officers represented by Senior-General Min Aung Hlaing, who graduated from the nineteenth intake of the prestigious Defense Services Academy,[13] seems determined to continue on the path of "power-sharing" with civilians. Thus, in a society at war with itself for so many years, resistance to reform is more likely to come from the huge state bureaucracy and from certain contending intellectual and political elites either excluded from the transition as it was "pacted" in 2011–12 or growing dissatisfied with it, including the dominant NLD.

Furthermore, the depth of social change needed in Myanmar is staggering—infrastructure, education, banking, taxation, civil liberties, transportation, demobilization of bloated armed forces and rebel ethnic groups, and so on. As during the early years of independence, the Burmese elites are constantly debating and clashing over which model of development the country should ultimately adopt. Myanmar has been coming out of its relative isolation since the early 2010s, and foreign investors are rushing in to better understand this new Asian El Dorado, trying to grasp how to invest in it, in which sectors and with whom. This is becoming a great source of worry for Burmese society and policy elites, highly xenophobic for many decades.

The Burmese have never been great capitalists. Even before Ne Win set up a Marxist-style dictatorship in 1962, intellectuals and political leaders as well as army officials—including Aung San Suu Kyi's father, Bogyoke Aung San—had already vaunted the merits of Fabian or Saint-Simonian, but not liberal, economic policies. For a long time, capitalism, competition and foreign investment were associated with the British colonial enterprise, when Westerners,

Indians and Chinese dominated the province's economy to the detriment of the Burmese majority. The same pattern was repeated in the 1950s prior to the big waves of nationalization in 1963 and 1965, which saw thousands of Indians, Chinese and Westerners pack their bags and leave the country. Since the 1990s and the development of closer relations with Myanmar's Asian neighbors, China in the lead, the liberal development model has once again become associated in the Burmese imaginary with out-and-out plundering of its resources, monopolized by a handful of large foreign state companies, particularly from China and Thailand.

Since 2011, the commercial opening up and revamping of early 1990s foreign investment laws proposed by Thein Sein's economic advisors have been the subject of much debate among military and policy circles in Naypyitaw.[14] The early postcolonial temptation of socialism and the resistance to capitalism seem almost to have vanished, as recently claimed by a member of the government-appointed Myanmar Investment Commission (a sixteen-member body scrutinizing economic policies). However, a broad and diffuse reluctance to fully open the national economy to foreigners still lingers in the stately avenues of Naypyitaw and Yangon.[15]

Myanmar thus risks being gradually torn apart between, on the one hand, its emerging private sector—the small fish as well as the handful of Burmese financial moguls, or cronies—wanting to take advantage of the national wealth and of deeper integration into the modern world's major trade flows and, on the other hand, Myanmar's very nationalistic intellectual and bureaucratic circles, trained in the interventionist and Bamar-focused policy school of preceding decades, who will resist an unbridled opening-up to foreign powers. The latter's role in Myanmar's long process of development and democratization will thus prove very delicate, even if it is actually up to the Burmese themselves to bring their country into a modernity they have chosen. The speaker of the upper house has acknowledged that the country's new elites are eager to learn from the outside world, even while stipulating that this should be a selective learning process: "We will only take the best of what the world has to offer."[16] This seems ultimately to be the path the Burmese are taking.

The political path to be followed by the upcoming Burmese leadership, especially after the 2015 elections won by Aung San Suu Kyi, will certainly be even more decisive for the country's stability than that brought to power by the controversial 2010 polls. The loose pact and political settlement established directly after the disbanding of the SPDC in 2011 was not openly contested between these two post-junta elections. Nor was the outcome of

Khin Nyunt's 2003 seven-step roadmap successfully challenged in the first five years of transition. It is, therefore, the political negotiations to be held from 2016, conducted by a new NLD-led administration, that will show whether the transition—as pacted in 2011—can be meaningfully consolidated. In other words, it remains to be seen whether there can be a real transfer of power from the old, powerful generation of Burmese leaders, army officials and state bureaucrats, trained during the pre-2011 era of direct military rule, to a new generation of civilian leaders, who bring with them new aspirations, and a novel view of the world and of Myanmar's place in it.

NOTES

FOREWORD AND ACKNOWLEDGMENTS

1. Egreteau, Renaud, *Toward a Reorganization of the Political Landscape in Burma (Myanmar)*, Paris: Les Etudes du CERI No. 197b, 2013.

INTRODUCTION: DEMOCRATIZATION FROM ABOVE?

1. For details, see *Time Magazine*, "John Yettaw: Suu Kyi's Unwelcome Visitor", 20 May 2009; and Skidmore, Monique, "The Lady and the 'Wretched American': Burma's Trial of Aung San Suu Kyi", *Anthropology News* 50, 6 (2009), p. 30.
2. Taylor, Robert H., "Myanmar in 2009: On the Cusp of Normality?", *Southeast Asian Affairs* (2010), pp. 201–4.
3. The State Law and Order Restoration Council (SLORC, or *Na Wa Ta* in its Burmese acronym) between 1988 and 1997, and the State Peace and Development Council (SPDC, or *Na Ah Pa*) between 1997 and 2011.
4. Reflecting its scores in the 1990 elections (ICG, *The Myanmar Elections: Results and Implications*, Yangon/Brussels: Asia Report No. 147, 9 December 2015).
5. Interview with the author, Yangon, December 2015.
6. This term was used by and in O'Donnell, Guillermo and Philippe C. Schmitter, *Transition from Authoritarian Rule: Tentative Conclusions about Uncertain Democracies*, Baltimore, MD: The Johns Hopkins University Press, 1986, p. 3.
7. These seven steps were: (1) Reconvening the National Convention adjourned in 1996; (2) Step-by-step implementation of the process necessary for the emergence of a genuine and disciplined democratic system; (3) Drafting of a new constitution; (4) Holding of a nationwide referendum to approve the constitutional text; (5) Holding general elections for legislative bodies; (6) Convening the newly elected legislative bodies; and (7) Building of a modern, developed and democratic nation by the state leaders and government elected by the legislative bodies. For a more detailed analysis, see Taylor, Robert H., "One Day, One Fathom, Bagan Won't Move: On the Myanmar Road to Constitution", in Wilson, Trevor (ed.), *Myanmar's Long Road to National Reconciliation*, Singapore: ISEAS Publications, 2006, pp. 3–28.
8. In late 2015, Myanmar counted an impressive 36 million mobile subscribers, against a few

hundred thousand just five years before (*The Myanmar Times*, "Myanmar named fourth-fastest growing mobile market in the world by Ericsson", 20 November 2015).

9. Created in 2000 and based in Mae Sot, Thailand, the Assistance Association of Political Prisoners (Burma), or AAPP, carries out monthly surveys (http://aappb.org/, last accessed 21 March 2016).
10. Aung San Suu Kyi remained under house arrest between July 1989 and July 1995, between September 2000 and May 2002 and between September 2003 and November 2010.
11. As the titles of two recent books suggest: Russell, Rosalind, *Burma's Spring: Real Lives in Turbulent Times*, London: Thistle, 2014; and Pedersen, Rena, *The Burma Spring: Aung San Suu Kyi and the New Struggle for the Soul of a Nation*, New York: Pegasus, 2014. See also, among other reports: *Foreign Policy*, "The Burma Spring", 13 October 2011; *Newsweek*, "The Burmese Spring", 12 December 2011; *Harvard Political Review*, "The Burmese Spring", 19 March 2012; *The New Yorker*, "The Burmese Spring", 6 August 2012; Reporters without Borders, "Burmese Media Spring", December 2012; *The Economist*, "A Burmese Spring", 25 May 2013.
12. For instance: Htet Khaung Linn, "Myanmar parliament gets mixed score for performance", *Myanmar Now*, 13 December 2015; *The Myanmar Times*, "Hluttaw committees inefficient, ignored", 28 January 2016.
13. See, for instance, Maung Thawnghmung, Ardeth, "The Politics of Everyday Life in 21st Century Myanmar", *The Journal of Asian Studies* 70, 3 (2011), pp. 641–70, and Egreteau, Renaud and François Robinne (eds), *Metamorphosis: Studies in Social and Political Change in Myanmar*, Singapore: NUS Press, 2015.
14. Przeworski, Adam, *Democracy and the Limits of Self-Government*, Cambridge: Cambridge University Press, 2010, p. xii.
15. Among the most recent broad scholarly analyses, see in particular a series of edited volumes: Steinberg, David I. (ed.), *Myanmar: The Dynamics of an Evolving Polity*, Boulder, CO: Lynne Rienner, 2014; Cheesman, Nick, Nicholas Farrelly and Trevor Wilson (eds), *Debating Democratization in Myanmar*, Singapore: ISEAS Publications, 2014; Duell, Kerstin (ed.), *Myanmar in Transition: Polity, People and Processes*, Singapore: Select Books, 2013; Cheesman, Nick, Monique Skidmore and Trevor Wilson (eds), *Myanmar's Transition: Openings, Obstacles, and Opportunities*, Singapore: ISEAS Publications, 2012; and the monograph by Hong Kong University professor Ian Holliday, *Burma Redux: Global Justice and the Quest for Political Reform in Myanmar*, New York: Columbia University Press, 2012.
16. Wilson, Trevor, "Debating Democratization in Myanmar", in Cheesman, Nick, Nicholas Farrelly and Trevor Wilson, (eds), *Debating Democratization, op. cit.*, pp. 12–17.
17. Interview with the author, Yangon, January 2014.
18. Taylor, Robert H., "The Evolving Military Role in Burma", *Current History* 89, 545 (1990), p. 107.
19. Taylor, Robert H., *The Armed Forces in Myanmar's Politics: A Terminating Role?*, Singapore: ISEAS Trends No. 2, 2015, p. 5. See also an earlier piece: Taylor, Robert H., "Myanmar: From Army Rule to Constitutional Rule?", *Asian Affairs* 43, 2 (2012), pp. 221–36.
20. Quoted in Kyaw Yin Hlaing, "Understanding Recent Political Changes in Myanmar", *Contemporary Southeast Asia* 34, 2 (2012), p. 204.
21. Callahan, Mary P., "The Generals Loosen their Grip", *Journal of Democracy* 23, 4 (2012), p. 120.

22. Slater, Dan, "The Elements of Surprise: Assessing Burma's Double-Edged Détente", *South East Asia Research* 22, 2 (2014), p. 177.
23. As quoted in the *Working People's Daily* (10 June 1989), following the SLORC's forty-third press conference, held the day before.
24. Min Maung Maung, *The Tatmadaw and its Leadership Role in National Politics,* Yangon: News & Periodicals Enterprise (Ministry of Information), 1993, pp. 293 and 299.
25. SLORC Order No. 13/92, 2 October 1992.
26. After an internal purge staged in November 1997, the junta changed its name from SLORC to SPDC.
27. See note 7 above.
28. Maung Aung Myoe, "The Soldier and the State: The *Tatmadaw* and Political Liberalization in Myanmar since 2011", *South East Asia Research* 22, 2 (2014), pp. 233–49.
29. Skidmore, Monique and Trevor Wilson, "Interpreting the Transition in Myanmar", in Cheesman, Skidmore and Wilson (eds), *Myanmar's Transition, op. cit.*, pp. 3–20.
30. Maung Aung Myoe, *The Soldier and the State*, p. 233.
31. Croissant, Aurel and J. Kamerling, "Why Do Military Regime Institutionalize? Constitution-making and Elections as Political Survival Strategy in Myanmar", *Asian Journal of Political Science* 21, 2 (2013), pp. 105–25.
32. Bünte, Marco, "Burma's Transition to Quasi-Military Rule: From Rulers to Guardians?, *Armed Forces & Society* 40, 4 (2014), pp. 757–8.
33. Chambers, Paul, "Constitutional Change and Security Forces in Southeast Asia: Lessons from Thailand and Myanmar", *Contemporary Southeast Asia* 36, 1 (2014), p. 118.
34. As stressed in: Aung-Thwin, Maitrii, "Reassessing Myanmar's Glasnost", *Kyoto Review of Southeast Asia* 14 (2013); and Egreteau, Renaud, "The Continuing Political Salience of the Military in Post-SPDC Myanmar", in Cheesman, Farrelly and Wilson (eds), *Debating Democratisation, op. cit.*, pp. 259–84.
35. Clapp, Priscilla, *Myanmar: Anatomy of a Political Transition*, Washington, D.C.: USIP Special Report No. 369, 2015.
36. Min Zin and Brian Joseph, "The Democrats' Opportunity", *Journal of Democracy* 23, 4 (2012), p. 112.
37. Taylor, Robert H., "Myanmar's 'Pivot' Toward the Shibboleth of 'Democracy'", *Asian Affairs* 44, 3 (2013), p. 394.
38. Jones, Lee, "Explaining Myanmar's Regime Transition: The Periphery is Central", *Democratization* 21, 5, (2014), p. 784; and Pedersen, Morten, "Myanmar's Democratic Opening: The Process and Prospects for Reform", in Cheesman, Farrelly and Wilson (eds), *Debating Democratization, op. cit.*, pp. 23–5.
39. Pedersen, Morten, "Understanding Myanmar's Democratic Opening'", *East Asia Forum*, 3 April 2013.
40. Ganesan, N., "Interpreting Recent Developments in Myanmar as an Attempt to Establish Political Legitimacy", *Asian Journal of Peacebuilding* 1, 2 (2013), p. 254.
41. Interview with a retired lieutenant-colonel and DSA graduate, Yangon, February 2015.
42. Bünte, Marco, "Burma's Transition to Quasi-Military Rule", op. cit., pp. 757–8.
43. Jones, Lee, "The Political Economy of Myanmar's Transition", *Journal of Contemporary Asia* 44, 1 (2014), pp. 144–70.
44. *Ibid.* p. 167.

45. Maung Zarni, "A Three Insecurities Perspective for the Changing Myanmar", *Kyoto Review of Southeast Asia* 14 (2013).
46. Min Zin and Brian Joseph, *op. cit.*, pp. 107–8.
47. Khin Zaw Win, "Myanmar in Political Transition", in Duell, Kerstin (ed.), *Myanmar in Transition: Polity, People and Processes*, Singapore: Select Books, 2013, p. 10.
48. Fink, Christina, "How Real Are Myanmar's Reforms?", *Current History* 113, 764 (2014), p. 229.
49. Horsey, Richard, "Myanmar's Political Landscape Following the 2010 Elections: Starting with a Glass Nine-Tenths Empty?", in Cheesman, Skidmore and Wilson (eds), *Myanmar's Transition, op. cit.*, pp. 39–51.
50. "Praetorianism" is a concept taken from the political history of Ancient Rome. The term—from the Latin *praetorianus*, "of the praetor"—describes the action of a "Praetorian Guard", a military unit directly assigned to the protection of the Emperor, or, during the Roman Republic, of the *Praetor* (an elected magistrate). By extension, a modern praetorian system is a regime in which the armed forces regularly intrude into the civilian and political realms. See, among others, Perlmutter, Amos, *Egypt: The Praetorian State*, New Brunswick: Transaction Publishers, 1974 and Huntington, Samuel P., *The Soldier and the State*, Cambridge, MA: Belknap Press, 1957.
51. Interview with the author, Naypyitaw, August 2013.
52. Interview with the author, Yangon, January 2014.

1. MILITARY GUARDIANSHIP AND THE SEARCH FOR A PACTED TRANSITION

1. Looking at the first and second waves of democratic transition in 1970s and 1980s Europe and Latin America, Guillermo O'Donnell and Philippe C. Schmitter have argued that a "forced" breakdown of military regimes (either from within, or through external intervention) has been a far more commonly observed "transitional opening" (*Transition from Authoritarian Rule: Tentative Conclusions about Uncertain Democracies*, Baltimore, MD: The Johns Hopkins University Press, 1986, pp. 17–18). However, subsequent literature on the third and even fourth waves of democratization since the end of the Cold War has demonstrated that "pacted" transitions and negotiated political change have increasingly been achieved around the world. See, for instance, Hagopian, Frances, "Democracy by Undemocratic Means? Elites, Political Pacts and Regime Transition in Brazil", *Comparative Political Studies* 23, 2 (1990), pp. 147–70; Linz, Juan J. and Alfred Stepan, *Problems of Democratic Transition and Consolidation: Southern Europe, South America and Post-Communist Europe*, Baltimore, MD: The John Hopkins University Press, 1996; Hunter, Wendy, *Eroding Military Influence in Brazil: Politicians against Soldiers*, Chapel Hill, NC: University of North Carolina Press, 1997; and Munck, Gerardo L. and Carol S. Leff, "Modes of Transition and Democratization: South America and Eastern Europe in Comparative Perspective", *Comparative Politics* 29, 3 (1997), pp. 343–62.
2. Welch, Claude E., *No Farewell to Arms: Military Disengagement from Politics in Africa and Latin America*, Boulder, CO: Westview Press, 1987; see also Hagopian, *op. cit.*, and Ensalaco, Mark, "Military Prerogatives and the Stalemate of Chilean Civil-Military Relations", *Armed Forces & Society* 21, 2 (1995), pp. 255–70.
3. Studies published since the 2000s have explored the persistent salience of the Tatmadaw's political role: Selth, Andrew, *Burma's Armed Forces: Power without Glory*, Norwalk, CT:

EastBridge, 2002; Win Min, "Looking inside the Burmese Military", *Asian Survey* 48, 6 (2008), pp. 1018–37; Callahan, Mary P., "Myanmar's Perpetual Junta: Solving the Riddle of the *Tatmadaw's* Long Reign", *New Left Review* 60 (2009), pp. 27–63; Maung Aung Myoe, *Building the Tatmadaw: Myanmar Armed Forces since 1948*, Singapore: ISEAS Publications, 2009; Callahan, Mary P., "The Endurance of Military Rule in Burma: Not Why, But Why Not?", in Levenstein, Susan L. (ed.), *Finding Dollars, Sense and Legitimacy in Burma*, Washington, D.C.: Woodrow Wilson Center, 2010, pp. 54–76; Prager-Nyein, Susanne, "The Armed Forces of Burma: The Constant Sentinel", in Mietzner, Marcus (ed.), *The Political Resurgence of the Military in Southeast Asia: Conflict and Leadership*, London: Routledge, 2011, pp. 24–44; Egreteau, Renaud and Larry Jagan, *Soldiers and Diplomacy in Burma: Understanding the Foreign Policies of the Burmese Praetorian State*, Singapore: NUS Press, 2013; and Farrelly, Nicholas, "Discipline without Democracy: Military Dominance in Post-Colonial Burma", *Australian Journal of International Affairs* 67, 3 (2014), pp. 312–26.

4. Discussion with the author, Naypyitaw, February 2013.
5. Huntington, Samuel P., *The Soldier and the State*, Cambridge, MA: Belknap, 1957, and *Political Order in Changing Societies*, New Haven, CT: Yale University Press, 1968.
6. Janowitz, Morris, *The Professional Soldier: A Social and Political Portrait*, Glencoe, IL: The Free Press, 1960; Finer, Samuel E., *The Man on Horseback: The Role of the Military in Politics* (revised edn), New York: Praeger, 1975 [1962]; Perlmutter, Amos, "The Praetorian State and the Praetorian Army: Toward a Taxonomy of Civil-Military Relations in Developing Countries", *Comparative Politics* 1, 3 (1969), pp. 382–404; Nordlinger, Eric, *Soldiers in Politics: Military Coups and Governments*, London: Prentice Hall, 1977; and Perlmutter, Amos, *Political Roles and Military Rulers*, London: Frank Cass, 1981.
7. Perlmutter, "The Praetorian State", *op. cit.*, p. 392 and Nordlinger, op. cit., pp. 22–7.
8. While Perlmutter initially defined two types ("arbitrator" and "ruler"), Nordlinger presented a threefold typology ("moderator", "guardian" and "ruler"), which Muthiah Alagappa completed with a fourth ideal type ("referee", "guardian", "participant ruler" and "praetorian ruler"), but I consider Alagappa's referee and guardian types too similar to each other, hence my threefold typology. See Alagappa, Muthiah, "Investigating and Explaining Change: An Analytical Framework", in Alagappa, Muthiah (ed.), *Coercion and Governance: The Declining Political Role of the Military in Asia*, Stanford, CA: Stanford University Press, 2001, p. 34.
9. Alagappa, *op. cit.*, p. 34.
10. *Ibid.*
11. Finer, *The Man on Horseback*, *op. cit.*, pp. 183–4.
12. Finer, Samuel E., "The Retreat to the Barracks. Notes on the Practice and the Theory of Military Withdrawal from the Seats of Power", *Third World Quarterly* 7, 1 (1985), pp. 16–30.
13. Guyot, James F., "Burmese Praetorianism", in Gartner, Uta and Jens Lorenz (eds), *Tradition and Modernity in Myanmar*, Berlin: LIT Verlag, 1994, pp. 129–48.
14. See, for instance: A Tatmadaw Researcher, *A Concise History of Myanmar and the Tatmadaw's Role, 1948–1988 (Vol. I and II)*, Rangoon: Ministry of Information Printing & Publishing Press, 1991; Mya Win, *Tatmadaw's Traditional Role in National Politics*, Yangon: News and Periodicals Enterprises, 1992; and Min Maung Maung, *The Tatmadaw and its Leadership Role in National Politics*, Yangon: News & Periodicals Enterprise, 1993.
15. For details, see Butwell, Richard, "Civilians and Soldiers in Burma", *Studies in Asia* 1, 2 (1961), pp. 74–85 and Dupuy, Trevor N. "Burma and its Army: A Contrast in Motivations and Characteristics", *The Antioch Review* 20, 4 (1960), pp. 428–40.

16. The Tatmadaw itself produced an unashamedly apologetic report of the caretaker government: *Is Trust Vindicated? A Chronicle of the Various Accomplishments of the Government Headed by General Ne Win during the Period of Tenure from November 1958 to February 6, 1960*, Rangoon: Director of Information, Government of the Union of Burma, 1960.
17. A Tatmadaw Researcher, *op. cit.*, (Volume I), pp. 35–6; Mya Win, *op. cit.*, pp. 22–33; and Min Maung Maung, *op. cit.*, pp. 118–23.
18. On the contrasting understandings of military-led socialist revolution in the Burmese context, see Taylor, Robert H., "Burmese Concepts of Revolution", in Hobart, Mark and Robert H. Taylor (eds), *Context, Meaning, and Power in Southeast Asia*, Ithaca, NY: SEAP, 1986, pp. 79–92, and Wiant, Jon A., "Tradition in the Service of Revolution: The Political Symbolism of *Taw-hlan-ye-khit*", in Lehman, F. K. (ed.), *Military Rule in Burma since 1962*, Singapore: Maruzen Asia, 1981, pp. 59–72.
19. The first postcolonial constitution, adopted in 1947, was annuled by the 1962 coup d'état.
20. Silverstein, Josef, "From Soldiers to Civilians: The New Constitution of Burma in Action", in Silverstein, Josef (ed.), *The Future of Burma in Perspective: A Symposium*, Athens, OH: Center of International Studies, University of Ohio, 1974, pp. 80–92.
21. For more details on the Ne Win regime, see the thorough studies by Yoshihiro Nakanishi, *Strong Soldiers, Failed Revolution: The State and Military in Burma, 1962–88*, Singapore: NUS Press, 2013 and Robert H. Taylor, *General Ne Win: A Political Biography*, Singapore: ISEAS Publications, 2015.
22. The constitution of 1974 had been abrogated by the 1988 coup.
23. See Chapter One, note 7.
24. For detailed exploration of the constitutional text and its controversies: Taylor, Robert H., "One Day, One Fathom, Bagan Won't Move: On the Myanmar Road to Constitution", in Wilson, Trevor (ed.), *Myanmar's Long Road to National Reconciliation*, Singapore: ISEAS Publications, 2006, pp. 3–28. Williams, David C., "What's So Bad about Burma's 2008 Constitution? A Guide for the Perplexed", in Crouch, Melissa and Tim Lindsey (eds), *Law, Society and Transition in Myanmar*, Oxford: Hart Publishing, 2014, pp. 117–40; Taylor, Robert H., "The Third Constitution of the Union of Myanmar", in Kyaw Yin Hlaing (ed.), *Prisms on the Golden Pagoda: Perspectives on National Reconciliation in Myanmar*, Singapore: NUS Press, 2014, pp. 132–51.
25. Hla Min was replaced by Lt-Gen. Wai Lwin in August 2012; Thein Htay was replaced by Lt-Gen. Thet Naing Win in February 2013.
26. Horsey, Richard, *Who's Who in the New Myanmar Government*, New York: SSRC Conflict Prevention and Peace Forum Briefing Paper, 14 April 2011.
27. Kyaw Yin Hlaing, "Understanding Recent Political Changes in Myanmar", *Contemporary Southeast Asia*, 34, 2 (2012), p. 211.
28. Interview with an army brigadier general, Naypyitaw, February 2015.
29. General Saw Maung was deposed in April 1992 by General Than Shwe, who remained in charge of the junta until 2011.
30. O'Donnell and Schmitter, *op. cit.*, p. 3.
31. *Ibid.*, p. 26.
32. Karl, Terry L., "Dilemmas of Democratization in Latin America", *Comparative Politics* 23, 1 (1990), p. 13; Linz and Stepan, *op. cit.*, p. 65.
33. O'Donnell and Schmitter, *op. cit.*, p. 37.
34. Linz and Stepan, *op. cit.*, pp. 57 and 64.

35. O'Donnell and Schmitter, *op. cit.*, pp. 39–40.
36. Hagopian, *op. cit.*, pp. 147–70.
37. As in Venezuela or Russia in the 2000s, for instance; see Schmitter, Philippe C., "Twenty-Five Years, Fifteen Findings", *Journal of Democracy* 21, 1 (2010), p. 23.
38. Among analyses released since the 2000s, see: Reynolds, Andrew et al.,"How Could Burma Democratize?", *Journal of Democracy* 12, 4 (2001), p. 106; Thawnghmung, Ardeth Maung, "Preconditions and Prospects for Democratic Transition in Burma/Myanmar", *Asian Survey* 43, 3 (2003), pp. 443–60; Holliday, Ian, "Voting and Violence in Myanmar: Nation Building for a Transition to Democracy", *Asian Survey* 48, 6 (2008), p. 1051; and Kyaw Yin Hlaing, "Problems with the Process of Reconciliation", in Rieffel, Lex (ed.), *Myanmar/Burma: Inside Challenges, Outside Interests*, Washingon, D.C.: Brookings Institution Press, 2010, p. 36.
39. Stipulating that it was too early to consider lifting them (National League for Democracy, *Sanctions against Burma. A Review by the National League for Democracy*, 8 February 2011).
40. *New Light of Myanmar*, 26 July 2011, p. 9.
41. Jagan, Larry, "What Thein Sein promised Suu Kyi", *Asia Times*, 30 September 2011.
42. Kyaw Yin Hlaing, "Understanding Recent Political Changes in Myanmar", *Contemporary Southeast Asia* 34, 2 (2012), pp. 206–7.
43. Reuters, *Myanmar court rejects Suu Kyi party ban appeal*, 29 January 2011.
44. Kyaw Yin Hlaing, "The Unexpected Arrival of a New Political Era in Myanmar", in Kyaw Yin Hlaing (ed.), *Prisms on the Golden Pagoda: Perspectives on National Reconciliation in Myanmar*, Singapore: NUS Press, 2014, pp. 221–2.
45. The 2008 constitution contains no provisions as to how and when a legislator should be replaced if s/he is removed, passes away or resigns.
46. Interview with Tin Oo, NLD patron, Yangon, December 2015.
47. Steinberg, David I., *The Significance of Burma/Myanmar's By-Elections*, Washington, D.C.: East-West Center Asia-Pacific Bulletin No. 156, 2 April 2012, pp. 1–2.
48. ICG, *Myanmar: A New Peace Initiative*, Yangon/Brussels: Asia Report No. 214, 30 November 2011.
49. Author's discussions with KIO leadership, August 2011.
50. Diamond, Larry, "The Need for a Political Pact", *Journal of Democracy* 23, 4 (2012), pp. 138–49.
51. Callahan, Mary P., *Drivers of Political Change in Post-junta, Constitutional Burma*, Washington, D.C.: USAID, 2012, p. 4.
52. O'Donnell and Schmitter, *op. cit.*, p. 38.
53. Regular discussions with several of these Burmese individuals over the years, in Myanmar or abroad, during international conferences, workshops or one-on-one interviews.
54. On the formation of Egress in 2006 and the Myanmar Peace Center in 2011, see Ganesan, Narayanan, "The Myanmar Peace Center: Its Origins, Activities, and Aspirations", *Asian Journal of Peacebuilding* 2, 1 (2014), pp. 130–1.
55. Interview with Khin Maung Swe, Yangon, May 2013.
56. Interview with Thu Wai, Yangon, January 2014.
57. Not necessarily hand in hand with other actors of the "Third Force", though. Discussion with the author, Hong Kong, June 2012.
58. Khin Zaw Win, "A Burmese Perspective on Prospects for Progress", in Skidmore, Monique and Trevor Wilson (eds), *Myanmar: The State, Community and the Environment*, Canberra: ANU E-Press, 2007, p. 33. See also Khin Zaw Win, "Reality Check on the Sanctions Against

Myanmar", in Ganesan, Narayanan and Kyaw Yin Hlaing (eds), *Myanmar: State, Society, and Ethnicity*, Singapore: ISEAS Publications, 2007, pp. 278–88.

59. "He's a traitor. I don't like him", one NLD veteran simply put it. Interview with the author, Naypyitaw, May 2013.
60. Thant Myint-U, "What to do about Burma", *London Review of Books* 9, 3 (2007), pp. 31–3; Thant Myint-U, "The Burma Dilemma", *The New York Times*, 21 May 2008.
61. See an early analysis: Zaw Oo, "Exit, Voice, and Loyalty in Burma: The Role of Overseas Burmese in Democratising their Homeland", in Wilson, Trevor (ed.), *Myanmar's Long Road to National Reconciliation*, Singapore: ISEAS Publications, 2006, pp. 231–62.
62. Notes on discussions at the Myanmar Peace Center, Yangon, April 2015.
63. Interview with Bo Kyaw Nyein, Yangon, July 2014.
64. See Aung Naing Oo's views: "Peace, hope, optimism: ingredients for peace", *The Myanmar Times*, 31 March 2015. See also a Kachin perspective: Naw, Stella, "The peace that we envision", *The Irrawaddy*, 15 October 2015.
65. Interview with a leader of the 88 Generation movement, Yangon, January 2014.
66. For instance, Harn Yawnghwe joined a round table I organized in Paris in the aftermath of Cyclone Nargis in 2008, while Lian Sakhong was part of a panel I co-convened with Dr. Julie Baujard during the 10th Burma Studies Conference held in 2010.
67. Interview, Shalom Foundation, Yangon, December 2015.
68. See his doctoral thesis, *Contrasting Pathways to Change in Burma/Myanmar: From Bullets to Bribery*, unpublished PhD dissertation, Bangkok: Mahidol University, 2013, p. 100.
69. Christian Science Monitor, *Burma Elections. Are activists the new Third Force in politics?*, 28 June 2010.
70. Mratt Kyaw Thu, "Lack of Election Complaints Smoothes NLD Transition", *Frontier Myanmar*, 29 January 2016.
71. The Myanmar Times, *Ceasefire pact is 'historic gift': president*, 16 October 2015.
72. Interview with the author, Yangon, June 2013.
73. Interview with the author, Yangon, May 2013.

2. THE BROADENING OF SOCIOPOLITICAL SPACES

1. Among others, O'Donnell and Schmitter, *Transition from Authoritarian Rule: Tentative Conclusions about Uncertain Democracies*, Baltimore, MD: The Johns Hopkins University Press, 1986, p. 48.
2. Khin Zaw Win, "Myanmar in Political Transition", in Duell, Kerstin (ed.), *Myanmar in Transition: Polity, People and Processes*, Singapore: Select Books, 2013, p. 9.
3. As observed, for instance, during my various interactions with presiding officers at the Union parliament or even with officials from the Ministry of Defense in Naypyitaw (2013–15).
4. A strong reminder of those times can be found in Christina Fink's excellent account of Myanmar under military rule, *Living Silence in Burma: Surviving under Military Rule* (1st edition), London: Zed Books, 2001.
5. *The Economist*, "Yangon's digital spring", 3 March 2012.
6. For an overview of the role of activist media after the Burmese monks' revolt (2007) and Cyclone Nargis (2008), see Humphries, Richard, "Saffron-robed Monks and Digital Flash Cards: The Development and Challenges of Burmese Exile Media", in Nault, Derrick M. (ed.), *Development in Asia: Interdisciplinary, Post-neoliberal and Transnational Perspectives*, Boca Raton, FL: Brown Walker, 2009, pp. 237–58.

7. AFP, "Tech sector sizzles as Myanmar embraces Internet for the masses", 28 September 2014.
8. *The Irrawaddy*, "Private dailies still struggling with Govt competition, production costs", 6 May 2015.
9. *The New York Times* interviewed its last director, Tint Swe: "Chief censor in Myanmar caps his red pen", 21 September 2012.
10. Discussion with Ross Dunkley, *MT* founder, Yangon, December 2002.
11. Discussion with one of *MT*'s editors, Yangon, January 2014. *The Myanmar Times* evolved into a daily paper in March 2015.
12. All incidents happened in early 2015, in an increasingly volatile pre-electoral context: *AFP*, "Photographer arrested for Myanmar military Facebook satire", 28 February 2015; Mizzima News, "Myanmar Post journalists jailed for two months", 19 March 2015; and *Democratic Voice of Burma*, "Myanmar Times apologises for land grab cartoon", 31 March 2015.
13. Human Rights Watch, *Burma: activists charged for mocking military online*, 17 October 2015.
14. Ko Htwe and Gene Williams, "Old ties to Myanmar's new media (corrected version)", *Asia Times*, 10 January 2014.
15. *The Myanmar Times*, "Press freedom: a long and winding road", 17 March 2015.
16. The Irrawaddy, "Burma's military appoints point men to media relations", 15 October 2014.
17. As deputy defense minister; discussion with the author, Naypyitaw, February 2015.
18. AFP, "Myanmar workers win rights to vote", 14 October 2011; AFP, "Myanmar president signs protest bill", 3 December 2011.
19. *The Myanmar Times*, "Ministry enacts protest by-laws", 16–22 July, 2012.
20. See, for instance, Patrick Strefford's argument, "Myanmar's Transition and its Protest Movements", *Asia Journal of Global Studies* 6, 1 (2014), pp. 4–15. One should notice, though, that monk and activist demonstrations were severely repressed in Letpadaung in November 2012: *Reuters*, "Myanmar's deep mine of old troubles", 27 December 2012.
21. AFP, "Myanmar protests: inquiry to be held into security force's crackdown on student protesters", 25 March 2015; see also Selth, Andrew, "Burma: the return of the 'vigilantes'", *The Lowy Interpreter*, 22 April 2015.
22. Selth, Andrew, "Second thoughts on the civil unrest in Burma", *The Lowy Interpreter*, 14 April 2015.
23. AP, "Myanmar frees 14,600, but few political prisoners", 17 May 2011.
24. Zarganar had been jailed since 2008 for his activism after the passage of Cyclone Nargis, and Su Su Nway has long spearheaded labor and women's rights movements with the help of the NLD in her native township of Kawhmu, in the Irrawaddy delta: AFP, "Myanmar frees scores of political prisoners", 12 October 2011.
25. *The Myanmar Times*, "More amnesties planned, says Thura U Shwe Mann", 18–24 October 2011.
26. Thein Nyunt later left the NDF to found his own party. Interview, NDF headquarters, Yangon, May 2013.
27. *The New Light of Myanmar*, 27 August 2011.
28. Beech, Hannah, "The Barefoot Diplomat", *TIME*, 1 December 2011.
29. Discussion with the author, Yangon, June 2013.
30. *The Myanmar Times*, "Miles to go: Gambira 7 years on from Saffron", 3 November 2014.
31. Discussion with Ko Ko Gyi, Yangon, January 2014.
32. Most of these activists, however, requested anonymity when interviewed.

33. Discussion with Aung Naing Oo, a director at the Myanmar Peace Center and a former exile in the US and Thailand, Yangon, March 2015.
34. AFP, "Myanmar: Political prisoners freed", 17 May 2013.
35. *The Irrawaddy*, "Burma releases 41 more political prisoners", 11 December 2013.
36. Giving their names, age, jail registration numbers, and reasons and date of punishment: see *The New Light of Myanmar*, 1 November 2014, pp. 4–7 and 10–12.
37. AAPPB, "Monthly Chronology of November 2015 and Remaining Political Prisoners List and Facing Trial List", http://aappb.org/2015/12/monthly-chronology-of-november–2015-and-remaining-political-prisoners-listand-facing-trial-list, last accessed 13 December 2015.
38. See one of his many interviews: *The Bangkok Post*, "In his own words; the rise and fall of Khin Nyunt", 8 April 2012. Khin Nyunt has since released his memoirs (in Burmese).
39. Interview with a former Tatmadaw lieutenant-colonel who joined the Ministry of Information after retirement, Naypyitaw, July 2014.
40. *The Myanmar Times*, "If they call me, I will work: U Thein Swe", 10 October 2014. Ex-Brig.-Gen. Thein Swe's son, Sonny Swe, used to be one of the owners of *The Myanmar Times*—he now owns *Frontier Magazine*.
41. *The Irrawaddy*, "2 political prisoners among thousands to be freed", 7 October 2014.
42. *The Myanmar Times*, "Committee rejects military intelligence prisoner proposal", 22 December 2013.
43. Reuters, "Myanmar frees 69 political prisoners", 15 November 2013.
44. See the obituaries in several Western media: *The New York Times*, "Ne Win, ex-Burmese military strongman, dies at 91", 6 December 2002; *TIME*, "The Puppet Master of Burma", 16 December 2002; and *The Economist*, "Ne Win, destroyer of Burma, died on December 5th aged 91", 12 December 2002.
45. Steinberg, David I., "Myanmar: Reconciliation—Progress in the Process?", *Southeast Asian Affairs* 2003, pp. 175–6.
46. Interview with the author, Yangon, July 2014.
47. For further theoretical discussions, see Diamond, Larry and Richard Gunther (eds), *Political Parties and Democracy*, Baltimore, MD: The Johns Hopkins University Press, 2001.
48. ICG, *The Myanmar Elections*, Yangon/Brussels: Asia Briefing No. 105, 2010, p. 3.
49. Interview with Khin Maung Swe, Yangon, July 2014.
50. Interview with an SNDP legislator, Naypyitaw, August 2013.
51. Interview with RNDP legislators, Naypyitaw, January 2014. The ALD and RNDP would reunite in the run-up of the 2015 elections to split again early 2016.
52. *The New Light of Myanmar*, 14 August 2010, p. 1.
53. Interview with Han Shwe, NUP spokesman, Yangon, January 2014.
54. Interview with Cho Cho Kyaw Nyein, Yangon, July 2014.
55. Interviews with both of them, Yangon, January 2014.
56. Interview with Than Than Nu, Yangon, January 2014.
57. *The Guardian*, "Burma's 'three princesses' prepare for election they have no chance of winning", 22 July 2010.
58. Despite the KIO's repeated claims Dr. Tu Ja had long moved away from the movement; interview with KIO members, August 2011.
59. Discussion with a Baptist pastor and Kachin community leader, Myitkyina, February 2013.
60. Interview with Hkyet Hting Nan, UDPKS chairman, Naypyitaw, February 2015.

61. *The Myanmar Times*, "Kachin candidates campaign for peace, federalism", 7 November 2015.
62. For a deeper analysis, see Wade, Francis, "West Bank of the East: Burma's Social Engineering Project", *Los Angeles Review of Books*, 7 November 2015.
63. Interview, Yangon, May 2013.
64. As, for instance, the United National Development Party (UNDP); interview with the author, Yangon, May 2013.
65. Mizzima News, "UEC rejects Muslim parliamentary candidates", 2 September 2015.
66. Interview with the author, Yangon, August 2015.
67. Interview with a newly-elected NLD parliamentarian, Yangon, May 2013.
68. Interview with UEC commissioners, Naypyitaw, August 2015.
69. See earlier note 6, as well as International Crisis Group (ICG), *Myanmar's Post-Election Landscape*, Brussels: Asia Briefing No. 118, 2011; and Tin Maung Maung Than. "Myanmar's 2010 Elections: Continuity and Change", *Southeast Asian Affairs* 2011, pp. 190–207.
70. Richard Horsey, *Outcome of the Myanmar Elections*, New York: SSRC Conflict Prevention and Peace Forum Briefing, November 17, 2010.
71. See, for instance, Englehart, Neil A., "Two Cheers for Burma's Rigged Elections", *Asian Survey* 52, 4 (2012), pp. 666–86.
72. However, the argument, made after only one electoral exercise, remains pretty fragile. See Macdonald, Adam P., "From Military Rule to Electoral Authoritarianism: The Reconfiguration of Power in Myanmar and its Future", *Asian Affairs* 40, 1 (2013), pp. 20–36.
73. For a comparative, and speculative, view on the 2015 elections, see Marston, Hunter, "Myanmar's Electoral System: Reviewing the 2010 and 2012 Elections and Looking Ahead to the 2015 General Elections", *Asian Journal of Political Science* 21, 3 (2013), pp. 268–84.
74. However, this was in the absence of the newly elected NLD representatives, who had not as yet agreed to swear the oath to the 2008 constitution. See Min Zin, "Picking the wrong battle", *Foreign Policy*, 20 April 2012. The transcript of Ban Ki-moon's public speech is available online at: http://www.un.org/apps/news/infocus/sgspeeches/statments_full.asp?statID=1526#.VW69s6ZgSJ0 (last accessed 22 June 2015).
75. The USDP and the SNDP secured the two other seats (*The Economist*, "By-elections in Myanmar: the Lady of all landslides", 7 April 2012).
76. ICG, *The Myanmar Elections: Results and Implications*, Yangon/Brussels: Asia Report No. 147, 2015.
77. In January 2012, one Amyotha Hluttaw MP from the USDP passed away, as did one Pyithu Hluttaw legislator from the RNDP in March 2012.
78. As described by long-time activist Min Zin, "In a flawed election, Burma's people will have their say at last", *Foreign Policy*, 4 November 2015.
79. Interview with a first-time elected NLD Union-level legislator who had campaigned (unsuccessfully) in 2010 for another party, Yangon, December 2015.
80. Interview with Tin Aye, Chairman of the UEC, Naypyitaw, August 2015.
81. *The Myanmar Times*, "Final results confirm scale of NLD election victory", 23 November 2015.
82. Interview with Tin Oo, NLD patron, Yangon, December 2015.
83. Egreteau, Renaud, "The (few) generals that don't exit in Myanmar", *The Diplomat*, 20 November 2015.
84. See Richard Horsey's analysis in Transnational Institute, "The 2015 General Election in

Myanmar: What Now for Ethnic Politics?", *Myanmar Policy Briefing No. 17*, December 2015.

85. See, for instance, the post-election report by the Carter Center, one of the US institutions allowed by the Myanmar authorities to independently monitor the electoral process: *Election Observation Mission Preliminary Statement*, Yangon, 10 November 2015.
86. Among others: *The Economist*, "Myanmar: The lose-lose election", 18 July 2015; Human Rights Watch, "Burma: election fundamentally flawed", 4 November 2015; and Burma Campaign UK, *Burma's 2015 Elections and the 2008 Constitution*, London: Burma Briefing No. 41, October 2015.
87. On recent debates following that argument: Putnam, Robert, *Making Democracy Work*, Princeton, NJ: Princeton University Press, 1993; Diamond, Larry, *Developing Democracy: Towards Consolidation*, Baltimore, MD: Johns Hopkins University Press, 1999; and Burnell, Peter and Peter Calvert (eds), *Civil Society in Democratization*, London: Frank Cass, 2004.
88. See Muthiah Alagappa's tentative explanations using the context of post-Cold War Asia, "Civil Society and Democratic Change: Indeterminate Connection, Transforming Relations", in Alagappa, Muthiah (ed.), *Civil Society and Political Change in Asia: Expanding and Contracting Democratic Space*, Stanford: Stanford University Press, 2004, pp. 478–508; for Southeast Asia, see Weiss, Meredith L., "Civil Society and Democratisation in Southeast Asia: What Is the Connection?", in Case, William (ed.), *The Routledge Handbook of Southeast Asian Democratization*, London: Routledge, 2015, pp. 135–46.
89. Alagappa, *op. cit.*, p. 478.
90. Diamond, Larry J., "Toward Democratic Consolidation", *Journal of Democracy*, 5, 3 (1994), p. 16.
91. See the broader study: Cohen, Jean L. and Andrew Arato, *Civil Society and Political Theory*, Cambridge: Cambridge University Press, 1994.
92. Bernhard, Michael and Ekrem Karakoc, "Civil Society and the Legacies of Dictatorship", *World Politics* 59, 4, (2007), pp. 539–67.
93. O'Donnell and Schmitter, *op. cit.*, p. 26.
94. O'Donnell and Schmitter, *op. cit.*, pp. 49–55.
95. See two analyses of the situation in the 1990s: Steinberg, David I., "A Void in Myanmar: Civil Society in Burma", in Kramer, Tom and Pietje Vervest (eds), *Strengthening Civil Society in Burma: Possibilities and Dilemmas for International NGOs*, Chiang Mai: Silkworm Books, 1999, pp. 1–14; and Liddell, Zunnetta, "No Room to Move: Legal Constraints on Civil Society in Burma", in Kramer and Vervest (eds), *op. cit.*, pp. 54–68. For a global overview of social and personal life under the junta, see Fink, Christina, *Living Silence in Burma: Surviving under Military Rule* (1st edition), London: Zed Books, 2001.
96. ICG, *Myanmar: The Role of Civil Society*, Yangon/Brussels: Asia Report No. 27, 2001.
97. Kyaw Ying Hlaing, "Associational Life in Myanmar: Past and Present", in Ganesan, Narayanan and Kyaw Yin Hlaing (eds), *Myanmar: State, Society, and Ethnicity*, Singapore: ISEAS Publications, 2007, pp. 143–71.
98. South, Ashley, *Civil Society in Burma: The Development of Democracy amidst Conflict*, Washington, D.C.: East-West Center Policy Studies No. 51, 2008.
99. For instance: Lorch, Jasmin, "The (Re)-Emergence of Civil Society in Areas of State Weaknesses: The Case of Education in Burma/Myanmar", in Skidmore, Monique and Trevor Wilson (eds), *Dictatorship, Disorder and Decline in Myanmar*, Canberra: ANU E-Press, 2008, pp. 151–76.

100. On their activities in the 2000s, see *10 Years Metta*, Yangon: Metta Development Foundation, 2010.
101. Among others: Brees, Inge, "Burmese Refugee Transnationalism: What Is The Effect?", *Journal of Current Southeast Asian Affairs* 28, 2 (2009), pp. 23–46; Matelski, Maaike, "Civil Society and Expectations of Democratisation from Below: The Case of Myanmar", *Thammasat Review*, 16 (2012), pp. 153–66; Baujard, Julie, "Nous sommes des femmes dangereuses!...en danger. Mobilisation des réfugiées birmanes à Delhi", *Moussons*, 22 (2013), pp. 57–73; and Mullen, Matthew, *Contrasting Pathways to Change in Burma/Myanmar: From Bullets to Bribery*, unpublished PhD dissertation, Bangkok: Mahidol University, 2013.
102. Kyaw Ying Hlaing, "Burma: Civil Society Skirting Regime Rules", in Alagappa (ed.), *Civil Society and Political Change in Asia, op. cit.*, pp. 389–418.
103. Thawnghmung, Ardeth Maung and Paul Sarno, "Myanmar Impasses: Alternatives to Isolation and Engagement?" *Asian Journal of Political Science* 14, 1 (2006), pp. 40–63.
104. Interview with Devi Thant Sin, environmental activist and great-granddaughter of the last Burmese king, Yangon, July 2014.
105. Dorning, Karl, "Creating an Environment for Participation: International NGOs and the Growth of Civil Society in Burma", in Wilson, Trevor (ed.), *Myanmar's Long Road to National Reconciliation*, Singapore: ISEAS Publications, 2006, pp. 188–217. More recently, see Ware, Anthony, *Context-Sensitive Development: How International NGOs Operate in Myanmar*, Sterling, VA: Kumarian Press, 2012.
106. For a synthetic analysis, see Beatty, Linnea M., "Democracy Activism and Assistance in Burma: Sites of Resistance", *International Journal* 65, 3 (2010), pp. 619–36.
107. Interview, Yangon, January 2005.
108. Tegenfeldt, David, "International Non-Governmental Organizations in Burma", in Taylor, Robert H. (ed.), *Burma: Political Economy under Military Rule*, London: Hurst, 2001, pp. 109–18; five years later: Tegenfeldt, David, "More than Saving Lives: The Role of International Development Agencies in Supporting Change Processes in Burma/Myanmar", in Wilson, Trevor (ed.), *Myanmar's Long Road to National Reconciliation*, Singapore: ISEAS Publications, 2006, pp. 218–30.
109. For instance, Loeschmann, Heike (ed.), *Active Citizens under Political Wraps: Experiences from Myanmar/Burma and Vietnam*, Berlin: Heinrich Boell Foundation, 2006.
110. Moe Thuzar and Pavin Chachavalpongpun, *Myanmar: Life after Nargis*, Singapore: ISEAS Publications, 2009; Larkin, Emma, *Everything is Broken*, New York: Penguin Books, 2010.
111. Jaquet, Carine and Matthew J. Walton, "Buddhism and Relief in Myanmar: Reflections on Relief as a Practice of *Dāna*", in Kawanami, Hiroko and Geoffrey Samuel (eds), *Buddhism, International Relief Work, and Civil Society in Myanmar*, Basingstoke: Palgrave Macmillan, 2013, pp. 51–74.
112. One need only visit the Defence Services Museum in Naypyitaw, which has openly exhibited dozens of pictures illustrating the Tatmadaw's relief efforts and "commitment to the people in need" over the past years.
113. Prasse-Freeman, Elliott, "Power, Civil Society, and an Inchoate Politics of the Daily in Burma/Myanmar", *The Journal of Asian Studies* 71, 2 (2012), pp. 371–2.
114. Interview with a Myanmar Egress faculty member, Hong Kong, June 2011.
115. Lidauer, Michael, "Democratic Dawn? Civil Society and Elections in Myanmar (2010–2012)", *Journal of Current Southeast Asian Affairs* 31, 2 (2012), p. 96.

116. As illustrated by the splinter group of veteran NLD politicians who formed the National Democratic Force (NDF). Interview, NDF headquarters, Yangon, May 2013.
117. *The Straits Times*, "A 'third force' for reform in Myanmar", 22 June 2013.
118. Discussions with local peasants rehoused in a new village built about 6 miles south of Myitsone, February 2013.
119. Interview, upper house legislator from Kachin State, Naypyitaw, March 2015.
120. The full text of the statement is available online, and in Burmese, at <http://www.burmapartnership.org/wp-content/uploads/2011/08/Pages-from-Irrawaddy-Appeal-by-DASSK.pdf> (last accessed 30 March 2016).
121. *The New Light of Myanmar*, "The government is elected by the people and it has to respect people's will", 1 October 2011.
122. *The Economist*, "Myanmar's surprising government: damned if they don't", 4 October 2011.
123. Its local partner is the Tatmadaw-controlled Union of Myanmar Economic Holding Ltd (UMEHL).
124. *The Irrawaddy*, "Copper Mine Protest Earns Nationwide Support", 13 September 2012. Another detailed and conceptual analysis: Prasse-Freeman, Elliott, "Grassroots Protest Movements and Mutating Conceptions of 'the Political' in an Evolving Burma", in Egreteau, Renaud and François Robinne (eds), *Metamorphosis: Studies in Social and Political Change in Myanmar*, Singapore: NUS Press, 2015, pp. 69–100.
125. Reuters, "Myanmar's deep mine of old troubles", 27 December 2012.
126. *The Myanmar Times*, "Fury over Letpadaung copper mine report", 18–24 March 2013.
127. *The Irrawaddy*, "Rights activist back to Insein on peaceful assembly rap", 7 April 2015.
128. Discussion with members of the Tampadipa Institute headed by Khin Zaw Win, Naypyitaw, February 2013.
129. Kramer, Tom, *Civil Society Gaining Ground: Opportunities for Change and Development in Burma*, Amsterdam: TNI, 2011.

3. RESTORING PARLIAMENTARY DEMOCRACY

1. For recent scholarly work on the role of parliaments and parliamentarians, see Martin, Shane, Thomas Saalfeld and Kaare W. Strom (eds), *Oxford Handbook of Legislative Studies*, Oxford: Oxford University Press, 2014; Blomgren, Magnus and Olivier Rozenberg (eds), *Parliamentary Roles in Modern Legislatures*, London: Routledge, 2012.
2. This was the object of several studies in the 1970s and 1990s: Mezey, Michael L., *Comparative Legislatures*, Durham, NC: Duke University Press, 1979; Norton, Philip (ed.), *Legislatures*, Oxford: Oxford University Press, 1990; Olson, David M., *Democratic Legislative Institutions: A Comparative View*, Armonk, NY: M.E. Sharpe, 1994.
3. Mezey, *op. cit.*, p. 36. By the same author, on Asia's context of the 1970s, see Mezey, Michael L., "The Functions of Legislatures in the Third World", *Legislative Studies Quarterly* 8, 4 (1983), pp. 511–50.
4. Löwenberg, Gerhard, Peverill Squire and D. Roderick Kiewiet (eds), *Legislatures: Comparative Perspectives on Representative Assemblies*, Ann Arbor, MI: The University of Michigan Press, 2002; Fish, M. Steven, "Stronger Legislatures, Stronger Democracies", *Journal of Democracy* 17, 1 (2006), pp. 5–20; Fish, M. Steven and Matthew Kroenig, *The Handbook of National Legislatures*, Cambridge: Cambridge University Press, 2009; Arter, David (ed.), *Comparing and Classifying Legislatures*, London: Routledge, 2009.

5. Olson, David M. and Philip Norton (eds), *The New Parliaments of Central and Eastern Europe*, London: Frank Cass, 1996; Hahn, Jeffrey W. (ed.), *Democratization in Russia: The Development of Legislative Institutions*, Armonk, NY: M.E. Sharpe, 1996; Norton, Philip and David M. Olson (eds), *Post-Communist and Post-Soviet Parliaments: The Initial Decade*, London: Routledge, 2008; and Semenova, Elena, Michael Edinger and Heinrich Best (eds), *Parliamentary Elites in Central and Eastern Europe: Recruitment and Representation*, London: Routledge, 2014.
6. Power, Timothy J., "Elites and Institutions in Conservative Transitions to Democracy: Ex-Authoritarians in the Brazilian National Congress", *Studies in Comparative International Development* 31, 3 (1996), pp. 56–84; and Morgenstern, Scott and Benito Nacif (eds), *Legislative Politics in Latin America*, Cambridge: Cambridge University Press, 2002.
7. Baaklini, Abdo I., Guilain Denoeux and Robert Springborg, *Legislative Politics in the Arab World: The Resurgence of Democratic Institutions*, Boulder, CO: Lynne Rienner, 1999; Barkan, Joel D. (ed.), *Legislative Power in Emerging African Democracies*, Boulder, CO: Lynne Rienner, 2009.
8. Norton, Philip and Nizam Ahmed (eds), *Parliaments in Asia*, London: Frank Cass, 1999; Rüland, Jürgen, C. Jurgenmeyer, M. H. Nelson and Patrick Ziegenhain, *Parliaments and Political Change in Asia*, Singapore: ISEAS Publications, 2005; Ziegenhain, Patrick, *The Indonesian Parliament and Democratization*, Singapore: ISEAS Publications, 2008; Case, William, *Executive Accountability in Southeast Asia: The Role of Legislatures in New Democracies and Under Electoral Authoritarianism*, Honolulu, HI: East-West Center, Policy Studies No. 57, 2011; Kasuya, Yuko (ed.), *Presidents, Assemblies and Policy-making in Asia*, New York: Palgrave Macmillan, 2013; and Zheng, Yongnian, Lye Liang Fook and Wilhem Hofmeister (eds), *Parliaments in Asia: Institution Building and Political Development*, London: Routledge, 2014.
9. Norton, Philip and David M. Olson, "Parliaments in Adolescence", in Olson, David M. and Philip Norton (eds), *The New Parliaments of Central and Eastern Europe*, London: Frank Cass, 1996, pp. 231–43.
10. Horsey, Richard, *The Initial Functioning of Myanmar Legislatures*, New York: SSRC Conflict Prevention and Peace Forum Briefing, 17 May 2011; International Crisis Group (ICG), *"Not a Rubber Stamp": Myanmar's Legislature in a Time of Transition*, Brussels: Asia Briefing No. 142, 2013.
11. Moe Thuzar, "The Role of Parliament in Myanmar's Reforms and Transition to Democracy", in Duell, Kerstin (ed.), *Myanmar in Transition: Polity, People and Processes*, Singapore: Select Books, 2013, pp. 19–32; Kean, Tom, "Myanmar's Parliament: From Scorn to Significance", in Cheesman, Nick, N. Farrelly and T. Wilson, *Debating Democratisation in Myanmar*, Singapore: ISEAS Publications, 2014, pp. 43–74; Egreteau, Renaud, "(Re)-emerging Patterns of Parliamentary Politics", in Steinberg, David I. (ed.), *Myanmar: The Dynamics of an Evolving Polity*, Boulder, CO: Lynne Rienner, 2014, pp. 59–88; and Fink, Christina, "Myanmar's Proactive National Legislature", *Social Forces* 82, 2 (2015), pp. 327–54.
12. Egreteau, Renaud, "Legislators in Myanmar's First Post-Junta National Legislature (2010–2015): A Sociological Analysis", *Journal of Current Southeast Asian Affairs* 33, 2 (2014), pp. 91–124; "Who Are The Military Delegates in Myanmar's 2010–2015 Union Legislature?", *Sojourn* 30, 2 (2015), pp. 338–70.
13. However, provincial parliaments still lag behind in terms of autonomous workings and effectiveness; see Egreteau, "(Re)-emerging Patterns of Parliamentary Politics", in Steinberg (ed.),

Myanmar: The Dynamics of an Evolving Polity, op. cit., pp. 78–9; and Holliday, Ian, Maw Htun Aung and Cindy Joelene, "Institution Building in Myanmar: The Establishment of Regional and State Assemblies", *Asian Survey* 55, 4 (2015), pp. 641–64.

14. Past scholarly works were also mostly based on facts about post-independence electoral politics and parliamentary affairs, but were not comparative or theoretically-grounded. See, for instance: Maung Maung, "Portrait of the Burmese Parliament", *Parliamentary Affairs* 10, 2 (1956), pp. 204–9; Srinivasan, R., "A Decade of Parliamentary Life in Burma", *The Indian Journal of Social Science* 19, 3 (1958), pp. 291–304; Maung Maung, "New Parliament in Burma", *India Quarterly* 16, 2 (1960), pp. 139–44; Silverstein, Josef, "Politics, Parties and National Elections in Burma", *Far Eastern Survey* 25, 12 (1956), pp. 177–84; and Singh, Uma Shankar, "Parties and Politics in Burma during the Period 1948–1962", *India Quarterly* 11, 3 (1977), pp. 99–120.
15. Callahan, Mary P., "On Time Warps and Warped Time: Lessons from Burma's Democratic Era", in Rotberg, Robert (ed.), *Burma: Prospects for a Democratic Future*, Washington, D.C.: Brookings Institution Press, 1998, pp. 49–67; Kyaw Yin Hlaing, "Power and Factional Struggles in Post-Independence Burmese Governments", *Journal of Southeast Asian Studies* 39, 1 (2008), pp. 149–77.
16. Nakanishi, Yoshihiro, *Strong Soldiers, Failed Revolution: The State and Military in Burma, 1962–88*, Singapore: NUS Press, 2013, pp. 180–94; see also Taylor, Robert H., "Burma", in Ahmad, Zakaria Haji and Harold Crouch (eds), *Military-Civilian Relations in South-East Asia*, Singapore: Oxford University Press, 1985, pp. 40–1.
17. For more historical detail, see Taylor, Robert H., "Elections in Burma/Myanmar: For Whom and Why?", in Taylor, Robert H. (ed.), *The Politics of Elections in Southeast Asia*, Washington, D.C.: Woodrow Wilson Center Press, 1996, pp. 164–83.
18. Inter-ethnic conflict and the emerging civil war delayed the organization of the polls in many places throughout Myanmar. Elections to the lower house started in June 1951 and spanned seven months, until January 1952.
19. The representatives of these two Conventions were not elected, but appointed directly by the regime, while those elected in the parliamentary vote on 27 May 1990 were never able to convene.
20. Interviews with the speaker of the upper house (Naypyitaw, August 2013) and the deputy speaker of the lower house (Naypyitaw, July 2014).
21. *The New Light of Myanmar*, 21 January 2011, p. 9; Egreteau, Renaud, "Myanmar military chief revamps its parliamentary team", *Nikkei Asian Review*, 27 January 2016.
22. *The Irrawaddy*, 22 February 2011.
23. *The Economist*, "Myanmar's sham legislature", 27 January 2011.
24. Interview with NLD party representatives, Yangon, May 2013.
25. Win Tin passed away in April 2014 (*The Economist*, "Win Tin: Myanmar's conscience", 3 May 2014).
26. Interview, Naypyitaw, January 2014.
27. The polls were cancelled in three constituencies of northern Kachin State, still dreadfully mired in all-out civil war.
28. Tin Maung Maung Than, "Myanmar's 2012 By-Elections: Return of NLD", *Southeast Asian Affairs* 2013, pp. 204–19.
29. *The Bangkok Post*, "Suu Kyi makes parliamentary debut", 9 July 2012.
30. Nakanishi, *op. cit*.

31. Pitkin, Hanna F., *The Concept of Representation*, Berkeley, CA: University of California Press, 1967, p. 61. Pitkin makes the distinction between elected "descriptive" representatives who "stand for" their constituents—with whom they share similar characteristics (gender, ethnicity, social background)—and "substantive" representatives who "act for" their constituents, even if their own sociological profile does not mirror that of their voters (a white congressman representing the interests of the black community, for instance). Contemporary scholars still debate whether more "descriptive" representatives in an elected body leads to more beneficial representation than "substantive" representatives; for an introduction, see, for instance, Mansbridge, Jane, "Should Blacks Represent Blacks and Women Represent Women? A Contingent 'Yes'", *The Journal of Politics*, 61, 3 (1999), pp. 628–57.
32. For the English translation carried out by MCM Publishing Group (which owns, among others, *The Myanmar Times*), see: n.a., *The Parliaments of Myanmar*, Yangon: MCM, 2013. The translation is littered with typos, mistakes, and inconsistencies. Yet, the mini-biographies of the 658 MPs provide a wealth of information and anecdotal evidence for anyone able to pay attention to the details—particularly the dates of birth, ethnicities, religions, education levels and occupational backgrounds. For what it's worth and despite its flaws, this document is the first of its kind.
33. Interview, director of the Pyidaungsu Hluttaw office, Naypyitaw, August 2015.
34. Discussion, Ministry of Defense, Naypyitaw, February 2015.
35. For more details, see Egreteau, Renaud, *Legislators, op. cit.*; *Who Are The Military Delegates*, op. cit.
36. At the time of writing, Myanmar's latest official census, carried out in March 2014, has not yet revealed ethnic data (expected late 2016).
37. Selth, Andrew, *Burma's Armed Forces: Power without Glory*, Norwalk, CT: Eastbridge, 2002, p. 173; Maung Aung Myoe, *Building the Tatmadaw: Myanmar Armed Forces since 1948*, Singapore: ISEAS Publications, 2009, p. 199.
38. This has been demonstrated in Egreteau, Renaud, *Retired Military Officers in Myanmar's Parliament: An Emerging Legislative Force?*, Singapore: ISEAS Trends No. 17, 2015.
39. Putnam, Robert, *The Comparative Study of Political Elites*, Englewood Cliffs, NJ: Prentice Hall, 1976, p. 43.
40. *Ibid.*, p. 166.
41. On the announcement of the electoral results, only a few anecdotal details of the second post-SPDC legislature were known: the total absence of Muslim representatives, the doubling of the number of elected women MPs, and the fact that fewer than 14% of MPs elected in 2010 were re-elected, for instance. For more details, see Renaud Egreteau, "Myanmar parliament preserves old patterns", *Nikkei Asian Review*, 3 April 2016.
42. Reuters, "As Myanmar parliament opens, junta's shadow looms large", 31 January 2011 and *The Myanmar Times*, "First Parliament Sessions Conclude in Nay Pyi Taw", 28 March–3 April, 2011. For an objective assessment of the first session of the Union parliament, see Horsey, Richard, "The Initial Functioning of the Myanmar Legislature", *SSRC Conflict Prevention and Peace Forum Briefing Paper*, New York, 17 May 17, 2011.
43. Reuters, "In Myanmar, a 'sham' parliament stirs to life", 26 January 2012; *The Irrawaddy*, "Old Burma meets new in parliament", 20 July 2012; and Kean, Tom, "Burma's biggest win: its legislature", *The Diplomat*, 1 February 2013.
44. *The Myanmar Times*, "Trepidation, speculation as commission gets to work", 24 February 2016.

45. *The Global New Light of Myanmar*, 20 January 2015, p. 2.
46. *The Myanmar Times*, "The hluttaws flexes its muscles", 21–27 May 2012.
47. Interviews with a USDP legislator, head of Magwe region's land seizure sub-commission, Naypyitaw, July 2014.
48. See for instance, concurring analyses: Moe Thuzar, *op. cit.*; Kean, *Myanmar's Parliament, op. cit.*; Egreteau, "(Re)-emerging Patterns of Parliamentary Politics", *op. cit.*; and Fink, *op. cit.*
49. *The Myanmar Times*, "Man of the House", 21–27 November 2011.
50. Interviews with several elected legislators of the lower house, Naypyitaw, February and August 2013.
51. On the role of the speaker in post-war America, see Green, Matthew N., *The Speaker of the House: A Study in Leadership*, New Haven, CT: Yale University Press, 2010.
52. Interview with the deputy speaker of the lower house, Naypyitaw, July 2014.
53. This, though, did not prevent him from facing a humiliating defeat in the 2015 elections.
54. Interview with Khin Aung Myint, speaker of the upper house, Naypyitaw, August 2013.
55. *The Myanmar Times*, "MPs pass impeachment motion despite warnings", 3 September 2012.
56. *The Myanmar Times*, "Electoral change to be examined by new body", 13 June 2014.
57. This was an issue for which the NDF had long campaigned. Interview with Khin Maung Swe, NDF founder, Yangon, July 2014.
58. *The Irrawaddy*, "Lower House chairman rejects PR system proposal", 14 November 2014.
59. Interviews with various Bamar and ethnic representatives in the upper house, Naypyitaw, 2013–2015.
60. *The Myanmar Times*, "Hluttaw refuses human rights body budget", 26 March–1 April 2012.
61. ICG, *Myanmar's Military: Back to the Barracks?*, Brussels: Asia Briefing No. 143, 22 April 2014, pp. 15–16.
62. For a theoretical reference, see Martin, Shane, "Committees", in Shane, Saalfeld and Strom, *op. cit.*, pp. 352–70.
63. Namely: the Bill Committee, the Hluttaw Rights Committee, the Public Accounts Committee and the Government's Guarantees, Pledges and Undertaking Vetting Committee (art. 115a and 147a). A Defense and Security Committee can be convened, according to the constitution, but this has to be decided upon by the commander-in-chief of the armed forces.
64. Interview, secretary of the lower house's Public Accounts Committee, Naypyitaw, August 2013.
65. Interview, secretary of the Rule of Law, Peace and Tranquility committee, Naypyitaw, August 2015.
66. Interview, acting chair of the lower house's Hluttaw Rights Committee, Naypyitaw, February 2015.
67. Norton, Philip and David M. Olson, "Parliaments in Adolescence", in Olson, David M. and Philip Norton (eds), *The New Parliaments of Central and Eastern Europe*, London: Frank Cass, 1996.
68. Egreteau, "(Re)-emerging Patterns of Parliamentary Politics", *op. cit.*, pp. 74–9.
69. Interview with Nanda Kyaw Zwa, deputy speaker of the lower house, Naypyitaw, July 2014.
70. Discussion with the NDI country director, Naypyitaw, February 2015.
71. Interview with a consultant working as electoral expert for the European Commission in Naypyitaw, July 2014. However, Article 121g of the 2008 constitution prevents any active or would-be Burmese lawmaker and his/her party from receiving funding or any kind of material support from foreign organizations and/or governments.

72. Interview, chair of the International Relations Committee (Pyithu Hluttaw), Naypyitaw, August 2015.
73. Notable exceptions: Srinivasan, *op. cit.* and Furnivall, John S., *The Governance of Modern Burma*, New York: Institute of Pacific Relations, 1960.
74. In stark contrast, many incumbent military appointees were re-installed in the House by the army chief: see Egreteau, "Myanmar military chief revamps its parliamentary team", *op. cit.*
75. Interview with an octogenarian Rakhine legislator from the lower house, whose elder son has proved more than helpful to him, Naypyitaw, July 2014.
76. *The Irrawaddy*, "Parliament votes in favor of tripling lawmakers' salaries", 22 January 2015. In December 2015, US$1 = K1,300.
77. Interviews with Rawang, Chin, Shan and Kachin legislators, Naypyitaw, July 2014 and February 2015.
78. As indicated by discussions I had with ethnic legislators from the Shan and Chin States, Naypyitaw, January and July 2014. It should be noted that the small minority of post-SPDC MPs—largely Kokang and Wa individuals—who still have not mastered the Burmese language are those who have spent decades in isolation near or across the Chinese and Thai borders, unable or unwilling to join Myanmar's education system.
79. ICG, *op. cit.*, p. 14.
80. See, for instance, Remington, Thomas F. (ed.), *Parliaments in Transition: The New Legislative Politics in the Former USSR and Eastern Europe*, Boulder, CO: Westview Press, 1994; and Hahn, Jeffrey W. (ed.), *Democratization in Russia: The Development of Legislative Institutions*, Armonk, NY: M.E. Sharpe, 1996.
81. Among others, Paul Hutchcroft has comparatively examined the oligarchic and patrimonial state systems in place in post-Marcos Philippines and in post-coup Thailand in the 1990s, arguing that the more entrenched clientelism is in a society, the more limited the democratizing institutional developments. See Hutchcroft, Paul, "After the Fall: Prospects for Political and Institutional Reform in Post-Crisis Thailand and the Philippines", *Government and Opposition* 34, 4 (1999), pp. 473–97.
82. Sherlock, Stephen, *Struggling to Change: The Indonesian Parliament in an Era of Reformasi*, Canberra: Centre for Democratic Institutions, 2003; Ziegenhain, *op. cit.*
83. Interview with Khin Maung Swe, founder of the NDF, Yangon, August 2015.
84. Mizzima News, "NDF MPs rejoin NLD", 9 April 2012.
85. Interview with an elected SNDP representative, Naypyitaw, August 2013.
86. Interview with Hkun Htun Oo, Yangon, June 2013. The SNLD came second, behind the NLD, in this vote.
87. Interview with an SNDP lower-house MP, Naypyitaw, February 2015.
88. Interview with a member of the Kayin People's Party (KPP), Yangon, May 2013.
89. Interview with a CPP legislator from the lower house, Naypyitaw, February 2015.
90. Interview with the ZCD general secretary, Yangon, December 2015.
91. *The Myanmar Times*, "Rakhine National Party in 'chaos'", 26 June 2015.
92. For a Burmese view, see: Aung Aung (RI), *Promoting Democracy in Myanmar: Political Party Capacity Building*, Stockholm: ISDP Asia Paper, 2013; and Stokke, Kristian, Khine Win and Soe Myint Aung, "Political Parties and Popular Representation in Myanmar's Democratisation Process", *Journal of Current Southeast Asian Affairs* 34, 3 (2015), pp. 3–35.
93. For an introduction: Holliday, Maw Htun Aung and Joelene, *op. cit.*

94. The speaker and his deputy pride themselves on this. Interview with the author, Yangon, March 2015.
95. Chin News Group, "Survey on starvation by Chin state hluttaw member", 13 February 2013; and Mizzima News, "More must be done to tackle poverty in Rakhine, state hluttaw told", 10 September 2014.
96. International Mon News Agency, 12 December 2014. However, the tenth regular session of the Mon state *hluttaw*—during which the law was adopted—lasted for only three days, in December 2014. Provincial assemblies convene for far shorter periods than the Union parliament.
97. Interviews with UDPKS legislators, Naypyitaw, January 2014.
98. However, the selection of the fourteen chief ministers by the provincial legislative assemblies appeared to be one of the few potential constitutional amendments that could draw quite broad support from all Union-level parliamentarians—military excluded—according to interviews I carried out with members of the constitutional review parliamentary committee in Naypyitaw, July 2014 and February 2015.
99. See, for instance, Mietzner, Marcus, "Indonesia's Decentralization: The Rise of Local Identities and the Survival of the Nation-State", in Hill, Hal (ed.), *Regional Dynamics in Decentralized Indonesia*, Singapore: ISEAS, 2014, pp. 45–67.
100. Htet Khaung Linn, "Myanmar parliament gets mixed score for performance", *Myanmar Now*, 13 December 2015.
101. Egreteau, "(Re)-emerging Patterns of Parliamentary Politics", *op. cit.*
102. The case of post-Suharto Indonesia offers an interesting parallel, as emphasized in Horowitz, Donald L., *Constitutional Change and Democracy in Indonesia*, Cambridge: Cambridge University Press, 2013; and Ziegenhain, *op. cit.*.

4. PATTERNS OF PERSISTENT PRAETORIAN BEHAVIORS

1. Interview, deputy defense minister, Naypyitaw, February 2015.
2. On the Tatmadaw's construction of "national security" (*amyotha loun-kyoun-yeh*) and "state security" (*naing-ngan-daw loun-kyoun-yeh*), see Callahan, Mary P., "National Security and the Military in Post-junta, Constitutional Myanmar", in Sasakawa Peace Foundation USA, *The United States and Japan: Assisting Myanmar Development*, Washington, D.C.: Sasakawa Peace Foundation USA, 2015, pp. 41–55.
3. For recent studies on the Tatmadaw's self-perceptions: Steinberg, David I., "The Persistence of Military Dominance", in Steinberg, David I. (ed.), *Myanmar: The Dynamics of an Evolving Polity*, Boulder, CO: Lynne Rienner, 2014, pp. 37–58; Bünte, Marco, "Burma's Transition to Quasi-Military Rule: From Rulers to Guardians?, *Armed Forces & Society* 40, 4 (2014), pp. 742–64; Egreteau, Renaud, "The Continuing Political Salience of the Military in Post-SPDC Myanmar", in Cheesman, Nick, Nicholas Farrelly and Trevor Wilson (eds), *Debating Democratisation in Myanmar*, Singapore: ISEAS Publications, 2014, pp. 259–84. For a contrasting and highly critical view, see Ko Ko Thett, "The Myth of the Indispensability of the Military in Burmese Political Culture: Totalitarian Discourse in the State of Myanmar", in Crauwells, Geert et al. (eds), *Totalitarian and Authoritarian Discourses: A Global and Timeless Phenomenon?*, Bern: Peter Lang, 2014, pp. 263–92.
4. As confirmed, to the letter, by the Tatmadaw commander-in-chief's January 2015 interview

on a Singaporean TV channel: Channel News Asia, "Myanmar not ready for reduced military role in Parliament: Army chief", 20 January 2015.

5. Interview with an active brigadier general, Naypyitaw, February 2015.
6. *The Myanmar Times*, "'The army does not need to change'", 11 November 2013.
7. See, for instance *The New Light of Myanmar*, 28 March 2012, p. 1; 28 March 2013, p. 1; 28 March 2014, p. 3; and Channel News Asia, *op. cit.*
8. Maung Aung Myoe, "The Military and Political Liberalisation in Myanmar", in Duell, Kerstin (ed.), *Myanmar in Transition: Polity, People and Processes*, Singapore: Select Books, 2013, pp. 63–4.
9. Nordlinger, Eric, *Soldiers in Politics: Military Coups and Governments*, London: Prentice Hall, 1977, pp. 22–7; Alagappa, Muthiah, "Investigating and Explaining Change: An Analytical Framework", in Alagappa, Muthiah (ed.), *Coercion and Governance: The Declining Political Role of the Military in Asia*, Stanford, CA: Stanford University Press, 2001, p. 34.
10. Callahan, *op. cit.*, p. 47.
11. Interview with a retired army lieutenant-colonel, Naypyitaw, July 2014.
12. Steinberg, David I., "The Persistence of Military Dominance", in Steinberg, David I. (ed.), *Myanmar: The Dynamics of an Evolving Polity*, Boulder, CO: Lynne Rienner, 2014, pp. 42–4.
13. *Ibid.*, p. 9.
14. Callahan, Mary P., "The Generals Loosen their Grip", *Journal of Democracy* 23, 4 (2012), p. 120.
15. Interview with the author, Yangon, May 2013.
16. See Andrew Selth's views on police reform: "Myanmar's Coercive Apparatus: The Long Road to Reform", in Steinberg, David I. (ed.), *Myanmar: The Dynamics of an Evolving Polity*, Boulder, CO: Lynne Rienner, 2014, p. 23.
17. A recent analysis by Christine C. Fair shows how an increasingly independent Pakistani judiciary has positively affected democratization and the rule of law in recent years: "Democracy on the Leash in Pakistan", in Fair, C. Christine and Sarah J. Watson (eds), *Pakistan's Enduring Challenges*, Philadelphia, PA: University of Pennsylvania Press, 2015, pp. 131–55.
18. Interview with a retired lieutenant-colonel in the infantry, Yangon, February 2015.
19. Interview with Khin Aung Myint, Naypyitaw, August 2013.
20. *The Myanmar Times*, "Order to end attacks puts ceasefire back on the table", 19 December 2011.
21. ICG, *A Tentative Peace in Myanmar's Kachin Conflict*, Brussels/Yangon: Asia Report No. 140, 2013, pp. 9–10.
22. *The Myanmar Times*, "Myanmar declares ceasefire in Kachin", 21 January 2013.
23. Interview with a Kachin pastor, Myitkyina, February 2013.
24. *Time Magazine*, "Inside the Kachin War against Burma", 21 November 2014.
25. Aung Zaw, "Putting a New Face on Myanmar's Military", *The Irrawaddy*, 12 July 2013.
26. The Irrawaddy, "Tension mounts as clock ticks for student demonstrators", 3 March 2015; and *The Myanmar Times*, "Students in Bago ignore government deadline", 4 March 2015.
27. *The Myanmar Times*, "New chief minister to face close scrutiny from MPs", 4 July 2014. The major-general, however, resigned from the army soon after his nomination as chief minister.
28. Discussions with Rakhine Union-level legislators, Naypyitaw, February 2015.
29. See the 2015 report by Matthew and Amy Smith's human rights-focused NGO, Fortify Rights: "Midnight Intrusions", Chiang Mai: Fortify Rights Report, March 2015.

30. Mizzima News, "Key legislation passed in third Parliament session", 27 March 2012.
31. For more on the Ministry of Home Affairs' dreaded General Administration Department, see Kyi Pyar Chit Saw and Matthew Arnold, *Administering the State in Myanmar*, Yangon: MDRI-Asia Foundation Discussion Paper No. 6, October 2014.
32. *The Myanmar Times*, "Ward, village law could disrupt elections: activists", 25 December 2014.
33. Min Zin, "The Return of Myanmar's Military?", *The New York Times*, 17 November 2014.
34. Reuters, "Myanmar journalist killed by army was former bodyguard of Suu Kyi", 28 October 2014; *The Irrawaddy*, "Does Burma's Army Still Hold a License to Kill?", 27 October 2014.
35. *The Myanmar Times*, CSOs condemn journalist killing, 27 October 2014.
36. Heinemann, Tim, "Misunderstanding Myanmar's Military", *Asia Times*, 11 February 2015.
37. Cheesman, Nick, *Opposing the Rule of Law: How Myanmar's Courts Make Law and Order*, Cambridge: Cambridge University Press, 2015.
38. *Ibid.*, p. 76.
39. Democratic Voice of Burma, "Army denies murder of Kachin teachers", 29 January 2015.
40. Taylor, Robert H., *The Armed Forces in Myanmar's Politics: A Terminating Role?*, Singapore: ISEAS Trends No. 2, 2015, pp. 18–9.
41. Author's discussions held at the Ministry of Defence, Naypyitaw, February 2015.
42. *The Irrawaddy*, "Rare civilian trial for soldier accused of rape", 25 September 2014.
43. Interview with the author, Naypyitaw, March 2015.
44. As demonstrated in the case of Pakistan in Siddiqa, Ayesha, *Military Inc.: Inside Pakistan's Military Economy*, London & Ann Arbor, MI: Pluto Press, 2007.
45. ICG, *Myanmar: The Politics of Economic Reform*, Asia Report No. 231, 27 July 2012, p. 11.
46. For a more comprehensive analysis, see Tin Maung Maung Than, *State Dominance in Myanmar: The Political Economy of Industrialization*, Singapore: ISEAS Publications, 2007.
47. Among others: McCartan, Brian, "Myanmar Military in the Money", *Asia Times*, 28 February 2012; Freeman, Nick J., "Navigating the Economic Reform Process", *Southeast Asian Affairs* 2014, pp. 224–40; ICG, *Myanmar's Military: Back to the Barracks?*, Brussels: Asia Briefing No. 143, 22 April 2014, pp. 10–11; and *Nikkei Asian Review*, "What will become of military-owned corporate behemoths?", 1 December 2015.
48. More details in Egreteau, Renaud, *Military Delegates in Myanmar's Legislature: What Do They Do, What Will They (Continue) To Do?*, Singapore: ISEAS Perspectives No. 21, 28 April 2015.
49. *The Global New Light of Myanmar*, 26 June 2015, p. 1.
50. Article 109b of the 2008 constitution indeed stipulates that "not more than 110" representatives of the armed forces shall be appointed to the Pyithu Hluttaw. Constitutionally, therefore, the army commander can nominate fewer than 110 military legislators in the lower house, without any prior constitutional reform. If this were to happen, the army's constitutional veto would vanish.
51. As a matter of fact, it was the USDP that brought the first ever constitutional amendment bill, in June 2015.
52. Interview with the author, Naypyitaw, August 2013.
53. Mya Win, *Tatmadaw's Traditional Role in National Politics*, Yangon: News and Periodicals Enterprises, 1992, pp. 77–8.
54. Interview with a deputy defense minister, Naypyitaw, February 2015.
55. Alagappa, *op. cit.*, p. 34.

56. See, for instance, Chambers, Paul, "Superfluous, Mischievous, or Emancipating? Thailand's Evolving Senate Today", *Journal of Current Southeast Asian Affairs* 28, 3 (2009), pp. 9–10.
57. Mietzner, Marcus, "The Political Marginalization of the Military in Indonesia", in Mietzner, Marcus (ed.), *The Political Resurgence of the Military in Southeast Asia: Conflict and Leadership*, London: Routledge, 2011, p. 131.
58. As illustrated by the regular conversations I've held with Burmese legislators from various parties, and with party leaders, since 2013.
59. Reuters, "Myanmar's military moves amid Suu Kyi no-show", 25 April 2012.
60. Callahan, *op. cit.*, p. 128.
61. Interview with a deputy defense minister, Naypyitaw, February 2015.
62. The equivalent of West Point, Sandhurst and Saint-Cyr. *The Myanmar Times*, "In Hluttaws, more green shoots", 2–8 January 2012.
63. Interview with a military legislator in the upper house, Naypyitaw, February 2015.
64. The salary for civilian MPs is scheduled to increase threefold, from 300,000 kyats to 1 million at the start of the 2015–16 fiscal year. *The Myanmar Times*, "MPs ignore president on pay rises", 26 January 2015.
65. Interview with the author, Naypyitaw, February 2015.
66. A more detailed examination can be found in Egreteau, Renaud, "Soldiers as Lawmakers? Assessing the Legislative Role of the Burmese Armed Forces (2010–2015)", in Egreteau, Renaud and François Robinne (eds), *Metamorphosis: Studies in Social and Political Change in Myanmar*, Singapore: NUS Press, 2015, pp. 15–42.
67. Interview with a brigadier-general, army representative in the upper house, Naypyitaw, February 2015.
68. See, for instance, the case of India's national legislature: Spary, Carole, "Disrupting Rituals of Debate in the Indian Parliament", *The Journal of Legislative Studies* 16, 3 (2010), pp. 338–51.
69. AFP, *Myanmar army bristles against constitutional change*, 18 November 2014.
70. *The Global New Light of Myanmar*, 27 June 2015, p. 1.
71. *The Myanmar Times*, "MPs pass impeachment motion despite warnings", 3 September 2012.
72. *The Myanmar Times*, "Tribunal resigns to avoid impeachment", 10 September 2012.
73. Nardi, Dominic J., "After impeachment, a balancing act", *The Myanmar Times*, 1 October 2012.
74. Interview with two retired lieutenant-colonels elected as USDP Union-level legislators in 2010, Naypyitaw, January and July 2014.
75. The motion was drafted by a legislator from the NDF. Interview with an NDF representative in the lower house, Yangon, May 2013.
76. *Irrawaddy-on-Line*, "Myanmar Parliament approves controversial defense budget", 29 March 2013.
77. Interviews with Union legislators from the SNDP, NUP and USDP, Naypyitaw, July 2014 and February 2015.
78. Interview with a retired navy commander, Yangon, March 2015.
79. Interview with the author, Naypyitaw, January 2014.
80. Interview with the author, Naypyitaw, July 2014.
81. Interview with a former army colonel sitting in the lower house as a legislator from Bago region, Naypyitaw, August 2013.

82. Dr. Nyo Nyo Thinn then sent flowers to these four army majors; interview with the author, Yangon, May 2013.
83. Interview with a brigadier from the upper house, Naypyitaw, February 2015.
84. *New Light of Myanmar*, 9 September 2011, p. 10.
85. *New Light of Myanmar*, 28 September 2011, p. 8.
86. Yola Verbruggen, "The bloc in the system", *Mizzima Business Weekly*, 23 October 2014.

5. THE SALIENCE OF ETHNIC AND RELIGIOUS CLEAVAGES

1. Other publications which have underscored this salience include Silverstein, Josef, "The Federal Dilemma in Burma", *Far Eastern Survey* 28, 7 (1959), pp. 97–105; Taylor, Robert H., "Perceptions of Ethnicity in the Politics of Burma", *Southeast Asian Journal of Social Science* 10, 1 (1982), pp. 1–22; Smith, Martin, *Burma: Insurgency and the Politics of Ethnicity*, London: Zed Books, 1991; and, more recently, Gravers, Mikael, "Introduction: Ethnicity against the State—State against Ethnic Diversity?", in Gravers, Mikael (ed.), *Exploring Ethnic Diversity in Burma*, Copenhagen: NIAS Press, 2007, pp. 1–33; and South, Ashley, *Ethnic Politics in Burma: States of Conflict*, London: Routledge, 2008.
2. Very few academics have proposed possible power-sharing schemes that differ from the usual frameworks of centralization/decentralization or unitary/federal state. Among the recent exceptions, see the "liberal integrationist" policy alternative in Thawnghmung, Ardeth Maung, "The Dilemmas of Burma's Multinational Society", in Bertrand, Jacques and André Laliberté (eds), *Multination States in Asia: Accommodation or Resistance*, Cambridge: Cambridge University Press, 2010, pp. 136–63.
3. On the Bamar hegemony, see: Yawnghwe, Chao-Tzang, "Burma: Depoliticization of the Political", in Alagappa, M. (ed.), *Political Legitimacy in Southeast Asia: The Quest for Moral Authority*, Stanford, CA: Stanford University Press, 1995, pp. 170–92; Houtman, Gustaaf, *Mental Culture in Burmese Crisis Politics: Aung San Suu Kyi and the National League for Democracy*, Tokyo: ILCAA Monograph Series, 1999; and Gravers, Mikael, *Nationalism as Political Paranoia in Burma*, London: Curzon Press, 1999.
4. Rajah, Ananda, "Ethnicity and Civil War in Burma: Where is the Rationality?", in Rotberg, R. (ed.), *Burma: Prospects for a Democratic Future*, Washington, D.C.: Brookings Institution Press, 1998, p. 137.
5. Boutry, Maxime, "How Far From National Identity? Dealing with the Concealed Diversity of Myanmar", in Egreteau, Renaud and François Robinne (eds), *Metamorphosis: Studies in Social and Political Change in Myanmar*, Singapore: NUS Press, 2015, pp. 103–26.
6. Horowitz, Donald L., *Ethnic Groups in Conflict*, Berkeley, CA: University of Berkeley Press, 1985, pp. 230–2.
7. For instance:, Taylor, Robert H., "Refighting Old Battles, Compounding Misconceptions: The Politics of Ethnicity in Myanmar Today", *ISEAS Perspectives* 12 (2015), p. 3.
8. The two best accounts to date on these developments remain: Lintner, Bertil, *Burma in Revolt: Opium and Insurgency since 1948*, Chiang Mai: Silkworm Books, 1999; and Smith, *op. cit*.
9. With the Shalom Foundation and Reverend Saboi Jum liaising, among others; notes on discussions at the Shalom Foundation, Yangon, December 2015.
10. Interview with representatives of the Karen National Union (KNU), Karenni National Progressive Party (KNPP) and Shan State Army-South (SSA-S), Thailand, September 2008.

11. Discussions with a KIA spokesperson, August 2011.
12. Its 5th Brigade, though, refused the plan and broke away from the DKBA. The splinter group re-joined the KNU and became better known as the Kloh Htoo Baw group; see Transnational Institute, "Ending Burma's Cycle Conflicts: Prospects for Ethnic Peace", Burma Policy Briefing No. 8, February 2012, p. 5.
13. In 1995, by the Karenni National Progressive Party (KNPP); interview with KNPP Joint-Secretary Mae Hong Son, September 2008.
14. *The Irrawaddy*, "Amnesty offer to Kokang troops—Leaders face manhunt", 1 September 2009.
15. See the exploration of Kachin narratives: Jaquet, Carine, "Unwanted War, Unachievable Peace: Examining Some Kachin Narratives in Times of Conflict", in Egreteau, Renaud and François Robinne (eds), *Metamorphosis: Studies in Social and Political Change in Myanmar*, Singapore: NUS Press, 2015, pp. 179–206.
16. Discussions with Kachin community leaders, Myitkyina, February 2013. Since 2011, however, while the KIA has opted for the path of war, the local Kachin civil society scene has tried to develop and expand to the best of its abilities. See, for instance, *The Economist*, "Myanmar's Kachins: eager mindsets", 3 January 2015.
17. If not thousands on the Tatmadaw side. See Davis, Anthony, "Pyrrhic victory in Myanmar", *Asia Times*, 30 January 2013; and Beech, Hannah, "Inside the Kachin War against Burma", *Time*, 21 November 2014.
18. Personal observation in KIA-controlled IDP camps, August 2011.
19. ICG, *A Tentative Peace in Myanmar's Kachin Conflict*, Brussels/Yangon: Asia Report No. 140, 2013, pp. 12–13.
20. These interests include, especially, Burmese jade mined principally in Kachin State, which the Chinese are wild about; timber and illegal logging; and the double pipeline between Yunnan and the Rakhine coastline, completed by the China National Petroleum Corporation in May 2013. See, for instance, Yun Sun, "The Guilty and the Innocent: China and Illegal Logging in Myanmar", *The Irrawaddy*, 22 January 2015; Egreteau, Renaud, "Jade or JADE? Debating International Sanctions on Burma's Gem Industry?", *Asia-Pacific Bulletin No. 132*, 2011; and Yun Sun, "Gas pains for China and Myanmar", *Asia Times*, 14 October 2014.
21. See his own assessment of his role, four years later: Aung Min, "Perception, misperception in the Myanmar peace process", *Nikkei Asian Review*, 14 October 2015.
22. Reuters, "Myanmar govt, rebels sign draft nationwide ceasefire accord", 31 March 2015.
23. Discussions with a director at MPC, Yangon, March 2015.
24. For a positive assessment of the peace process, see South, Ashley, "Governance and Political Legitimacy in the Peace Process", in Steinberg, David I. (ed.), *Myanmar: The Dynamics of an Evolving Polity*, Boulder, CO: Lynne Rienner, 2014, pp. 159–90. Ashley South has been a regular consultant on Myanmar's ethnic affairs for the past twenty years. For a less enthusiastic perspective, in the same edited volume, see Smith, Martin, "Ethnic Politics in a Time of Change", pp. 135–57.
25. Interview with a retired police officer and KPP member, Yangon, May 2013.
26. Interview with Ja Nan Lahtaw, Shalom Foundation Executive Director, Yangon, December 2015.
27. Thant Myint-U, "Myanmar's best hope for peace", *The New York Times*, 18 August 2015.
28. Transnational Institute, *op. cit.*, p. 7.
29. Interview with one Shan and one Chin elected representative, Naypyitaw, February 2015.

30. *The Irrawaddy*, "Fighting on 3 fronts in wake of ceasefire deals: ethnic armies", 8 April 2015.
31. *The Economist*, "Myanmar: the periphery cannot hold", 14 March 2015.
32. Discussions with KIA officials, August 2011.
33. *AFP*, "Myanmar's powerful Wa rebels seek their own state", 29 May 2013.
34. *The Myanmar Times*, "Internal pressures take their toll on the peace process", 28 July 2013.
35. Interviews, Naypyitaw, July 2014 and February 2015.
36. Interview, Naypyitaw, January 2014.
37. Discussion with a veteran Burmese politician, Yangon, July 2014.
38. Jolliffe, Kim, "Playing with Peace in Myanmar", *Foreign Policy in Focus*, 7 April 2015; and *Ethnic Conflict and Social Services in Myanmar's Contested Regions*, San Francisco, CA: The Asia Foundation, 2014.
39. Wright, Joseph and Matthew Winters, "The Politics of Effective Foreign Aid", *Annual Review of Political Science*, 13 (2010), pp. 61–80.
40. *The Myanmar Times*, "Kayin groups slam KNU over signing of ceasefire agreement", 6 October 2015.
41. See the public statement online at: http://womenofburma.org/a-non-inclusive-nationwide-ceasefire-agreement-will-not-bring-peace-statement-by-the-womens-league-of-burma/ (last accessed 19 December 2015).
42. Interview with Kachin NGO leaders, Myitkyina, February 2013.
43. Jagan, Larry, "Myanmar: ceasefire marks flawed first steps to peace", *The Bangkok Post*, 14 October 2015.
44. ICG, *Myanmar's Peace Process: A Nationwide Ceasefire Remains Elusive*, Brussels/Yangon: Asia Briefing No. 146, September 2015.
45. Mizzima News, "Peace accord is approved, but holdout armies mean fighting will continue", 9 December 2015.
46. Min Zin, "Why there's less to Burma's peace process than meets the eye", *Foreign Policy*, 26 May 2015.
47. Mya Win, *op. cit.*, p. 77.
48. Holliday, Ian, Maw Htun Aung and Cindy Joelene, "Institution Building in Myanmar: The Establishment of Regional and State Assemblies", *Asian Survey* 55, 4 (2015).
49. Interview with a minister of the Yangon regional government, also a legislator in Yangon's regional parliament, Yangon, January 2014.
50. Nixon, Hamish et al., *State and Region Governments in Myanmar*, Yangon: MDRI-Asia Foundation, 2013, p. 61. The 2008 constitution also limits their legislative focus to social, economic and technical matters.
51. For instance, between 2011 and 2013 the Ayeyarwaddy Hluttaw convened for a total of sixty-nine days, while the Mon Hluttaw and Shan Hluttaw only convened for twenty and twenty-nine days respectively. Nixon, et al., *op. cit.*, p. 63.
52. Author's discussions with Kachin, Rakhine, Karen and Chin elected legislators, Yangon and Naypyitaw, February–April 2015.
53. Interview with the author, Yangon, February 2015.
54. For a comparative perspective on the relationship between democratization and decentralization in Indonesia in the 2000s, see Choi, Nankyung, *Local Politics in Indonesia: Pathways to Power*, London: Routledge, 2011.
55. For more details, see Kyaw Yin Hlaing, "Challenging the Authoritarian State: Buddhist

Monks and Peaceful Protests in Burma", *The Fletcher Forum of World Affairs* 32, 1 (2008), pp. 125–44.

56. ICG, *The Dark Side of Transition: Violence against Muslims in Myanmar*, Brussels/Yangon: Asia Report No. 251, 2013; and Frydenlund, Iselyn, "Are Myanmar's Monks Hindering Democratisation?", *East Asia Forum*, 4 November 2015.
57. The movement emerged around 2012. Walton, Matthew and Susan Hayward, *Contesting Buddhist Narratives: Democratization, Nationalism and Communal Violence in Myanmar*, Washington, D.C.: East-West Center Policy Studies No. 71, 2014, pp. 12–14.
58. Walton, Matthew J., "Buddhism turns violent in Myanmar", *Asia Times*, 2 April 2013.
59. See two reports by Human Rights Watch (HRW): HRW, *'The Government Could Have Stopped This': Sectarian Violence and Ensuing Abuses in Burma's Arakan State*, Washington, D.C.: HRW Publications, 2012; and HRW, *'All You Can Do Is Pray': Crimes Against Humanity and Ethnic Cleansing of Rohingya Muslims in Burma's Arakan State*, Washington, D.C.: HRW Publications, 2013.
60. Interview with a veteran Rohingya community leader in exile, Ruili (Yunnan), July 2014.
61. *The Myanmar Times*, "Meiktila erupts", 25 March 2013; *The Myanmar Times*, "Muslims fear further attacks in riot-hit Lashio", 29 May 2013.
62. Reuters, "Tensions boil in riot-hit Myanmar city", 5 July 2014; *The New York Times*, "Mandalay's Chinese Muslims chilled by riots", 12 July 2014.
63. Further information can be found in Yegar, Moshe, *The Muslims of Burma: A Study of a Minority Group*, Wiesbaden: Otto Harrassowith, 1972; and in Lintner, *op. cit.*, p. 491 and Smith, *Burma*, op. cit., pp. 125–9.
64. Most of the country's Muslims are Sunnis. As of March 2016, the results of the 2014 national census had yet to be released. However, one estimates that the Burmese Muslims may represent some 5 to 8 per cent of Myanmar's total population today. A soon-to-be-released edited volume covers various aspects of these communities at the dawn of the twenty-first century: Crouch, Melissa (ed.), *Islam and the State in Myanmar: Muslim-Buddhist Relations and the Politics of Belonging*, New Delhi: Oxford University Press, forthcoming June 2016.
65. A substantial majority of the Muslim populations of western Rakhine State have long identified themselves as such, and not as Rohingya; interview with an imam from Buthidaung exiled in Yunnan, August 2011.
66. For a factual account of the recent (mis)fortunes of the Burmese Muslims, see Berlie, Jean A., *The Burmanization of Myanmar's Muslims*, Bangkok: White Lotus, 2008.
67. The central mosque of Toungoo was burnt down in 2001. As of 2012, its tumbling walls and half-destroyed minarets, covered under tree roots, stand on Merchant Street (Personal observation, Toungoo, November 2012).
68. As recently stressed by Holliday, Ian, "Addressing Myanmar's Citizenship Crisis", *Journal of Contemporary Asia* 44, 3 (2014), pp. 404–21.
69. See for instance, the analysis of how a single social media post inflamed Mandalay in July 2014: *The Myanmar Times*, "Mandalay: from mouse clicks to mob rule in 24 hours", 5 July 2014.
70. Interview with a Rohingya official in the Union National Development Party (UNDP), Yangon, May 2013.
71. Interview with an elected representative for a Rohingya-majority constituency, Yangon, August 2015.

72. Interviews with the leadership of the Rakhine National Party (RNP), Naypyitaw, February 2015.
73. Interviews with NLD elected representatives, Naypyitaw, August 2013, July 2014 and February 2015.
74. *The Irrawaddy*, "UNHCR rejects Rohingya resettlement suggestion", 13 July 2012.
75. Reuters, "Don't exaggerate the problems: Suu Kyi on Myanmar's persecuted Rohingyas", 5 November 2015.
76. ICG, *The Dark Side of Transition*, *op. cit.*, pp. 8–10.
77. Interview with a Muslim USDP legislator from Rakhine State, Yangon, August 2015. During the 2010 polls, the USDP succeeded in co-opting members of the Rohingya community (provided they registered as "Bamar Muslim", but neither as "Rohingya" nor "Bengali"—which would have barred them from contesting elections).
78. Ghosh, Nirmal, "Buddhism's right-wing face in Myanmar", *The Straits Times*, 30 March 2015.
79. *TIME*, "The Face of Buddhist Terror", 1 July 2013.
80. Walton and Hayward, *Contesting Buddhist Narratives*, *op. cit.*, p. 14.
81. Min Zin, "The People vs. The Monks", *The New York Times*, 6 June 2014.
82. *New Light of Myanmar*, 11 March 2014.
83. *New Light of Myanmar*, 27 November 2014.
84. Interview, Shalom Foundation, Yangon, December 2015.
85. Among others: Amnesty International, *Myanmar: Parliament must reject discriminatory 'race and religion' laws*, 3 March 2015; and Human Rights Watch, *Burma: Reject Discriminatory Marriage Bill*, 9 July 2015.
86. Matt Walton et al., "Why Are Women Supporting Myanmar's Religious Protection Laws?", *East Asia Forum*, 9 September 2015.
87. Interview with Kachin, Lisu and Chin Christian parliamentarians, Naypyitaw, February, April and August 2015.
88. Rakhine MPs were especially active in its favor, given the long legacy of distrust between this Buddhist community of western Myanmar and the Rohingya (or "Bengali") Muslim minority. Author's discussion with the chairman of the Rakhine National Party, Naypyitaw, February 2015.
89. *The Myanmar Times*, "First monogamy law charge hits Muslim masonry worker", 18 September 2015.
90. Basu, Amrita, *Violent Conjunctures in Democratic India*, Cambridge: Cambridge University Press, 2015.

6. ENDURING BURMESE REALITIES

1. Przeworski, Adam et al., *Democracy and Development: Political Institutions and Well-Being in the World, 1950–1990*. New York: Cambridge University Press, 2000, p. 81.
2. Shah, Aqil, *Army and Democracy in Pakistan*, Cambridge, MA: Harvard University Press, 2014, p. 2. See also Siddiqa, Ayesha, *Military Inc.: Inside Pakistan's Military Economy*, London & Ann Arbor, MI: Pluto Press, 2007, pp. 60–1.
3. Hepple, Leslie W., "Geopolitics, Generals and the State in Brazil", *Political Geography Quarterly* 5, 4 (1986), pp. 79–90.
4. Houtman, Gustaaf, *Mental Culture in Burmese Political Crisis: Aung San Suu Kyi and the National League for Democracy*, Tokyo: ICLAA Monograph No. 33, 1999.

5. Hicken, Allan, "Clientelism", *Annual Review of Political Science* 14 (2011), pp. 289–310.
6. Among others, see one reader still of great theoretical significance: Schmidt, Steffen W. et al. (eds), *Friends, Followers and Factions*, Berkeley, CA: University of California Press, 1977.
7. Scott, James C., "Patron-Client Politics and Political Change in Southeast Asia", *The American Political Science Review*, 66, 1 (1972), pp. 91–113.
8. Przeworski et al., *op. cit.*
9. Abente-Brun, Diego and Larry Diamond (eds), *Clientelism, Social Policy and the Quality of Democracy*, Baltimore, MD: The Johns Hopkins University Press, 2014.
10. Hilgers, Tina, "Democratic Processes, Clientelistic Relationships, and the Material Good Problems", in Hilgers, Tina (ed.), *Clientelism in Everyday Latin American Politics*, New York: Palgrave Macmillan, 2012, pp. 3–24.
11. Chandra, Kanchan, *Why Ethnic Parties Succeed: Patronge and Ethnic Head Counts in India*, Cambridge: Cambridge University Press, 2004; more recently, "Patronage, Democracy and Ethnic Politics in India", in Abente-Brun and Diamond (eds), *op. cit.*, pp. 135–72.
12. Tomsa, Dick and Andreas Ufen (eds), *Party Politics in Southeast Asia: Clientelism and Electoral Competition in Indonesia, Thailand and the Philippines*, London: Routledge, 2013.
13. Houtman, *op. cit.*, p. 176.
14. Looking at two small villages located in the Buddhist- and Bamar-dominated rural areas near Mandalay and Sagaing, Nash examined the patterns of traditional Burmese local leadership. He highlighted two interesting features of Burmese local politics in the 1950s: the weaknesses of local party organizations and civil associations intimately linked to the fate of local individuals boasting a fluctuant *awza*, and the parallel clout of the military, presenting itself as the sole organized agency that could "fill the breach" in the absence of strong associations at the local level; see Nash, Manning, "Party Building in Upper Burma", *Asian Survey* 3, 4 (1963), pp. 197–202.
15. Using fieldwork conducted in 1961–2, Spiro complements Nash's argument by stressing the significance of the concept of *ana* (power). Most Burmese people, he claims, speak of "*awza-ana*" when referring to political power. Spiro, Melford E., "Ethnographic Notes on Conceptions and Dynamics of Political Power in Upper Burma (Prior to the 1962 Military Coup)", *Ethnology* 36, 1 (1997), pp. 31–47.
16. Maung Maung Gyi, *Burmese Political Values: The Socio-Political Roots of Authoritarianism*, New York: Praeger, 1983.
17. Taylor, Robert H., "Finding the Political in Myanmar, a.k.a Burma", *Journal of Southeast Asian Studies* 39, 2 (2008), p. 232.
18. Selth, Andrew, *Burma's Armed Forces: Power without Glory*, Norwalk: EastBridge, 2002, p. 267; Callahan, Mary P., "Of *kyay-zu* and *kyet-su*: The Military in 2006", in Skidmore, Monique and Trevor Wilson (eds), *Myanmar: The State, Community and Environment*, Canberra: ANU E-Press, 2007, pp. 36–53; and Win Min, "Looking Inside the Burmese Military", *Asian Survey* 48, 6 (2008), p. 1020.
19. Interview with a retired lieutenant-colonel turned USDP legislator, Naypyitaw, July 2014. He lost his seat in the 2015 polls.
20. Interview, Yangon, February 2015. He also ran in the 2015 elections, but lost.
21. Nash, *op. cit.*, p. 202.
22. See, for instance, Mya Win, *Tatmadaw's Traditional Role*, Yangon: News and Periodicals Enterprises, 1992; and Min Maung Maung, *The Tatmadaw and its Leadership Role in National Politics*, Yangon: News & Periodicals Enterprise, 1993.

23. Among others, see Silverstein, Josef, "The Evolution and Salience of Burma's National Political Culture", in Rotberg, Robert I. (ed.), *Burma: Prospects for a Democratic Future*, Washington, D.C.: Brookings Institution Press, 1998, pp. 11–32; Callahan, Mary P., "On Time Warps and Warped Time: Lessons from Burma's Democratic Era", in Rotberg (ed.), *op. cit.*, pp. 49–67; Kyaw Yin Hlaing, "Power and Factional Struggles in Post-Independence Burmese Governments", *Journal of Southeast Asian Studies* 39, 1 (2008), pp. 149–77; and Walton, Matthew J., "The Disciplining Discourse of Unity in Burmese Politics", *The Journal of Burma Studies*, 19, 1 (2015), pp. 11–14.
24. Trager, Frank N., "The Political Split in Burma", *Far Eastern Survey* 27, 10 (1958), p. 154.
25. Maung Maung, "Burma at the Crossroads", *India Quarterly* 14, 4 (1958), pp. 380–8.
26. Badgley, John H., "Burmese Communist Schisms", in Wilson, John (ed.), *Peasant Rebellion and Communist Revolution in Asia*, Stanford, CA: Stanford University Press, 1974, pp. 151–68.
27. Hoffman, Ralf, "Traditional Political Culture and the Prospects for Democracy in Burma", in Gartner, Uta and Jens Lorenz (eds), *Tradition and Modernity in Myanmar*, Berlin: LIT Verlag, 1994, pp. 175–87.
28. Interview with Tin Oo, Yangon, December 2015.
29. Interview with Khin Maung Swe, Yangon, August 2015.
30. Interview with Hkun Htun Oo, SNLD's patron, Yangon, June 2013.
31. Interview with an SNDP legislator from the lower house, Naypyitaw, February 2015.
32. Interview with a CPP legislator from the lower house who had just joined the CNDP at the request of his "saya", Naypyitaw, February 2015.
33. Interview with the author, Naypyitaw, February 2015.
34. Interview with the ZCD's general secretary, Yangon, December 2015.
35. Interview with Thu Wai, Yangon, January 2014.
36. Interviews, Yangon, January 2014.
37. Interview, Yangon, December 2015.
38. For more details, see McAllister, Ian, "The Personalization of Politics", in Dalton, Russell J. and Hans-Dieter Klingemann (eds), *The Oxford Handbook of Political Behaviour*, Oxford: Oxford University Press, 2007, pp. 571–88.
39. As explained in detail in Steinberg, David I., *Turmoil in Burma: Contested Legitimacies in Myanmar*. Norwalk, CT: EastBridge, 2006.
40. Maung Maung Gyi. *op. cit.*, p. 174. For a more recent Burmese view, see Aung Aung (RI), *Promoting Democracy in Myanmar: Political Party Capacity Building*, Stockholm: ISDP Asia Paper, 2013.
41. At the same time, the USDP, a vast heterogeneous platform created out of the USDA in 2010, is also yet to show whether it can cohesively survive its first massive electoral defeat (November 2015).
42. See, among others in the 1990s: Diamond, Larry J., "Toward Democratic Consolidation", *Journal of Democracy*, 5, 3 (1994), pp. 5–17; and Linz, Juan J. and Alfred Stepan, *Problems of Democratic Transition and Consolidation*, Baltimore, MD: The Johns Hopkins University Press, 1996.
43. Callahan, Mary P., *Drivers of Political Change in Post-junta, Constitutional Burma*, Washington, D.C.: USAID, 2012, pp. 18–19.
44. Thant Myint U, *Where China Meets India: Burma and the New Crossroads of Asia*, New York: Farrar, Straus & Giroux, 2012.

45. Lintner, Bertil, *Great Game East: India, China, and the Struggle for Asia's Most Volatile Frontier*, New Delhi: HarperCollins, 2012.
46. Feit, Edward, *The Armed Bureaucrats: Military-Administrative Regimes and Political Development*, New York: Houghton Mifflin, 1972, p. 7.
47. Perlmutter, Amos, *Political Roles and Military Rulers*, London: Frank Cass, 1981, p. 258.
48. As explained by Lewis J. Edinger in "Military Leaders and Foreign Policy", *The American Political Science Review* 57, 2 (1963), pp. 392–405.
49. Huntington, Samuel, *The Soldier and the State*, Cambridge, MA: Belknap Press, 1957, p. 92.
50. Shah, *op. cit.*
51. Egreteau, Renaud and Larry Jagan, *Soldiers and Diplomacy in Burma: Understanding the Foreign Policies of the Burmese Praetorian State*, Singapore: NUS Press, 2013, pp. 50–4.
52. K. Yhome, "Myanmar's military diplomacy", *The New Indian Express*, 9 August 2012.
53. Callahan, Mary P., *National Security and the Military in Post-junta, Constitutional Myanmar*, in Sasakawa Peace Foundation USA, *The United States and Japan: Assisting Myanmar Development*, Washington, D.C.: Sasakawa Peace Foundation USA, 2015, pp. 47–8.
54. Interview with Hla Myint Oo, Chair of the International Relations Committee of the lower house, Naypyitaw, April 2015.
55. On the much-discussed India-China "rivalry" in Myanmar, see Egreteau, Renaud, "Burmese Tango: Indian and Chinese Games and Gains in Burma (Myanmar) since 1988", in Devare, Sudhir T., Swaran Singh and Reena Marwah (eds), *Emerging China: Prospects of Partnership in Asia*, New Delhi: Routledge, 2012, pp. 269–92.
56. Among others: Taylor, Robert H., "Myanmar's 'Pivot' Toward the Shibboleth of 'Democracy'", *Asian Affairs* 44, 3 (2013), p. 394; Ganesan, N., "Interpreting Recent Developments in Myanmar as an Attempt to Establish Political Legitimacy", *Asian Journal of Peacebuilding* 1, 2 (2013); and Jones, Lee, "The Political Economy of Myanmar's Transition", *Journal of Contemporary Asia* 44, 1 (2014), pp. 144–70.
57. See my earlier analysis: Egreteau, Renaud, "Continuity and Change: Myanmar's Foreign Policy", *The Myanmar Times*, 15 September 2013.
58. See Yun Sun's most recent assessment: "China and Myanmar: Moving beyond Mutual Dependence", in Steinberg, David I. (ed.), *Myanmar: The Dynamics of an Evolving Polity*, Boulder, CO: Lynne Rienner, 2014, pp. 267–88.
59. See two recent analyses: Lynn Kuok, *Promoting Peace in Myanmar: US Interests and Role*, Washington, D.C.: CSIS, 2014 and Haacke, Jürgen, "US-Myanmar Relations: Developments, Challenges, and Implications", in Steinberg (ed.), *op. cit.*, pp. 289–318.
60. Lintner, Bertil, "Myanmar morphs to US-China battlefield", *Asia Times*, 2 May 2013. See also Dai Yonghong and Liu Hongchao, *Rivalry and Cooperation: A New "Great Game" in Myanmar*, Stockholm: Institute for Security and Development Policy Asia Paper, 2014.
61. *The Burman*, '"Our Union Is Like A Tender Gourd', Says Premier U Nu", 24 December 1954, p. 1.

CONCLUSION: *GLASNOST* WITHOUT *PERESTROIKA*

1. *The Economist*, "A Burmese Spring", 25 May 2013.
2. Interview with NLD patron Tin Oo, Yangon, December 2015.
3. See, for instance, Aung-Thwin, Maitrii, "Reassessing Myanmar's Glasnost", *Kyoto Review of Southeast Asia* 14 (2013); and Egreteau, Renaud, "Réformes en Birmanie: *Glasnost* sans

Perestroika?", in Racine, Jean-Luc (ed.), *Asie: Mondes Emergents, 2013–2014*, Paris: La Documentation Française, 2013, pp. 75–87.

4. Channel News Asia, "Myanmar not ready for reduced military role in Parliament: Army chief", 20 January 2015.
5. Thant Myint U, "White Elephants and Black Swans: Thoughts on Myanmar's Recent History and Possible Futures", in Cheesman, Nick, Monique Skidmore and Trevor Wilson (eds), *Myanmar's Transition: Openings, Obstacles and Opportunities*, Singapore: ISEAS Publications, 2012, p. 25.
6. For details, see a quantitative analysis by Michael Albertus and Victor Menaldo: "Dealing with Dictators: Negotiated Democratization and the Fate of Outgoing Autocrats", *International Studies Quarterly* 58, 3 (2014), pp. 550–65.
7. As explained in Bermeo, Nancy G., "Myth of Moderation: Confrontation and Conflict in Democratic Transitions", *Comparative Politics* 29, 3 (1997), pp. 305–22.
8. Reuters, "Aung San Suu Kyi says boycott of Myanmar elections an option", 3 April 2015.
9. A more detailed examination of the various metamorphoses the country has undergone since the early 2000s can be found in this collection of essays by thirteen Myanmar scholars: Egreteau, Renaud and François Robinne (eds), *Metamorphosis: Studies in Social and Political Change in Myanmar*, Singapore: NUS Press, 2015.
10. Rieffel, Lex, "Can the NLD Reform Myanmar's Economy?" *East Asia Forum*, 25 January 2016.
11. AFP, *Aung San Suu Kyi cleaning up Myanmar*, 13 December 2015.
12. Discussion with a retired air force officer, Naypyitaw, February 2015.
13. Whereas President Thein Sein graduated from the ninth intake, and Thura Shwe Mann from the eleventh.
14. See, for instance, Tin Maung Maung Than, "Introductory Overview: Myanmar's Economic Reforms", *Journal of Southeast Asian Economies* 31, 2 (2014), pp. 165–72; and an early assessment of the potential resource curse in Bissinger, Jared, "Foreign Investment in Myanmar: A Resource Boom but a Development Bust?", *Contemporary Southeast Asia* 34, 1 (2012), pp. 23–52.
15. Interview with the author, Naypyitaw, February 2015.
16. Interview with Khin Aung Myint, Naypyitaw, 15 August 2013.

SELECTIVE BIBLIOGRAPHY

n. a., *Constitution of the Republic of the Union of Myanmar*, Yangon: Printing and Publishing Enterprise, Ministry of Information, 2008.

n. a., *Is Trust Vindicated? A Chronicle of the Various Accomplishments of the Government Headed by General Ne Win during the Period of Tenure from November 1958 to February 6, 1960*, Rangoon: Director of Information, Government of the Union of Burma, 1960.

n. a., *The Parliaments of Myanmar*, Yangon: MCM, 2013.

Abente-Brun, Diego and Larry Diamond (eds), *Clientelism, Social Policy and the Quality of Democracy*, Baltimore, MD: The Johns Hopkins University Press, 2014.

Alagappa, Muthiah, "Investigating and Explaining Change: An Analytical Framework", in Alagappa, Muthiah (ed.), *Coercion and Governance: The Declining Political Role of the Military in Asia*, Stanford, CA: Stanford University Press, 2001, pp. 29–66.

——— "Civil Society and Democratic Change: Indeterminate Connection, Transforming Relations", in Alagappa, Muthiah (ed.), *Civil Society and Political Change in Asia: Expanding and Contracting Democratic Space*, Stanford, CA: Stanford University Press, 2004, pp. 478–508.

Albertus, Michael and Victor Menaldo, "Dealing with Dictators: Negotiated Democratization and the Fate of Outgoing Autocrats", *International Studies Quarterly* 58, 3 (2014), pp. 550–65.

Arter, David (ed.), *Comparing and Classifying Legislatures*, London: Routledge, 2009.

Aung Aung (RI), *Promoting Democracy in Myanmar: Political Party Capacity Building*, Stockholm: ISDP Asia Paper, 2013.

Aung-Thwin, Maitrii, "Reassessing Myanmar's Glasnost", *Kyoto Review of Southeast Asia* 14 (2013).

Baaklini, Abdo I., Guilain Denoeux and Robert Springborg, *Legislative Politics in the Arab World: The Resurgence of Democratic Institutions*, Boulder, CO: Lynne Rienner, 1999.

Badgley, John H., "Burmese Communist Schisms", in Wilson, John (ed.), *Peasant Rebellion and Communist Revolution in Asia*, Stanford, CA: Stanford University Press, 1974, pp. 151–68.

Barkan, Joel D. (ed.), *Legislative Power in Emerging African Democracies*, Boulder, CO: Lynne Rienner, 2009.

Baujard, Julie, "Nous sommes des femmes dangereuses!...en danger. Mobilisation des réfugiées birmanes à Delhi", *Moussons* 22 (2013), pp. 57–73.

Beatty, Linnea M., "Democracy Activism and Assistance in Burma: Sites of Resistance", *International Journal* 65, 3, (2010), pp. 619–36.

Berlie, Jean A., *The Burmanization of Myanmar's Muslims*, Bangkok: White Lotus, 2008.

Bermeo, Nancy G., "Myth of Moderation: Confrontation and Conflict in Democratic Transitions", *Comparative Politics* 29, 3 (1997), pp. 305–22.

Bernhard, Michael and Ekrem Karakoc. "Civil Society and the Legacies of Dictatorship", *World Politics* 59, 4, (2007), pp. 539–67.

Bissinger, Jared, "Foreign Investment in Myanmar: A Resource Boom but a Development Bust?", *Contemporary Southeast Asia* 34, 1 (2012), pp. 23–52.

Blomgren, Magnus and Olivier Rozenberg (eds), *Parliamentary Roles in Modern Legislatures*, London: Routledge, 2012.

Brees, Inge. "Burmese Refugee Transnationalism: What Is The Effect?", *Journal of Current Southeast Asian Affairs* 28, 2 (2009), pp. 23–46.

Bünte, Marco, "Burma's Transition to Quasi-Military Rule: From Rulers to Guardians?", *Armed Forces & Society* 40, 4, (2014), pp. 742–64.

Burnell, Peter and Peter Calvert (eds), *Civil Society in Democratization*, London: Frank Cass, 2004.

Butwell, Richard, "Civilians and Soldiers in Burma," *Studies in Asia* 1, 2 (1961), pp. 74–85.

Callahan, Mary P., "On Time Warps and Warped Time: Lessons from Burma's Democratic Era", in Rotberg, Robert (ed.), *Burma: Prospects for a Democratic Future*, Washington, D.C.: Brookings Institution Press, 1998, pp. 49–67.

——— "Of *kyay-zu* and *kyet-su*: The Military in 2006", in Skidmore, Monique and Trevor Wilson (eds), *Myanmar: The State, Community and Environment*, Canberra: ANU E-Press, 2007, pp. 36–53.

——— "Myanmar's Perpetual Junta: Solving the Riddle of the *Tatmadaw*'s Long Reign", *New Left Review* 60 (2009), pp. 27–63.

——— "The Endurance of Military Rule in Burma: Not Why, But Why Not?", in Levenstein, Susan L. (ed.), *Finding Dollars, Sense and Legitimacy in Burma*, Washington, D.C.: Woodrow Wilson Center, 2010, pp. 54–76.

——— "The Generals Loosen their Grip", *Journal of Democracy* 23, 4 (2012), pp. 120–31.

——— *Drivers of Political Change in Post-junta, Constitutional Burma*, Washington, D.C.: USAID, 2012.

—— "National Security and the Military in Post-junta, Constitutional Myanmar", in n.a. (ed.), *The United States and Japan: Assisting Myanmar Development*, Washington, D.C.: Sasakawa Peace Foundation USA, 2015, pp. 41–55.

Case, William, *Executive Accountability in Southeast Asia: The Role of Legislatures in New Democracies and Under Electoral Authoritarianism*, Honolulu HI: East-West Center Policy Studies No. 57, 2011.

Chambers, Paul, "Superfluous, Mischievous, or Emancipating? Thailand's Evolving Senate Today", *Journal of Current Southeast Asian Affairs* 28, 3 (2009), pp. 3–38.

—— "Constitutional Change and Security Forces in Southeast Asia: Lessons from Thailand and Myanmar", *Contemporary Southeast Asia* 36, 1, (2014), pp. 101–27.

Chandra, Kanchan, *Why Ethnic Parties Succeed: Patronage and Ethnic Head Counts in India*, Cambridge: Cambridge University Press, 2004.

—— "Patronage, Democracy and Ethnic Politics in India", in Abente-Brun, Diego and Larry Diamond (eds), *Clientelism, Social Policy and the Quality of Democracy*, Baltimore, MD: The Johns Hopkins University Press, 2014, pp. 135–72.

Cheesman, Nick, *Opposing the Rule of Law: How Myanmar's Courts Make Law and Order*, Cambridge: Cambridge University Press, 2015.

Cheesman, Nick, Nicholas Farrelly and Trevor Wilson (eds), *Debating Democratization in Myanmar*, Singapore: ISEAS Publications, 2014.

Cheesman, Nick, Monique Skidmore and Trevor Wilson (eds), *Myanmar's Transition: Openings, Obstacles, and Opportunities*, Singapore: ISEAS Publications, 2012.

Choi, Nankyung, *Local Politics in Indonesia: Pathways to Power*, London: Routledge, 2011.

Cohen, Jean L. and Andrew Arato. *Civil Society and Political Theory*, Cambridge: Cambridge University Press, 1994.

Croissant, Aurel and J. Kamerling, "Why Do Military Regimes Institutionalize? Constitution-making and Elections as Political Survival Strategy in Myanmar", *Asian Journal of Political Science* 21, 2, (2013), pp. 105–25.

Crouch, Melissa (ed.), *Islam and the State in Myanmar: Muslim-Buddhist Relations and the Politics of Belonging*, New Delhi: Oxford University Press, 2016 (forthcoming).

Dai Yonghong and Liu Hongchao, *Rivalry and Cooperation: A New "Great Game" in Myanmar*, Stockholm: Institute for Security and Development Policy Asia Paper, 2014.

Diamond, Larry J., "Toward Democratic Consolidation", *Journal of Democracy* 5, 3 (1994), pp. 5–17.

—— *Developing Democracy: Towards Consolidation*, Baltimore, MA: Johns Hopkins University Press, 1999.

—— "The Need for a Political Pact", *Journal of Democracy* 23, 4 (2012), pp. 138–49.

Diamond, Larry and Richard Gunther (eds), *Political Parties and Democracy*, Baltimore, MD: The Johns Hopkins University Press, 2001.

Dorning, Karl, "Creating an Environment for Participation: International NGOs and the Growth of Civil Society in Burma", in Wilson, Trevor (ed.), *Myanmar's Long Road to National Reconciliation*, Singapore: ISEAS Publications, 2006, pp. 188–217.

Duell, Kerstin (ed.), *Myanmar in Transition: Polity, People and Processes*, Singapore: Select Books, 2013.

Dupuy, Trevor N., "Burma and its Army: A Contrast in Motivations and Characteristics," *The Antioch Review* 20, 4 (1960), pp. 428–40.

Edinger, Lewis J., "Military Leaders and Foreign Policy", *The American Political Science Review* 57, 2 (1963), pp. 392–405.

Egreteau, Renaud, *Jade or JADE? Debating International Sanctions on Burma's Gem Industry*, Washington, D.C.: East-West Center Asia-Pacific Bulletin No. 132, 2011.

——— "Burmese Tango: Indian and Chinese Games and Gains in Burma (Myanmar) since 1988", in Devare, Sudhir T., Swaran Singh and Reena Marwah (eds), *Emerging China: Prospects of Partnership in Asia*, New Delhi: Routledge, 2012, pp. 269–92.

——— *Toward a Reorganization of the Political Landscape in Burma (Myanmar)*, Paris: Les Etudes du CERI No. 197b, 2013.

——— "Réformes en Birmanie: *Glasnost* sans *Perestroïka*?", in Racine, Jean-Luc (ed.), *Asie: Mondes Emergents, 2013–2014*, Paris: La Documentation Française, 2013, pp. 75–87.

——— "The Continuing Political Salience of the Military in Post-SPDC Myanmar", in Cheesman, Nick, Nicholas Farrelly and Trevor Wilson (eds), *Debating Democratisation in Myanmar*, Singapore: ISEAS Publications, 2014, pp. 259–84.

——— "(Re)-emerging Patterns of Parliamentary Politics", in Steinberg, David I. (ed.), *Myanmar: The Dynamics of an Evolving Polity*, Boulder, CO: Lynne Rienner, 2014, pp. 59–88.

——— "Legislators in Myanmar's First Post-Junta National Legislature (2010–2015): A Sociological Analysis", *Journal of Current Southeast Asian Affairs* 33, 2 (2014), pp. 91–124.

——— *Military Delegates in Myanmar's Legislature: What Do They Do, What Will They (Continue) To Do?*, Singapore: ISEAS Perspectives No. 21, 28 April 2015.

——— "Who Are The Military Delegates in Myanmar's 2010–2015 Union Legislature?", *Sojourn* 30, 2 (2015), pp. 338–70.

——— "Soldiers as Lawmakers? Assessing the Legislative Role of the Burmese Armed Forces (2010–2015)", in Egreteau, Renaud and François Robinne (eds), *Metamorphosis: Studies in Social and Political Change in Myanmar*, Singapore: NUS Press, 2015, pp. 15–42.

——— *Retired Military Officers in Myanmar's Parliament: An Emerging Legislative Force?*, Singapore: ISEAS Trends No. 17, 2015.

Egreteau, Renaud and Larry Jagan, *Soldiers and Diplomacy in Burma: Understanding the Foreign Policies of the Burmese Praetorian State*, Singapore: NUS Press, 2013.

Egreteau, Renaud and François Robinne (eds), *Metamorphosis: Studies in Social and Political Change in Myanmar*, Singapore: NUS Press, 2015.

Englehart, Neil A., "Two Cheers for Burma's Rigged Elections", *Asian Survey* 52, 4 (2012), pp. 666–86.

Ensalaco, Mark, "Military Prerogatives and the Stalemate of Chilean Civil-Military Relations", *Armed Forces & Society* 21, 2 (1995), pp. 255–70.

Fair, C. Christine, "Democracy on the Leash in Pakistan", in Fair, C. Christine and Sarah J. Watson (eds), *Pakistan's Enduring Challenges*, Philadelphia, PA: University of Pennsylvania Press, 2015, pp. 131–55.

Farrelly, Nicholas, "Discipline without Democracy: Military Dominance in Post-colonial Burma", *Australian Journal of International Affairs* 67, 3 (2014), pp. 312–26.

Feit, Edward, *The Armed Bureaucrats: Military-Administrative Regimes and Political Development*, New York: Houghton Mifflin, 1972.

Finer, Samuel E., *The Man on Horseback: The Role of the Military in Politics (revised edition)*, New York: Praeger, 1975 [1962].

——— "The Retreat to the Barracks. Notes on the Practice and the Theory of Military Withdrawal from the Seats of Power," *Third World Quarterly* 7, 1 (1985), pp. 16–30.

Fink, Christina, *Living Silence in Burma: Surviving under Military Rule* (1st edn), London: Zed Books, 2001.

——— "How Real Are Myanmar's Reforms?", *Current History* 113, 764 (2014), pp. 224–30.

——— "Myanmar's Proactive National Legislature", *Social Forces* 82, 2 (2015), pp. 327–54.

Fish, M. Steven, "Stronger Legislatures, Stronger Democracies", *Journal of Democracy* 17, 1 (2006), pp. 5–20.

Fish, M. Steven and Matthew Kroenig, *The Handbook of National Legislatures*, Cambridge: Cambridge University Press, 2009.

Freeman, Nick J., "Navigating the Economic Reform Process", *Southeast Asian Affairs* 2014, pp. 224–40.

Furnivall, John S., *The Governance of Modern Burma*, New York: Institute of Pacific Relations, 1960.

Ganesan, Narayanan, "Interpreting Recent Developments in Myanmar as an Attempt to Establish Political Legitimacy", *Asian Journal of Peacebuilding* 1, 2 (2013), pp. 253–74.

——— "The Myanmar Peace Center: Its Origins, Activities, and Aspirations", *Asian Journal of Peacebuilding* 2, 1 (2014), pp. 127–41.

Gravers, Mikael, *Nationalism as Political Paranoia in Burma*, London: Curzon Press, 1999.

——— "Introduction: Ethnicity against the State—State against Ethnic Diversity?", in Gravers, Mikael (ed.), *Exploring Ethnic Diversity in Burma*, Copenhagen: NIAS Press, 2007, pp. 1–33.

Green, Matthew N., *The Speaker of the House: A Study in Leadership*, New Haven, CT: Yale University Press, 2010.

Guyot, James F., "Burmese Praetorianism," in Gartner, Uta and Jens Lorenz (eds), *Tradition and Modernity in Myanmar*, Berlin: LIT Verlag, 1994, pp. 129–48.

Haacke, Jürgen, "US-Myanmar Relations: Developments, Challenges, and Implications", in Steinberg, David I. (ed.), *Myanmar: The Dynamics of an Evolving Polity*, Boulder, CO: Lynne Rienner, 2014, pp. 289–318.

Hagopian, Frances, "Democracy by Undemocratic Means? Elites, Political Pacts and Regime Transition in Brazil", *Comparative Political Studies* 23, 2 (1990), pp. 147–70.

Hahn, Jeffrey W. (ed.), *Democratization in Russia: The Development of Legislative Institutions*, Armonk, NY: M.E. Sharpe, 1996.

Hicken, Allan, "Clientelism", *Annual Review of Political Science* 14 (2011), pp. 289–310.

Hilgers, Tina, "Democratic Processes, Clientelistic Relationships, and the Material Good Problems", in Hilgers, Tina (ed.), *Clientelism in Everyday Latin American Politics*, New York: Palgrave Macmillan, 2012, pp. 3–24.

Hoffman, Ralf, "Traditional Political Culture and the Prospects for Democracy in Burma", in Gartner, Uta and Jens Lorenz (eds), *Tradition and Modernity in Myanmar*, Berlin: LIT Verlag, 1994, pp. 175–87.

Holliday, Ian, "Voting and Violence in Myanmar: Nation Building for a Transition to Democracy", *Asian Survey* 48, 6 (2008), pp. 1038–58.

——— *Burma Redux: Global Justice and the Quest for Political Reform in Myanmar*, New York: Columbia University Press, 2012.

——— "Addressing Myanmar's Citizenship Crisis", *Journal of Contemporary Asia* 44, 3 (2014), pp. 404–21.

Holliday, Ian, Maw Htun Aung and Cindy Joelene, "Institution Building in Myanmar: The Establishment of Regional and State Assemblies", *Asian Survey* 55, 4 (2015), pp. 641–64.

Horowitz, Donald L., *Ethnic Groups in Conflict*, Berkeley, CA: University of Berkeley Press, 1985.

——— *Constitutional Change and Democracy in Indonesia*, Cambridge: Cambridge University Press, 2013.

Horsey, Richard, *Outcome of the Myanmar Elections*, New York: SSRC Conflict Prevention and Peace Forum Briefing, 17 November 2010.

——— *Who's Who in the New Myanmar Government*, New York: SSRC Conflict Prevention and Peace Forum Briefing Paper, 14 April 2011.

——— *The Initial Functioning of Myanmar Legislatures*, New York: SSRC Conflict Prevention and Peace Forum Briefing, 17 May 2011.

—— "Myanmar's Political Landscape Following the 2010 Elections: Starting with a Glass Nine-Tenths Empty?", in Cheesman, Nick, Monique Skidmore and Trevor Wilson (eds), *Myanmar's Transition: Openings, Obstacles and Opportunities*, Singapore: ISEAS Publications, 2012, pp. 39–51.

Houtman, Gustaaf, *Mental Culture in Burmese Political Crisis: Aung San Suu Kyi and the National League for Democracy*, Tokyo: ICLAA Monograph No. 33, 1999.

Human Rights Watch (HRW), *'The Government Could Have Stopped This': Sectarian Violence and Ensuing Abuses in Burma's Arakan State*, Washington, D.C.: HRW Publications, 2012.

—— *'All You Can Do Is Pray': Crime against Humanity and Ethnic Cleansing of Rohingya Muslims in Burma's Arakan State*, Washington, D.C.: HRW Publications, 2013.

Humphries, Richard, "Saffron-robed Monks and Digital Flash Cards: The Development and Challenges of Burmese Exile Media", in Nault, Derrick M. (ed.), *Development in Asia: Interdisciplinary, Post-neoliberal and Transnational Perspectives*, Boca Raton, FL: Brown Walker, 2009, pp. 237–58.

Hunter, Wendy, *Eroding Military Influence in Brazil: Politicians against Soldiers*, Chapel Hill, NC: University of North Carolina Press, 1997.

Huntington, Samuel P., *The Soldier and the State*, Cambridge, MA: Belknap, 1957.

—— *Political Order in Changing Societies*, New Haven, CT: Yale University Press, 1968.

Hutchcroft, Paul, "After the Fall: Prospects for Political and Institutional Reform in Post-Crisis Thailand and the Philippines," *Government and Opposition* 34, 4 (1999), pp. 473–97.

International Crisis Group (ICG), *Myanmar: The Role of Civil Society*, Yangon/Brussels: Asia Report No. 27, 2001.

—— *The Myanmar Elections*, Yangon/Brussels: Asia Briefing No. 105, 2010.

—— *Myanmar's Post-Election Landscape*, Brussels/Yangon: Asia Briefing No. 118, 2011a.

—— *Myanmar: A New Peace Initiative*, Yangon/Brussels: Asia Report No. 214, 2011b.

—— Myanmar: The Politics of Economic Reform, Yangon/Brussels: Asia Report No. 231, 2012.

—— *A Tentative Peace in Myanmar's Kachin Conflict*, Brussels/Yangon: Asia Report No. 140, 2013a.

—— *The Dark Side of Transition: Violence against Muslims in Myanmar*, Brussels/Yangon: Asia Report No. 251, 2013b.

—— *'Not a Rubber Stamp': Myanmar's Legislature in a Time of Transition*, Brussels/Yangon: Asia Briefing No. 142, 2013c.

—— *Myanmar's Military: Back to the Barracks?*, Brussels/Yangon: Asia Briefing No. 143, 2014.

—— *Myanmar's Peace Process: A Nationwide Ceasefire Remains Elusive*, Brussels/Yangon: Asia Briefing No. 146, 2015a.

—— *The Myanmar Elections: Results and Implications*, Brussels/Yangon: Asia Briefing No. 147, 2015b.

Janowitz, Morris, *The Professional Soldier: A Social and Political Portrait*, Glencoe, IL: The Free Press, 1960.

Jaquet, Carine, "Unwanted War, Unachievable Peace: Examining Some Kachin Narratives in Times of Conflict", in Egreteau, Renaud and François Robinne (eds), *Metamorphosis: Studies in Social and Political Change in Myanmar*, Singapore: NUS Press, 2015, pp. 179–206.

Jaquet, Carine and Matthew J. Walton, "Buddhism and Relief in Myanmar: Reflections on relief as a Practice of *Dāna*", in Kawanami, Hiroko and Geoffrey Samuel (eds), *Buddhism, International Relief Work, and Civil Society in Myanmar*, Basingstoke: Palgrave Macmillan, 2013, pp. 51–74.

Jolliffe, Kim, *Ethnic Conflict and Social Services in Myanmar's Contested Regions*, San Francisco, CA: The Asia Foundation, 2014.

Jones, Lee, "The Political Economy of Myanmar's Transition", *Journal of Contemporary Asia* 44, 1 (2014), pp. 144–170.

—— "Explaining Myanmar's Regime Transition: The Periphery is Central", *Democratization* 21, 5 (2014), pp. 780–802.

Karl, Terry L., "Dilemmas of Democratization in Latin America", *Comparative Politics* 23, 1 (1990), pp. 1–21.

Kasuya, Yuko (ed.), *Presidents, Assemblies and Policy-making in Asia*, New York: Palgrave Macmillan, 2013.

Kean, Tom, "Myanmar's Parliament: From Scorn to Significance", in Cheesman, Nick, N. Farrelly and T. Wilson, *Debating Democratisation in Myanmar*, Singapore: ISEAS Publications, 2014, pp. 43–74.

Khin Zaw Win, "A Burmese Perspective on Prospects for Progress," in Skidmore, Monique and Trevor Wilson (eds), *Myanmar: The State, Community and the Environment*, Canberra: ANU E-Press, 2007, pp. 18–35.

—— "Reality Check on the Sanctions against Myanmar," in Ganesan, Narayanan and Kyaw Yin Hlaing (eds.), *Myanmar: State, Society, and Ethnicity*, Singapore: ISEAS Publications, 2007, pp. 278–88.

—— "Myanmar in Political Transition", in Duell, Kerstin (ed.), *Myanmar in Transition: Polity, People and Processes*, Singapore: Select Books, 2013, pp. 9–15.

Ko Ko Thett, "The Myth of the Indispensability of the Military in Burmese Political Culture: Totalitarian Discourse in the State of Myanmar", in Crauwells, Geert *et al.* (eds), *Totalitarian and Authoritarian Discourses: A Global and Timeless Phenomenon?*, Bern: Peter Lang, 2014, pp. 263–92.

Kramer, Tom, *Civil Society Gaining Ground: Opportunities for Change and Development in Burma*, Amsterdam: TNI, 2011.

Kyaw Ying Hlaing, "Burma: Civil Society Skirting Regime Rules", in Alagappa, Muthiah (ed.), *Civil Society and Political Change in Asia: Expanding and Contracting Democratic Space*, Stanford, CA: Stanford University Press, 2004, pp. 389–418.

—— "Associational Life in Myanmar: Past and Present", in Ganesan, Narayanan and Kyaw Yin Hlaing (eds), *Myanmar: State, Society, and Ethnicity*, Singapore: ISEAS Publications, 2007, pp. 143–71.

—— "Power and Factional Struggles in Post-Independence Burmese Governments", *Journal of Southeast Asian Studies* 39, 1 (2008a), pp. 149–77.

—— "Challenging the Authoritarian State: Buddhist Monks and Peaceful Protests in Burma", *The Fletcher Forum of World Affairs* 32, 1 (2008b), pp. 125–44.

—— "Problems with the Process of Reconciliation", in Rieffel, Lex (ed.), *Myanmar/ Burma: Inside Challenges, Outside Interests*, Washington, D.C.: Brookings Institution Press, 2010, pp. 33–51.

—— "Understanding Recent Political Changes in Myanmar," *Contemporary Southeast Asia* 34, 2 (2012), pp. 197–216.

—— "The Unexpected Arrival of a New Political Era in Myanmar", in Kyaw Yin Hlaing (ed.), *Prisms on the Golden Pagoda: Perspectives on National Reconciliation in Myanmar*, Singapore: NUS Press, 2014, pp. 218–31.

Kyi Pyar Chit Saw and Matthew Arnold, *Administering the State in Myanmar*, Yangon: MDRI-Asia Foundation Discussion Paper No. 6, 2014.

Larkin, Emma, *Everything is Broken*, New York: Penguin Books, 2010.

Lidauer, Michael, "Democratic Dawn? Civil Society and Elections in Myanmar (2010–2012)", *Journal of Current Southeast Asian Affairs* 31, 2 (2012), pp. 87–114.

Liddell, Zunnetta, "No Room to Move: Legal Constraints on Civil Society in Burma", in Kramer, Tom and Pietje Vervest (eds), *Strengthening Civil Society in Burma: Possibilities and Dilemmas for International NGOs*, Chiang Mai: Silkworm Books, 1999, pp. 54–68.

Lintner, Bertil, *Burma in Revolt: Opium and Insurgency since 1948*, Chiang Mai: Silkworm Books, 1999.

—— *Great Game East: India, China, and the Struggle for Asia's Most Volatile Frontier*, New Delhi: HarperCollins, 2012.

Linz, Juan J. and Alfred Stepan, *Problems of Democratic Transition and Consolidation: Southern Europe, South America and Post-Communist Europe*, Baltimore, MD: The Johns Hopkins University Press, 1996.

Loeschmann, Heike (ed.), *Active Citizens under Political Wraps: Experiences from Myanmar/Burma and Vietnam*, Berlin: Heinrich Boell Foundation, 2006.

Lorch, Jasmin, "The (Re)-Emergence of Civil Society in Areas of State Weaknesses: The Case of Education in Burma/Myanmar", in Skidmore, Monique and Trevor Wilson (eds), *Dictatorship, Disorder and Decline in Myanmar*, Canberra: ANU E-Press, 2008, pp. 151–76.

Löwenberg, Gerhard, Peverill Squire and D. Roderick Kiewiet (eds), *Legislatures: Comparative Perspectives on Representative Assemblies*, Ann Arbor, MI: The University of Michigan Press, 2002.

Lynn Kuok, *Promoting Peace in Myanmar: US Interests and Role*, Washington, D.C.: CSIS, 2014.

McAllister, Ian, "The Personalization of Politics", in Dalton, Russell J. and Hans-Dieter Klingemann (eds), *The Oxford Handbook of Political Behaviour*, Oxford: Oxford University Press, 2007, pp. 571–88.

Macdonald, Adam P., "From Military Rule to Electoral Authoritarianism: The Reconfiguration of Power in Myanmar and its Future", *Asian Affairs* 40, 1 (2013), pp. 20–36.

Mansbridge, Jane, "Should Blacks Represent Blacks and Women Represent Women? A Contingent "Yes", *The Journal of Politics* 61, 3 (1999), pp. 628–57.

Marston, Hunter, "Myanmar's Electoral System: Reviewing the 2010 and 2012 Elections and Looking Ahead to the 2015 General Elections", *Asian Journal of Political Science* 21, 3 (2013), pp. 268–84.

Martin, Shane, "Committees", in Martin, Shane, Thomas Saalfeld and Kaare W. Strom (eds), *Oxford Handbook of Legislative Studies*, Oxford: Oxford University Press, 2014, pp. 352–70.

Martin, Shane, Thomas Saalfeld and Kaare W. Strom (eds), *Oxford Handbook of Legislative Studies*, Oxford: Oxford University Press, 2014.

Matelski, Maaike, "Civil Society and Expectations of Democratisation from Below: The Case of Myanmar", *Thammasat Review* 16, (2012), pp. 153–66.

Maung Aung Myoe, *Building the Tatmadaw: Myanmar Armed Forces since 1948*, Singapore: ISEAS Publications, 2009.

——— "The Military and Political Liberalisation in Myanmar", in Duell, Kerstin (ed.), *Myanmar in Transition: Polity, People and Processes*, Singapore: Select Books, 2013, pp. 57–64.

——— "The Soldier and the State: The *Tatmadaw* and Political Liberalization in Myanmar since 2011", *South East Asia Research* 22, 2 (2014), pp. 233–49.

Maung Maung, "Portrait of the Burmese Parliament", *Parliamentary Affairs* 10, 2 (1956), pp. 204–9.

——— "Burma at the Crossroads", *India Quarterly* 14, 4 (1958), pp. 380–88.

——— "New Parliament in Burma", *India Quarterly* 16, 2 (1960), pp. 139–44.

Maung Maung Gyi, *Burmese Political Values: The Socio-Political Roots of Authoritarianism*, New York: Praeger, 1983.

Maung Zarni, "A Three Insecurities Perspective for the Changing Myanmar", *Kyoto Review of Southeast Asia* 14 (2013).

Mezey, Michael L., *Comparative Legislatures*, Durham, NC: Duke University Press, 1979.

——— "The Functions of Legislatures in the Third World", *Legislative Studies Quarterly* 8, 4 (1983), pp. 511–50.

Mietzner, Marcus, "The Political Marginalization of the Military in Indonesia", in Mietzner, Marcus (ed.), *The Political Resurgence of the Military in Southeast Asia: Conflict and Leadership*, London: Routledge, 2011, pp. 126–47.

——— "Indonesia's Decentralization: The Rise of Local Identities and the Survival of the Nation-State", in Hill, Hal (ed.), *Regional Dynamics in Decentralized Indonesia*, Singapore: ISEAS, 2014, pp. 45–67.

Min Maung Maung, *The Tatmadaw and its Leadership Role in National Politics*, Rangoon: Ministry of Information, News & Periodicals Enterprise, 1993.

Min Zin and Brian Joseph, "The Democrats' Opportunity", *Journal of Democracy* 23, 4 (2012), pp. 104–19.

Minoletti, Paul, *Women's Participation in the Subnational Governance of Myanmar*, Yangon: MDRI & Asia Foundation Discussion Paper No. 6, 2014.

Moe Thuzar, "The Role of Parliament in Myanmar's Reforms and Transition to Democracy", in Kerstin Duell (ed.), *Myanmar in Transition: Polity, People and Processes*, Singapore: Select Books, 2013, pp. 19–32.

Moe Thuzar and Pavin Chachavalpongpun, *Myanmar: Life after Nargis*, Singapore: ISEAS Publications, 2009.

Morgenstern, Scott and Benito Nacif (eds), *Legislative Politics in Latin America*, Cambridge: Cambridge University Press, 2002.

Mullen, Matthew, *Contrasting Pathways to Change in Burma/Myanmar: From Bullets to Bribery*, unpublished PhD dissertation, Bangkok: Mahidol University, 2013.

Munck, Gerardo L. and Carol S. Leff, "Modes of Transition and Democratization: South America and Eastern Europe in Comparative Perspective", *Comparative Politics* 29, 3 (1997), pp. 343–62.

Mya Win, *Tatmadaw's Traditional Role in National Politics*, Rangoon: Ministry of Information, News & Periodicals Enterprise, 1992.

Nakanishi, Yoshihiro, *Strong Soldiers, Failed Revolution: The State and Military in Burma, 1962–88*, Singapore: NUS Press, 2013.

Nash, Manning, "Party Building in Upper Burma", *Asian Survey* 3, 4 (1963), pp. 197–202.

Nixon, Hamish et al., *State and Region Governments in Myanmar*, Yangon: MDRI-Asia Foundation, 2013.

Nordlinger, Eric A., *Soldiers in Politics: Military Coups and Governments*, London: Prentice Hall, 1977.

Norton, Philip (ed.), *Legislatures*, Oxford: Oxford University Press, 1990.

Norton, Philip and Nizam Ahmed (eds), *Parliaments in Asia*, London: Frank Cass, 1999.

Norton, Philip and David M. Olson, "Parliaments in Adolescence", in Olson, David M. and Philip Norton (eds), *The New Parliaments of Central and Eastern Europe*, London: Frank Cass, 1996, pp. 231–43.

——— (eds), *Post-Communist and Post-Soviet Parliaments: The Initial Decade*, London: Routledge, 2008.

O'Donnell, Guillermo and Philippe C. Schmitter, *Transition from Authoritarian Rule: Tentative Conclusions about Uncertain Democracies*, Baltimore, MA: The Johns Hopkins University Press, 1986.

Olson, David M., *Democratic Legislative Institutions: A Comparative View*, Armonk, NY: ME Sharpe, 1994.

Olson, David M. and Philip Norton (eds), *The New Parliaments of Central and Eastern Europe*, London: Frank Cass, 1996.

Pedersen, Morten, "Myanmar's Democratic Opening: The Process and Prospects for Reform", in Cheesman, Nick, Nicholas Farrelly and Trevor Wilson (eds), *Debating Democratisation in Myanmar*, Singapore: ISEAS Publications, 2014, pp. 19–40.

Pedersen, Rena, *The Burma Spring: Aung San Suu Kyi and the New Struggle for the Soul of a Nation*, New York: Pegasus, 2014.

Perlmutter, Amos, "The Praetorian State and the Praetorian Army: Toward a Taxonomy of Civil-Military Relations in Developing Countries," *Comparative Politics* 1, 3 (1969), pp. 382–404.

—— *Egypt: The Praetorian State*, New Brunswick: Transaction Publishers, 1974.

—— *Political Roles and Military Rulers*, London: Frank Cass, 1981.

Pitkin, Hanna F., *The Concept of Representation*, Berkeley, CA: University of California Press, 1967.

Power, Timothy J., "Elites and Institutions in Conservative Transitions to Democracy: Ex-Authoritarians in the Brazilian National Congress", *Studies in Comparative International Development* 31, 3 (1996), pp. 56–84.

Prager-Nyein, Susanne, "The Armed Forces of Burma: The Constant Sentinel", in Mietzner, Marcus (ed.), *The Political Resurgence of the Military in Southeast Asia: Conflict and Leadership*, London: Routledge, 2011, pp. 24–44.

Prasse-Freeman, Elliott, "Power, Civil Society, and an Inchoate Politics of the Daily in Burma/Myanmar", *The Journal of Asian Studies* 71, 2 (2012), pp. 371–97.

—— "Grassroots Protest Movements and Mutating Conceptions of 'the Political' in an Evolving Burma", in Egreteau, Renaud and François Robinne (eds), *Metamorphosis: Studies in Social and Political Change in Myanmar*, Singapore: NUS Press, 2015, pp. 69–100.

Przeworski, Adam, *Democracy and the Limits of Self-Government*, Cambridge: Cambridge University Press, 2010.

Przeworski, Adam, Michael E. Alvarez, Jose Antonio Cheibub and Fernando Limongi, *Democracy and Development: Political Institutions and Well-Being in the World, 1950–1990*, New York: Cambridge University Press, 2000.

Putnam, Robert, *The Comparative Study of Political Elites*, Englewood Cliffs, NJ: Prentice Hall, 1976.

Putnam, Robert, *Making Democracy Work: Civic Traditions in Modern Italy*, Princeton, NJ: Princeton University Press, 1993.

Rajah, Ananda, "Ethnicity and Civil War in Burma: Where is the Rationality?", in

Rotberg, R. (ed.), *Burma: Prospects for a Democratic Future*, Washington, D.C.: Brookings Institution Press, 1998, pp. 135–50.

Remington, Thomas F. (ed.), *Parliaments in Transition: The New Legislative Politics in the Former USSR and Eastern Europe*, Boulder, CO: Westview Press, 1994.

Reynolds, Andrew et al., "How Could Burma Democratize?", *Journal of Democracy* 12, 4 (2001), pp. 95–108.

Rüland, Jürgen et al., *Parliaments and Political Change in Asia*, Singapore: ISEAS Publications, 2005.

Russell, Rosalind, *Burma's Spring: Real Lives in Turbulent Times*, London: Thistle, 2014.

Schmidt, Steffen W. et al., *Friends, Followers and Factions*. Berkeley CA: University of California Press, 1977.

Schmitter, Philippe C., "Twenty-Five Years, Fifteen Findings", *Journal of Democracy* 21, 1 (2010), pp. 17–28.

Scott, James C., "Patron-Client Politics and Political Change in Southeast Asia", *The American Political Science Review*, 66, 1 (1972), pp. 91–113.

Selth, Andrew, *Burma's Armed Forces: Power without Glory*, Norwalk, CT: EastBridge, 2002.

——— "Myanmar's Coercive Apparatus: The Long Road to Reform", in Steinberg, David I. (ed.), *Myanmar: The Dynamics of an Evolving Polity*, Boulder, CO: Lynne Rienner, 2014, pp. 13–35.

Semenova, Elena, Michael Edinger and Heinrich Best, eds. *Parliamentary Elites in Central and Eastern Europe: Recruitment and Representation*, London: Routledge, 2014.

Set Aung, Winston, "Myanmar: Reforms Gathering Momentum", in Cheesman, Nick, Nicholas Farrelly and Trevor Wilson (eds), *Debating Democratisation in Myanmar*, Singapore: ISEAS Publications, 2014, pp. 3–8.

Shah, Aqil, *Army and Democracy in Pakistan*, Cambridge, MA: Harvard University Press, 2014.

Sherlock, Stephen, *Struggling to Change: The Indonesian Parliament in an Era of Reformasi*, Canberra: Center for Democratic Institutions, 2003.

Siddiqa, Ayesha, *Military Inc.: Inside Pakistan's Military Economy*, London/Ann Arbor: Pluto Press, 2007.

Silverstein, Josef, "Politics, Parties and National Elections in Burma", *Far Eastern Survey* 25, 12 (1956), pp. 177–84.

——— "The Federal Dilemma in Burma", *Far Eastern Survey* 28, 7 (1959), pp. 97–105.

——— "From Soldiers to Civilians: The New Constitution of Burma in Action", in Silverstein, Josef (ed.), *The Future of Burma in Perspective: A Symposium*, Athens, OH: University of Ohio, Center of International Studies, 1974, pp. 80–92.

——— "The Evolution and Salience of Burma's National Political Culture", in Rotberg, Robert I. (ed.), *Burma: Prospects for a Democratic Future*, Washington, D.C.: Brookings Institution Press, 1998, pp. 11–32.

Singh, Uma Shankar, "Parties and Politics in Burma during the Period 1948–1962", *India Quarterly* 11, 3 (1977), pp. 99–120.

Skidmore, Monique, "The Lady and the 'Wretched American': Burma's Trial of Aung San Suu Kyi", *Anthropology News* 50, 6 (2009), p. 30.

Skidmore, Monique and Trevor Wilson, "Interpreting the Transition in Myanmar", in Cheesman, Nick, Monique Skidmore and Trevor Wilson (eds), *Myanmar's Transition: Openings, Obstacles and Opportunities*, Singapore: ISEAS Publications, 2012, pp. 3–20.

Slater, Dan, "The Elements of Surprise: Assessing Burma's Double-Edged Détente", *South East Asia Research* 22, 2 (2014), pp. 171–82.

Smith, Martin, *Burma: Insurgency and the Politics of Ethnicity*, London: Zed Books, 1991.

—— "Ethnic Politics in a Time of Change", in Steinberg, David I. (ed.), *Myanmar: The Dynamics of an Evolving Polity*, Boulder, CO: Lynne Rienner, 2014, pp. 135–57.

South, Ashley, *Civil Society in Burma: The Development of Democracy amidst Conflict*, Washington, D.C.: East-West Center Policy Studies No. 51, 2008.

—— *Ethnic Politics in Burma: States of Conflict*, London: Routledge, 2008.

—— "Governance and Political Legitimacy in the Peace Process", in Steinberg, David I. (ed.), *Myanmar: The Dynamics of an Evolving Polity*, Boulder, CO: Lynne Rienner, 2014, pp. 159–90.

Spary, Carole, "Disrupting Rituals of Debate in the Indian Parliament", *The Journal of Legislative Studies* 16, 3 (2010), pp. 338–51.

Spiro, Melford E., "Ethnographic Notes on Conceptions and Dynamics of Political Power in Upper Burma (Prior to the 1962 Military Coup)", *Ethnology* 36, 1 (1997), pp. 31–47.

Srinivasan, R., "A Decade of Parliamentary Life in Burma", *The Indian Journal of Social Science* 19, 3 (1958), pp. 291–304.

Steinberg, David I., "A Void in Myanmar: Civil Society in Burma", in Kramer, Tom and Pietje Vervest (eds), *Strengthening Civil Society in Burma: possibilities and Dilemmas for International NGOs*, Chiang Mai: Silkworm Books, 1999, pp. 1–14.

—— "Myanmar: Reconciliation—Progress in the Process?", *Southeast Asian Affairs* 2003, pp. 169–88.

—— *Turmoil in Burma: Contested Legitimacies in Myanmar*, Norwalk, CT: EastBridge, 2006.

—— *The Significance of Burma/Myanmar's By-Elections*, Washington, D.C.: East-West Center Asia-Pacific Bulletin No. 156, 2 April 2012, pp. 1–2.

—— (ed.), *Myanmar: The Dynamics of an Evolving Polity*, Boulder, CO: Lynne Rienner, 2014.

—— "The Persistence of Military Dominance", Steinberg, David I. (ed.), *Myanmar: The Dynamics of an Evolving Polity*, Boulder, CO: Lynne Rienner, 2014, pp. 37–58.

Stokke, Kristian, Khine Win and Soe Myint Aung, "Political Parties and Popular Representation in Myanmar's Democratisation Process", *Journal of Current Southeast Asian Affairs* 34, 3 (2015), pp. 3–35.

Strefford, Patrick, "Myanmar's Transition and its Protest Movements", *Asia Journal of Global Studies* 6, 1 (2014), pp. 4–15.

Tatmadaw Researcher, *A Concise History of Myanmar and the Tatmadaw's Role, 1948–1988*, Rangoon: Ministry of Information Printing & Publishing Press, 1991.

Taylor, Robert H., "Perceptions of Ethnicity in the Politics of Burma", *Southeast Asian Journal of Social Science* 10, 1 (1982), pp. 1–22.

——— "Burma", in Ahmad, Zakaria Haji and Harold Crouch (eds), *Military-Civilian Relations in South-East Asia*, Singapore: Oxford University Press, 1985, pp. 13–49.

——— "Burmese Concepts of Revolution", in Hobart, Mark and Robert H. Taylor (eds), *Context, Meaning, and Power in Southeast Asia*, Ithaca, NY: SEAP, 1986, pp. 79–92.

——— "The Evolving Military Role in Burma", *Current History* 89, 545 (1990), pp. 105–8, 134–5.

——— "Elections in Burma/Myanmar: For Whom and Why?", in Taylor, Robert H. (ed.), *The Politics of Elections in Southeast Asia*, Washington, D.C.: Woodrow Wilson Center Press, 1996, pp. 164–83.

——— "One Day, One Fathom, Bagan Won't Move: On the Myanmar Road to Constitution", in Wilson, Trevor (ed.), *Myanmar's Long Road to National Reconciliation*, Singapore: ISEAS Publications, 2006, pp. 3–28.

——— "Finding the Political in Myanmar, a.k.a Burma", *Journal of Southeast Asian Studies* 39, 2 (2008), pp. 219–37.

——— "Myanmar in 2009: On the Cusp of Normality?", *Southeast Asian Affairs* (2010), pp. 201–13.

——— "Myanmar: From Army Rule to Constitutional Rule?", *Asian Affairs* 43, 2 (2012), pp. 221–36.

——— "Myanmar's 'Pivot' Toward the Shibboleth of 'Democracy'", *Asian Affairs* 44, 3 (2013), pp. 392–400.

——— "The Third Constitution of the Union of Myanmar", in Kyaw Yin Hlaing (ed.), *Prisms on the Golden Pagoda: Perspectives on National Reconciliation in Myanmar*, Singapore: NUS Press, 2014, pp. 132–51.

——— *The Armed Forces in Myanmar's Politics: A Terminating Role?*, Singapore: ISEAS Trends No. 2, 2015.

——— *General Ne Win: A Political Biography*, Singapore: ISEAS Publications, 2015.

Tegenfeldt, David, "International Non-Governmental Organizations in Burma", in Taylor, Robert H. (ed.), *Burma: Political Economy under Military Rule*, London: Hurst, 2001, pp. 109–18.

——— "More than Saving Lives: The Role of International Development Agencies in Supporting Change Processes in Burma/Myanmar", in Wilson, Trevor (ed.),

Myanmar's Long Road to National Reconciliation, Singapore: ISEAS Publications, 2006, pp. 218–30.

Thant Myint-U, "What To Do About Burma," *London Review of Books* 9, 3 (2007), pp. 31–3.

——— *Where China Meets India: Burma and the New Crossroads of Asia*, New York: Farrar, Straus & Giroux, 2012.

——— "White Elephants and Black Swans: Thoughts on Myanmar's Recent History and Possible Futures", in Cheesman, Nick, Monique Skidmore and Trevor Wilson (eds), *Myanmar's Transition: Openings, Obstacles and Opportunities*, Singapore: ISEAS Publications, 2012, pp. 23–35.

Thawnghmung, Ardeth Maung, "Preconditions and Prospects for Democratic Transition in Burma/Myanmar", *Asian Survey* 43, 3 (2003), pp. 443–60.

——— "The Dilemmas of Burma's Multinational Society", in Bertrand, Jacques and André Laliberté (eds), *Multination States in Asia: Accommodation or Resistance*, Cambridge: Cambridge University Press, 2010, pp. 136–63.

——— "The Politics of Everyday Life in 21st Century Myanmar", *The Journal of Asian Studies* 70, 3 (2011), pp. 641–70.

Thawnghmung, Ardeth Maung and Paul Sarno. "Myanmar Impasses: Alternatives to Isolation and Engagement?", *Asian Journal of Political Science* 14, 1 (2006), pp. 40–63.

Thomson, John S., "Burmese Neutralism," *Political Science Quarterly* 72, 2 (1957), pp. 261–83.

Tin Maung Maung Than, *State Dominance in Myanmar: The Political Economy of Industrialization*, Singapore: ISEAS Publications, 2007.

——— "Myanmar's 2010 Elections: Continuity and Change", *Southeast Asian Affairs* 2011, pp. 190–207.

——— "Myanmar's 2012 By-Elections: Return of NLD", *Southeast Asian Affairs* 2013, pp. 204–19.

——— "Introductory Overview: Myanmar's Economic Reforms", *Journal of Southeast Asian Economies* 31, 2 (2014), pp. 165–72.

Tomsa, Dick and Andreas Ufen (eds), *Party Politics in Southeast Asia: Clientelism and Electoral Competition in Indonesia, Thailand and the Philippines*, London: Routledge, 2013.

Trager, Frank N., "The Political Split in Burma", *Far Eastern Survey* 27, 10 (1958), pp. 145–55.

Walton, Matthew J., "The Disciplining Discourse of Unity in Burmese Politics", *The Journal of Burma Studies* 19, 1 (2015), pp. 1–26.

Walton, Matthew J. and Susan Hayward, *Contesting Buddhist Narratives: Democratization, Nationalism and Communal Violence in Myanmar*, Washington, D.C.: East-West Center Policy Studies No. 71, 2014.

Ware, Anthony, *Context-Sensitive Development: How International NGOs Operate in Myanmar*, Sterling, VA: Kumarian Press, 2012.

Weiss, Meredith L., "Civil Society and Democratisation in Southeast Asia: What Is the Connection?", in Case, William (ed.), *The Routledge Handbook of Southeast Asian Democratization*, London: Routledge, 2015, pp. 135–46.

Welch, Claude E., *No Farewell to Arms: Military Disengagement from Politics in Africa and Latin America*, Boulder, CO: Westview Press, 1987.

Wiant, Jon A., "Tradition in the Service of Revolution: The Political Symbolism of *Taw-hlan-ye-khit*", in Lehman, F. K. (ed.), *Military Rule in Burma since 1962*, Singapore: Maruzen Asia, 1981, pp. 59–72.

Williams, David C., "What's So Bad about Burma's 2008 Constitution? A Guide for the Perplexed", in Crouch, Melissa and Tim Lindsey (eds), *Law, Society and Transition in Myanmar*, Oxford: Hart Publishing, 2014, pp. 117–40.

Wilson, Trevor, "Debating Democratization in Myanmar", in Cheesman, Nick, Nicholas Farrelly and Trevor Wilson (eds), *Debating Democratization in Myanmar*, Singapore: ISEAS Publications, 2014, pp. 12–17.

Win Min, "Looking inside the Burmese Military", *Asian Survey* 48, 6 (2008), pp. 1018–37.

Wright, Joseph and Matthew Winters, "The Politics of Effective Foreign Aid", *Annual Review of Political Science*, 13 (2010), pp. 61–80.

Yawnghwe, Chao-Tzang, "Burma: Depoliticization of the Political", in Alagappa, M. (ed.), *Political Legitimacy in Southeast Asia: The Quest for Moral Authority*, Stanford, CA: Stanford University Press, 1995, pp. 170–92.

Yegar, Moshe, *The Muslims of Burma: A Study of a Minority Group*, Wiesbaden: Otto Harrassowith, 1972.

Yun Sun, "China and Myanmar: Moving beyond Mutual Dependence", in Steinberg, David I., (ed.), *Myanmar: The Dynamics of an Evolving Polity*, Boulder, CO: Lynne Rienner, 2014, pp. 267–88.

Zaw Oo, "Exit, Voice, and Loyalty in Burma: The Role of Overseas Burmese in Democratising their Homeland," in Wilson, Trevor (ed.), *Myanmar's Long Road to National Reconciliation*, Singapore: ISEAS Publications, 2006, pp. 231–62.

Zheng, Yongnian, Lye Liang Fook and Wilhem Hofmeister (eds), *Parliaments in Asia: Institutions Building and Political Development*, London: Routledge, 2014.

Ziegenhain, Patrick, *The Indonesian Parliament and Democratization*, Singapore: ISEAS Publications, 2008.

INDEX